Disrupted Lives

Disrupted Lives

HOW PEOPLE CREATE MEANING
IN A CHAOTIC WORLD

GAY BECKER

UNIVERSITY OF CALIFORNIA PRESS
Berkeley   Los Angeles   London

University of California Press
Berkeley and Los Angeles, California

University of California Press, Ltd.
London, England

Library of Congress Cataloging-in-Publication Data

Becker, Gaylene.
    Disrupted lives : how people create meaning in a chaotic world /
Gay Becker.
        p. cm.
    Includes bibliographic references and index
    ISBN 0-520-20913-3 (cloth : alk. paper). — ISBN 0-520-20914-1 (pbk :
alk. paper)
        1. Life change events—United States.   2. Adjustment
(Psychology)—United States.   I. Title.   BF637.L53B43   1998
    302.5 —dc 21   96-52482

Printed in the United States of America
9 8 7 6 5 4 3 2 1

The paper used in this publication meets the minimum requirements of
American National Standards for Information Sciences—Permanence of
Paper for Printed Library Materials, ANSI z39.48-1984.

For my aunt, Hazel Perry,
and
in memory of my uncle, John Perry

Contents

Acknowledgments

My first thanks go to the hundreds of women and men who shared their stories of disruption to life. Their willingness to talk about their experiences, no matter how painful to describe or how difficult to reconcile, made this book possible.

Material that appeared in Gay Becker, "Metaphors in Disrupted Lives: Infertility and Cultural Constructions of Continuity," is reprinted with permission from *Medical Anthropology Quarterly* volume 8, number 4, copyright American Anthropological Association, 1994.

The National Institute on Aging (NIA), National Institutes of Health, provided funding for four of the five studies this book draws upon: (1) Gender and the Disruption of Life Course Structure, RO1 AGO8973, Gay Becker, Principal Investigator, Robert D. Nachtigall, Co-Principal Investigator; 1991–1995; (2) Sociocultural Mechanisms of Rehabilitation in Old Age, RO1 AG04053, Gay Becker, Principal Investigator, Sharon Kaufman, Co-Principal Investigator, 1983–1986; Chronicity and Life Reorganization in Old Age, Sharon Kaufman, Principal Investigator, Gay

Becker, Co-Principal Investigator, 1988–1991; (3) From Independence to Dependence among the Oldest Old, RO1 AGO9176, Gay Becker, Principal Investigator, Sharon Kaufman, Co-Principal Investigator, 1991–1994; (4) Cultural Responses to Illness in the Minority Aged, RO1 AG11144, Gay Becker, Principal Investigator, Yewoubdar Beyene and Denise Rodgers, Co-Principal Investigators, 1993–1998. Neither this book, which was written during the time the last-mentioned study was funded, nor the studies would have been possible without this funding.

I am indebted to Marcia Ory, who envisioned the potential of qualitative research to contribute to an understanding of aging and who initiated the NIA's emphasis on anthropological research on aging and the course of life. She has been a source of ongoing encouragement for my work. I am also grateful to Katrina Johnson, who served as project officer at NIA for several of these projects and was an important source of advice and support.

Many thanks are due to Yewoubdar Beyene, Sharon Kaufman, Robert Nachtigall, and Denise Rodgers, my research partners in these studies. Conducting research with them has been a creative, stimulating, and enjoyable process.

I owe special thanks to Edwina Newsom, project manager on several of these studies, for her sensitive interviews with people who participated in our research and for her creative management of the research projects, which freed me to spend more time in analysis and writing. I also thank Jeff Harmon, Seline Szkupinski Quiroga, and Eleanor Rosenberg, who skillfully conducted interviews on which some of the stories in this book are based.

I would like to acknowledge and thank the community organizations, agencies, and hospitals that helped to recruit people for these studies: Catholic Charities, Centro Latino, Lakeside Senior Health Services, Mount Zion Hospital and Medical Center, Northern California Resolve, North of Market Senior Services, the Over Sixty Clinic, PACT—An Adoption Alliance, San Francisco General Hospital, and the University of California, San Francisco/Mount Zion Home Care Services.

I am very grateful to the reviewers of this book, Virginia Oleson, Robert L. Rubinstein, and an anonymous reviewer. They made many valuable suggestions that I have tried to follow. I would also like to thank colleagues with whom I have had discussions that sparked my thinking in various ways: Mark Luborsky, Linda Pitcher, and Kathleen Slobin. The consistent enthusiasm for this book project voiced by Kristine Bertelsen and Arlene Van Craeynest has helped to keep me focused on it. I am grateful to the editors at the University of California Press with whom I worked: Naomi Schneider, whose enthusiasm and patience helped to carry the book along to completion, Erika Büky for careful oversight of the book's production, and Carlotta Shearson, who provided masterful copyediting.

Many thanks to Leilani Cuizon-Canalita and Nury Mayen, who printed innumerable drafts of the manuscript for me and who helped me to assemble the final product.

Finally, special thanks go to my husband, Roger Van Craeynest, with whom I have had an ongoing, stimulating dialogue about many of the ideas that appear in this book.

1 Mediating Disruption

This is the reason why I show it [a scrapbook] to you. It's easier to understand why I am here and how I became an old woman. This [picture] is a press conference in Budapest. And this is at the Parliament, the last time. My husband didn't want to leave Hungary. People lose their identity [when they leave]. But they came to arrest him, and we escaped. We hid in a chicken coop for two days. We decided we have to come [to the United States]. They put us in a van and drove us to a safe house that hid a Jewish family in World War II. Then we went through the border patrols. The car had an American sign on it. Russian soldiers everywhere. In eight days we landed in New York. It was the longest ride in my whole life. I woke up only in America, to know that we are not at home.

I lived two lives. It's two different lives. And sometimes they are fighting with each other. . . . And now, finally, I can go back to visit. And if I want to meet with my family, I have to go to the cemetery.

eighty-two-year-old refugee
from the 1956 Hungarian Revolution

At eighty-two, Mrs. Marya Zabor,[1] a refugee of the Hungarian Revolution, is painting her personal history, the canvas of her life. Small and fragile looking, her expressive hands move in the air as she moves from one picture to the next, in a continuous process of life reconstruction. She cannot afford to buy canvas, so she improvises; she paints on scraps of wood and pieces of cardboard. The walls of her single room are completely covered with her paintings. They are scenes from her life: some are dreams, some are memories. When she is not painting, she is inspecting her work for clues to self-knowledge. While she spends her days alone, painting, her mind is busy as she continuously sorts out the past and tries to find commonalities between it and the present. There are few.

> Life in America, it's a million persons different than in Europe and certainly different than in a smaller country like Hungary. And this is double work to get used to it and to accept it.

I tried to clarify what she meant: "You mean to find some common ground or something that you have in common with others?"

> Yes, that's right. And even so, I know many Hungarians in New York and here. Some of them died, some of them went back to Hungary. But the people are changed. They're not the same. We used to say, "When they put their feet on the ground of America, they are changing." They are lying so much. Everything I can tolerate. Just not to lie. If you met someone after the '56, you know, he wasn't a soldier, he was a lieutenant; it wasn't a person who served in a store, it was a manufacturer. And if it helps them, that's one thing. It's their problem. But I can't stand it. Because I came from the same place, and I know who they really were.
>
> I'm not blaming them, I'm blaming myself that I'm not able to try to get closer to them by changing my viewpoint of what is a whole life.

Mrs. Zabor's story highlights the major elements of a disrupted life—the disruption itself, a period of limbo, and a period of life reorganization. As she talks about her identity in the aftermath of change, other essential elements emerge that give the story depth and context. On the eve of the disruption, she was a member of the Hungarian intelligentsia, married to a man with great political power and considerable wealth. Today she is a widow who lives in poverty in a single room.

Nothing remains of her former life except a scrapbook, a couple of pieces of antique furniture, and her memories, translated onto scraps of paper and wood.

Mrs. Zabor's attempts to rediscover her whole life by painting scenes from it are manifestations of her intense, lifelong preoccupation with her sense of self. In reflecting on this preoccupation, she observes that she has developed a "viewpoint of what is a whole life." In her view, other refugees have lost their identities by portraying themselves as they would like to be seen rather than as they really are. Her story shows how disruption can bring about renewed efforts at self-discovery and highlight concerns about how the self is portrayed to others.

Throughout her narrative, Mrs. Zabor underscores differences: differences between Hungary and the United States, between the known and the unknown, between a picture of herself in a scrapbook and the picture of herself as an old woman. She tries to reconcile these differences, to create continuity, through metaphor, through words and art, an alternative system of metaphor in itself. She metaphorically captures the period of limbo she experienced during her eight-day flight from Hungary to the United States when she portrays that journey as "the longest ride in my whole life." Mrs. Zabor juxtaposes two metaphors—flight and fight—to illustrate the conflict between the two lives that she has lived, two lives that are "sometimes fighting with each other." In the flight metaphor, she depicts danger through a series of motifs: near arrest, escape, concealment in a chicken coop and in a safe house left over from another war, flight from soldiers and border patrols. Through this metaphor runs another metaphor: the car with an American sign on it—the car that transports her into another life—represents safety. The metaphorical fight is an internal one, a fight within the self. She draws attention to her realization of the profound changes at the end of the journey when she says "I woke up only in America, to know that we are not at home." Through metaphor, she thus elicits a haunting image of tension between the two lives, the one before the revolution and the other after, an image that is unlikely to dissipate.

Death also appears in Mrs. Zabor's story—the metaphorical death of the old way of life as well as actual deaths. Despite her efforts to unite past and present through her art work, the harsh truth remains, "If I want to meet with my family, I have to go to the cemetery."

Mrs. Zabor has condensed half a lifetime of disruption into a few powerful metaphors that convey the essential elements of the disruption in which she was caught: the enormous wrench of revolution disrupting her life; the period of limbo, of liminality, during which she waits to learn the outcome of her forced flight; and the laborious, forty-year effort to create a sense of continuity in the face of unwanted and irrevocable change. Her narrative reproduces the metaphors in her paintings, and she uses these metaphors to mediate the disruption to her life.

CREATING CONTINUITY

In this book I examine the process by which people attempt to create continuity after an unexpected disruption to life. People's efforts to create linkages with the past during times of disruptive changes—whether societal, such as those caused by a revolution, or individual, such as the onset of illness—have been readily observed. People maintain continuity with the past amid the facts of change by interpreting current events so that they are understood as part of tradition.[2] The ongoing interpretation of events and experiences enables people to make sense of their personal worlds; and a knowable world provides a framework for understanding major events as well as everyday experiences. A sense of continuity is captured in ordinary routines of daily life, the mundane and comforting sameness of repetitive activities, such as drinking a cup of coffee with the morning newspaper. These activities give structure and logic to people's lives.[3]

In all societies, the course of life is structured by expectations about each phase of life, and meaning is assigned to specific life events and the roles that accompany them. When expectations about the course of life are not met, people experience inner chaos and disruption. Such disruptions represent loss of the future. Restoring order to life necessitates reworking understandings of the self and the world, redefining the disruption and life itself.

The effort to create order is, in essence, what anthropologists study. Although the ways in which people strive to create order out of chaos and thereby render life meaningful have been an enduring focus of anthropological study, the majority of anthropological work has not focused specifically on disruptions to life.[4] When disruptions have been observed in the course of research, or "fieldwork," as it is referred to in anthropology, they have served to give point and form to anthropological observations of daily life by throwing cultural phenomena into relief. Some argue that a concept of culture must include those moments in social life when what is normal and habitual is disrupted and gives way to a new realm of possibilities.[5] The preoccupation with culture as a monolithic entity, which prevailed in the preceding era in anthropology, obscured the potential to understand what happens when things go wrong, when events fall outside of people's experiences of life and their expectations about it.

Although continuity is apparently a human need and a universal expectation across cultures,[6] continuity has a culture-specific shape. Western ideas about the course of life emphasize linearity. Metaphoric images of development and progress include gain and loss. The life span is seen as hierarchical, and aging as a "hill."[7] The underlying assumption that development occurs over the entire course of life has its roots in long-standing theories of evolution that inform notions of order and progress in the West. Western thought is organized to make sense of individual lives as orderly projects, but when this concept of the life course is translated into experiences of individual people, there is a great deal of slippage because real lives are more unpredictable than the cultural ideal.[8]

Anthropologists studying U.S. society have observed the need to preserve or reconstruct some semblance of continuity in the wake of disruptions to life.[9] Distress seems to be a major organizing factor in the way life stories are told in the United States;[10] these stories often focus on adversity and on the means for resolving unexpected disruptions among previously ordered events. The likely reasons for this focus are the aforementioned emphasis in the West, particularly in the United States, on the linear, orderly unfolding of life and the emphasis on the individual, the self, in relation to society.[11]

The way that order and chaos are thought of in the West has recently begun to change. Chaos has been negatively valued in the Western tradition because of the predominance of binary logic: if order is good, chaos must be bad because it is viewed as the opposite of order.[12] This attitude toward chaos has now begun to shift with the advent of chaos theory. Chaos theory suggests that deep structures of order are hidden within the unpredictability of chaotic systems, that chaotic systems exhibit orderly disorder rather than true randomness. The advent of chaos theory is part of a major paradigm shift, a shift from a Newtonian paradigm emphasizing predictability and linearity to a paradigm of "chaotics."[13] This latter paradigm celebrates unpredictability and nonlinearity and sees both as sources of new information.[14]

It takes time for new ways of thinking to pervade daily life, especially when the old paradigm has been particularly pervasive. Western understandings of order continue to revolve around linearity, and this book consciously reflects that tendency. We will get brief glimpses of the paradigm shift, but, for the most part, we will see just how deeply embedded is the traditional Western paradigm of predictability and order in people's lives. We will see how people organize stories of disruption into linear accounts of chaos that gradually turns to order.

The stories of disruption in this book thus capture a transitional moment in time. The future may hold a greater engagement with, and subsequent comfort with, notions of chaos, but we are not yet seeing people express that sentiment. Instead, people continue to draw on traditional cultural understandings of order and chaos in interpreting the disruptions in their lives. Because people are gradually integrating scientific models into their understanding of their everyday world, it is likely that with the passage of time the chaotics paradigm will take its place along with other explanations for why things go awry in life. We will see a few examples of this phenomenon among people who use biomedical technologies and consequently wrestle with disparities between old and new ways of seeing the world.

My studies of disruption to life are situated in a specific anthropological perspective: that each culture has its own expected "cultural life course." The course of life can be viewed as a cultural unit and a powerful collective symbol.[15] As a collectively shared image, the cultural life course may, through metaphor, provide people with images and motivations that guide their lives as members of society and as individuals.[16] For example, the "journey of life" metaphor is a root, or organizing, metaphor.[17] European representations of the life spiral portray another cultural conception of the life course.[18] Although the life course was traditionally portrayed as a life wheel, life bridge, or staircase, this iconography was allegorical and linked life stages to the dance of death, serving as a reminder that death could strike at any time. These portrayals, which date to the fifteenth century, referred to the basic insecurity of life. In the nineteenth century, these portrayals, in their secularized form, lost their reference to the dance of death, and the individualized life course emerged as the basic code for constructing experience in Western societies.[19] The contemporary Western conception of the life course as predictable, knowable, and continuous is thus a relatively recent phenomenon.

I view disruption as a part of the human condition. After analyzing hundreds of stories of people whose lives have been disrupted, I have come to see responses to disruption as cultural responses to change. These efforts to create continuity after a disruption emerge as a complex cultural process. When I began writing this book, I did not intend it to be primarily an analysis of U.S. culture; yet that is what it has become. The examination of disrupted lives and the efforts people make to regain a sense of continuity necessarily entails a close look at the cultural context in which disruption occurs and, ultimately, at those cultural dynamics that are at the root of the disruption. In this book, I explore this process through an examination of how disruption is both embodied and portrayed by people in the United States who have undergone a variety of disruptions to their lives. The strength of the ideal of continuity and its pervasiveness suggest that in the United States disruptions to life may seem all the more abrupt because of the tendency to view life as a predictable, continuous flow.[20] Expectations about continuity permeate responses to disruption as well as efforts to create continuity after disruption has occurred.

The study of disruption and people's efforts to create continuity does more, however, than simply unpack a pervasive assumption that there is continuity in life. Studying disruption enables us to examine the well-springs of many core tenets of U.S. society and to explore how deeply those core tenets are embedded in the cultural contours of people's lives. These tasks are part of what I undertake in this book.

FROM LIVING WITH DISRUPTION
TO STUDYING DISRUPTION

It has become commonplace for anthropologists to link themselves personally to their fieldwork, and this approach represents a shift from the approach of the previous era, in which I was trained, when "objectivity" was the primary goal of the social sciences. Despite this emphasis, I knew that my personal experience was at the core of my intellectual interest in disruption. My studies of disruption in people's lives have been fueled by my lifelong efforts to create a sense of continuity in my own life. I wanted to understand the process undergone by people who experience disruption so that I could apply what I learned to better cope with disruption in my own life.

My childhood was punctuated by a series of disruptions, some subtle yet profound, others seemingly cataclysmic. As I was growing up, my life seemed to be a sea of unforeseen changes, disruption, and uncertainty studded with islands of stability, brief periods in which life went on as normal. I struggled to stay afloat.

These disruptions were all the more potent because of the sociocultural and historical context in which they occurred. I grew up in the years of flux and change following World War II in an urban San Francisco neighborhood trying to cling steadfastly to its Jewish and Italian roots. My childhood world was a tiny island surrounded by a bustling Army base and two neighborhoods that were undergoing major population changes. Before the war, one of these neighborhoods had been populated by African Americans, Japanese Americans, and Jewish and Italian immigrants. World War II brought the migration of black southerners to work in the shipyards of California. Many Japanese Americans who had lived in rural California before their internment in concentration camps during the war did not return to their land: they came to San Francisco instead. The other neighborhood was one in which generations of Chinese Americans and Italian Americans had lived. Suddenly, in the wake the war and the Communist Revolution in China, that neighborhood became a mecca for thousands of refugees from Asia, primarily China.

Both neighborhoods filled up and overflowed their boundaries, pressing against the small, predominantly white, middle-class neighborhood in which I lived. Children of all colors filled the schools, bringing their cultural backgrounds with them. Their parents, who often spoke no English, filled the streets. No one ever said in front of me, "We must keep them out," but people in my neighborhood struggled to maintain a wall against these outsiders. A strong undertow pulled people in this postage stamp–sized neighborhood toward the staid, predictable patterns of the past.

I was the outsider inside the gates of my still white neighborhood. I was raised primarily by my grandparents, who as Christian Scientists were not even in the Protestant mainstream. Not only did they not go to doctors, but my grandmother was a faith healer, or, to use the parlance of Christian Science, a practitioner. I stood out in this neighborhood where every other family was Jewish or Catholic. I left the classroom when the science lesson started. I didn't go to mass or temple with my family. I didn't participate in the ethnic celebrations that were so much a part of the life of this community.

As I became an adult, the disruptions in my life became harder to ignore. At ten, I developed allergies and asthma. Unchecked by medical treatment, these conditions ruled my life. My eyelids would swell almost completely shut in the spring with the arrival of the pollen carried by seasonal winds; my lungs were congested every winter from colds and flu. I was absent from school often. When there, I was a liability in team sports: I ran slowly and wheezed audibly. I felt disfigured and grotesque.

When I was thirteen, a school counselor advised me to switch from a college preparatory track to a business track. My schoolmates all planned to go to college. Why had I been singled out as being different from them? College had always been my goal, and it was hard to let go of this lifelong expectation. I felt the sustaining dream of my short life begin to dissipate.

When I was fourteen, my grandfather died at the age of eighty-eight. He had hung on for over a year from the time his health had started to fail, and he died the day after I graduated from junior high school. I was so angry at this wholesale desertion when I needed him that no stranger would have recognized my response as grief; I was in a rage. He had been my pal. He taught me to read, first with blocks, then with newspapers. He walked the dog with me daily, took me on his newspaper route, cooked me truly inedible food, and bored me with baseball scores. He was good company. His going left a yawning, cavernous void.

I felt pushed out by society, disowned. I became more obviously marginal than I had been before. I became, for a brief time, an outlaw. I looked tough. I dressed mostly in black. I affected detachment, even callousness. Inside I was a mess. I practically lived on a street corner that was the turf of a "car club," a gang that stole cars. After being taken to the local juvenile detention center because of the company I kept, I decided being an outlaw was dangerous. I went to work at sixteen, which, for me, marked the full transition to adulthood.

I eventually began taking college courses while working full-time. I then went to work in an academic setting in which I worked with anthropologists as well as others in the social and health sciences. I discovered my niche in anthropology, where marginality was not only tolerated but accepted. Indeed, the abundance of books and papers on themes of marginality and being an outsider induced me to persist in my studies. Even more compelling was the affirmation of my identity I experienced each time I did fieldwork. My first fieldwork was with people who lived on the street and teenagers who had been labeled as delinquent. I instinctively started as an anthropologist where I had left off as an adolescent.

Although turmoil is often part of growing up, I attributed mine solely to the disruptions I had experienced. The staccato pattern of disruption, change, and return to normalcy I experienced in childhood forged my identity as an outsider. The search for answers to my seemingly aberrant life experience eventually made its way into my research. Over and over I asked how others responded to disruption, how it affected their identity, and how they viewed themselves and their lives when stability returned.

I tell my own story here not only because it has shaped my work but also for several other reasons. First, my story encapsulates many of the dimensions of disruption that appear in the other stories in this book. Specifically, it illustrates different contexts for continuity and discontinuity—family, class and ethnic background, and society more generally—and how those contexts shape people's experiences of disruption and continuity. For example, the family may diminish sense of disruption in some ways, as my grandfather's presence did in my childhood, and yet exacerbate it in other ways, as his death subsequently did.

Second, my story, like all of those in this book, is one of embodied distress. I felt the chaos of disruption at a visceral, bodily level long before my chronic illness—asthma—began to emerge when I was ten. I listened to my body continuously as I tried to monitor symptoms such as wheezing and swollen eyes that identified me as "sick." My struggles to breathe left indelible memories that were embodied in my subsequent actions. My bodily response to symptoms of asthma is informed by these memories even today.

I have omitted much of that distress from my account, however, because it resurrects old fears whenever I dwell on it. Moreover, the expression of distress is not culturally sanctioned in the United States. In the United States, there is an underlying ideology, born of Puritan beginnings, that values communication through mental rather than bodily activity, that values thinking more highly than feeling.[21] Bodily and emotional expression is suppressed. Indeed, the lack of acknowledgment of embodied distress heightens the difficulty people have in giving voice to bodily disruptions; embodied distress may be difficult to access through language and may remain muted and unarticulated.[22] At least when I was growing up, "toughing it out" was expected. Those cultural constraints make the distress I experienced difficult to articulate even now, and the validity of embodied distress is an issue that others in this book struggle with as well.

Third, I tell my story because it contains certain elements of narratives of disruption that appear in other stories in this book. Narratives, my own included, arise out of a desire to have life display coherence, integrity, fullness, and closure.[23] I can analyze my own narrative most easily simply because it is my own; I have told it to myself many times over the years. In the process, I have reshaped it so that it gives a sense of coherence to my life. Of course, I have not told all of it. Some parts of my story are omitted because they seem less directly related to the "story line." During my formative years, I was not aware that I was reshaping events to lend my life coherence; it is only recently, since I began this book, that I have seen how my own story fits this narrative convention.[24]

The plot of my story is something on the order of "disrupted life made good." The story thus has a moral authority similar to that of other stories of disruption that will be told in these pages. Indeed, the stories in this book speak directly to cultural notions in the United States of order and normalcy. Moral authority is embedded in a specific social reality, and the portrayal of a personal world in story form is necessary to the establishment of that authority.[25] The development of people's narratives of disruption is, preeminently, a cultural process.

THE DISTRESSED BODY

How are body and self affected by disruption? Order begins with the body.[26] That is, our understanding of ourselves and the world begins with our reliance on the orderly functioning of our bodies. This bodily knowledge informs what we do and say in the course of daily life. In addition, we carry our histories with us into the present through our bodies. The past is "sedimented" in the body; that is, it is embodied.[27] In order to examine the full range of the effects of disruption on people's lives, I start with bodily experience.[28]

To explain what I mean more thoroughly, I will use the example of the person who has asthma because I have already alluded to my own struggles with asthma and because doing so provides a concrete example of bodily distress.[29] Breathing is one of the body's most essential acts, and the ability to breathe is taken for granted.[30] People usually breathe without thinking,[31] but when breathing becomes difficult, they become self-consciously aware of their bodies, that is, of being a body. People who have asthma perennially "listen" to their bodies, anticipating as well as monitoring the symptoms of the illness, wheezing or shortness of breath. Bodily experience thus encompasses the past, the present, and the anticipated future.[32]

The body is the medium through which people experience their cultural world, and bodily experience can reflect the culture in which it occurs.[33] Breathing is a process that is not just physiological but also cultural. That is, when people with asthma listen for symptoms, they are engaging in a process that is culturally informed.[34] Cultural attitudes in the United States that value stoicism in the management of illness and individual responsibility for health inevitably affect the nature of embodied distress caused by asthma.[35] People in the United States deal with their asthma symptoms in ways that reflect these cultural attitudes; for example, they may ignore, diminish, or hide symptoms, use specific kinds of folk remedies to control symptoms, and delay seeking treatment.[36] An emphasis on bodily experience thus informs an understanding of people's activities and practices of everyday life.[37]

Our bodies, as sources of moral and political knowledge, are capable of generating categories of social analysis, a phenomenon I will try to demonstrate in this book. The body can be said to produce culture. People are able to ground their resistance to the power of cultural norms in bodily experience.[38] For example, a person with asthma may resist going to an emergency room (the recommended biomedical course of action for acute episodes of asthma) because they fear they will not receive appropriate treatment, but their resistance is tempered by their bodily knowledge: they listen to their bodies in deciding whether care is necessary.[39] Failure to listen for symptoms, or to gauge them accurately, may have serious and even fatal medical consequences. We will see in the examples in this book that bodily knowledge informs action, including resistance to the status quo.

Bodily experience is not restricted to individuals or small groups of people but encompasses large social collectivities.[40] Sharing experiences of embodied distress in asthma support groups, for example, may not only lead to greater bodily attention but also facilitate social action. When we view embodied experience of people in social groups, we gain insights about cultural phenomena because doing so gives us a window on a place where people and social institutions intersect, embodied experience in communal life.

In this book, I try to maintain a balance between explicit descriptions of the bodily experiences that people have and the stories that capture those experiences; it is not an easy task, however.[41] At times I emphasize the role of narrative in people's articulation and understanding of disruption simply because it is more difficult to portray the embodied distress that generates such narratives. It is not my intention, however, to divide them into separate realms. Instead, I want to show how, together, they make up a whole. Narrative is a conduit for emotion and a means through which embodied distress is expressed. Language gives access to a world of experience insofar as experience is brought to language.[42]

Nevertheless, narrative cannot completely capture the expression of emotion. Although there are other media, as illustrated by Mrs. Zabor's use of art as well as narrative to address her disrupted life, narrative is the primary expressive form for the mediation of disruption. Mrs. Zabor told her story to me with considerable intensity and, occasionally, extreme agitation. She showed me photographs from newspapers, mute testimonies to her former life. She visited her various paintings hanging on the walls, sometimes just looking at them, sometimes talking about them. She paced back and forth, she looked out the single window of her room, she cried. It is difficult to portray the kaleidoscope of emotion with which she conveyed her story or the embodied nature of its expression. Because narrative can be captured by a tape recorder and transcribed onto a printed page, however, it is through narratives that we gain access to embodied distress.

Bodily practices enact the past and, hence, embody cultural memory. Narrative, as the performance of bodily experience, can therefore be seen as practice. Such performances constitute action. People project images of themselves and the world to their audiences through performance, as Mrs. Zabor did.[43] In this book those images are projected through narrative.

WRESTLING WITH NORMALCY

I have found that people consciously wrestle with some cultural ethos that is at odds with their life situation.[44] This is particularly true when life circumstances do not fit with cultural ideas about what constitutes normalcy. We will look at the disjunction, as it is portrayed by people in the throes of disruption, between embodied distress and cultural expectations about order. We will also see how people's notions of order change as they attempt to come to grips with disruption to their lives. Efforts to create coherence and provide closure to situations that are at odds with their notions of order are shaped by complex cultural dynamics.

Narratives of disruption are people's efforts to integrate disruption and its aftermath with prevailing cultural sentiments. People define normalcy in terms of particular cultural images that have salience for them. From a phenomenological perspective, people themselves generate categories of normalcy, although they may later take issue with those categories when they no longer fit with life experience. Depending on the nature of the disruption, various cultural ideals of, for example, health, womanhood, manhood, parenthood, and the aging process emerge.

When we talk about disruption to life, we are also talking about stability, which is the flip side of disruption. Stability, however it is individually defined, has cultural contours. Studies of disrupted lives afford an opportunity to examine out-of-the-ordinary life experiences for what they can tell us about cultural constructs that are taken for granted. Stories of disruption in the United States reveal ideals about order and normalcy, but these ideals are just that, ideals; they do not necessarily reflect people's experience.

When I began my ethnographic studies, and, indeed, even when I began this book, I did not foresee the force with which certain cultural tenets concerning normalcy in the United States would dominate people's stories or the great extent to which they would be used by people to make sense of disruption.[45] What is most striking about the portrait of the issues that emerge when people wrestle with disruption is that in the United States core beliefs persist despite ongoing social change. Although ongoing social change may affect particular cultural norms and values, the sum of those values still articulates the cultural ethos that is characteristic of the United States. To be sure, individuals vary in their interpretations of normalcy. We will explore these variations—by ethnicity, gender, class, and age—as well as similarities that persist despite such heterogeneity. The juxtaposition of disruption, and embodied distress in particular, against cultural discourses on normalcy both highlights specific kinds of disruption and throws cultural phenomena into relief so that disparities become more visible.

People strive to be normal; however, the realities of life are very different from the ideal. People have compelling concerns and precious stakes to defend; and although they would be "quite helpless without the power of cultural templates to guide and sustain them," they live their lives uniquely.[46] In other words, events occur continuously that do not fit with a vision of how life should be, and when they do they affect people's individualized views of the world.[47]

Stories of disruption are, by definition, stories of difference. Disruption makes an individual feel different from others and can render social relationships uncomfortable and cumbersome.[48] The narratives in this book repeatedly attest to the emotional pain that difference causes and to the struggle to reduce or eliminate that sense of difference from others. Regardless of the phase of life they are in and the nature of the disruption, the people in this book view themselves as being at odds with what others—and they themselves—view as normal for their gender, age, and circumstances. They thus come into conflict with the social order as they understand it. They see themselves as marginal and may define themselves in terms of difference rather than normalcy.[49] The stories in this book show the conflict between the desire for normalcy and the acknowledgment of difference being enacted over and over again.

Rational determinism, a dominant cultural ethos in the United States, shapes cultural discourses on normalcy,[50] a number of which, such as the discourse on the family, the discourses on womanhood and manhood, the discourse on the self, and the discourse on aging, I discuss in this book. These discourses and others I allude to have one thing in common: they are all moral discourses. That is, they reflect dominant ideologies about how life should be lived. The news media's routine analysis of national news readily reveals how deeply these discourses are embedded, as well as one way in which they are continuously reinforced.

People's narratives of disruption are moral accounts of their lives. That is, the narratives reflect people's interpretations of these moral ideologies and their efforts to live up to them. Narratives can serve as moralizing judgments. A moralizing impulse is present in all narrative accounts; there is no other way that one's reality can be endowed with so much meaning.[51] In this book, the discourses people focus on highlight their divergence from normalcy, which thrusts them into the experience of otherness and thus requires a moralizing antidote to mediate the experience of becoming the other. Their stories have a moral authority that derives not only from invoking discourses on normalcy but also from demonstrating how attempts to live up to expectations about normalcy often fail despite protracted efforts.

By mapping culture, moral discourses help people to make sense of their world. Inability to live out moral discourses forces people to tease apart the different dimensions of phenomena they previously took for granted. People's narratives reflect the struggle to rethink those discourses after disruption to encompass their own experience. We will see people examining discourses on normalcy to find ways to fit their disparities into society's expectations.

Although the narratives in this book often express a longing for normalcy, they are also narratives of resistance to the status quo.[52] Examining the tensions that surround efforts to restore normalcy enables us to understand better how resistance develops. Although I say little directly about politics in this book, the narrators say a great deal. Indeed, narrative is always political because people choose which narrative to tell.[53] Although we will read narratives that muse about the possibilities in stream-of-consciousness fashion, we will also examine narratives that take a particular stance toward issues of normalcy and difference. Statements that say this is who I am or am not, statements that question the status quo, and statements that self-consciously proclaim some sort of difference are all statements of resistance. Resistance to the status quo can also be seen in descriptions of empowerment through community, for example, descriptions of participation in self-help groups, specific ethnic communities, religious organizations or in indigenous health-related activities.

The analysis of narrative is a primary means for uncovering how disruption is experienced and how continuity is created, and for examining disparities between cultural ideals and people's experiences. Narratives enable the narrator to reestablish a sense of continuity in life. This book is also concerned with the examination of the metaphors that unfold in the discourse on normalcy. The fluidity with which metaphorical images continuously replace one another in an ongoing, culturally informed process quickly becomes apparent when we read people's narratives. Anthropologists explore metaphor not for the metaphors themselves but for the cultural foundations of metaphor.[54] In this book, metaphor provides insights on the cultural foundations of U.S. society.[55]

STUDIES OF DISRUPTED LIVES

To illustrate how cultural meanings of continuity frame the experience of disruption to daily life, I draw on five studies of people in various phases of life in the United States. The five studies are about (1) the experience of infertility, (2) midlife disruption and change, (3) life reorganization after a stroke, (4) late-life transitions, and (5) the experience of chronic illness among older members of ethnic minority groups. These five studies are part of two long-term ethnographies I have been engaged in simultaneously, one on the experience of living with a chronic illness, especially in later life, and the other on the experience of infertility and related disruptions in midlife. Both of these ethnographies have been in progress for the past fifteen years and are likely to continue in one form or another for some time to come. Both are based on years of in-depth interviews, which are supported by observations of participants in a variety of settings and under a wide variety of circumstances.[56]

The five studies described below can be characterized in a word or two, and these characterizations will be used to refer to them throughout the book.

1.   *The Infertility Study* (Gender and the Disruption of the Life Course Structure). I began the infertility study after spending several years addressing my own infertility. It was the first time I had chosen a topic I was directly and personally involved with. The study, conducted with Robert Nachtigall, explored, first, how the discovery of infertility disrupts cultural expectations about the structure of life and, second, how men and women differ in their responses to unwanted childlessness.

After conducting a pilot study with 36 couples[57] we carried out a larger study with 134 couples and 9 women without their partners who were either undergoing medical treatment at the time of the first interview or had completed medical treatment during the preceding three years. The majority had undergone medical treatment for three or more years, although 20 persons had undergone medical treatment for a year or less. These women and men were recruited from medical practices, adoption counseling services, low-income clinics, and a self-help group and by others already in the study.[58]

2.   *The Midlife Study* (Midlife Disruption and Change). I began the midlife study at the conclusion of the pilot study on infertility because I wanted to understand the meanings associated with other disruptions in midlife. In the end, the infertility study turned out to be not just about infertility. The disruption of infertility triggers women's and men's rethinking not only of all the disruptions they had experienced in their lives but also of other disruptions that occurred during the course of the study, for example, deaths of family members, sudden job loss, and the onset of illness. I wanted to know whether disruption from infertility differed significantly from other kinds of disruptions for people in the same age group. I therefore explored the impact of a variety of disruptive events on the lives of twenty women and men between the ages of thirty-five and sixty-five. This research was shaped to some extent by issues that are common at this time of life. I recognized from studying infertility that disruption can be a catalyst for change. I wanted to understand how men and women interpreted changes, what

provoked them to change, what followed change, and how these changes affected their identity. These men and women were interviewed once or twice in great depth about disruptive events they had experienced, their interpretations of these events, and the impact these events had on their lives.

3.   *The Stroke Study* (Sociocultural Mechanisms of Rehabilitation in Old Age; Chronicity and Life Reorganization after a Stroke). The first of three studies of chronic illness in later life, the stroke study, which I conducted with Sharon Kaufman, explored the ways in which elderly persons' lives were altered by the abrupt onset of a chronic, disabling illness, namely, a stroke. This two-part study included (1) patterns of rehabilitation, which focused on acute care, rehabilitation, and the transition to home or institution after a stroke (102 persons over the age of forty-five), and (2) patterns of life course reorganization, which focused specifically on people who returned home after rehabilitation (115 persons over the age of fifty). Our total sample for the two studies was 214 persons, of whom 100 were interviewed three times over the course of a year. In the first study, respondents were recruited while they were inpatients in an acute care hospital; in the second study, they were recruited from the hospital's home care services after discharge from the hospital.

This was the only study in which respondents were not always able to tell a fully elaborated story. The serious medical problems that brought them into the study interfered with their ability to participate in interviews. Their symptoms included weakness and partial paralysis, memory losses, problems in comprehension, organic and reactive depression, uncontrollable emotions, speech impairment, disorientation or confusion, impaired judgment, and chronic fatigue or weakness. Despite the limitations these deficits imposed on their ability to communicate, people who had had a stroke struggled to share their experiences with us.

4.   *The Late-Life Transitions Study* (From Independence to Dependence among the Oldest Old). A second component of the ethnography of chronic illness in later life, the late-life transitions study, also

conducted with Sharon Kaufman, explored the transition from independence to dependence following physical impairment of loss of health among persons age eighty and older. After years of research on aging, I continued to have unanswered questions about older people's health transitions. What factors precipitated these transitions? Why did some lives seem to completely unravel, even after a precarious balance had been maintained, sometimes for years? Why did health transitions so often result in lessened independence? Why was there frequently such a wide disparity between elders' views of their impairments and autonomy and health professionals' views of those same impairments? [59]

This study had two distinct parts. In my portion of the study, forty-four people were interviewed two or more times. They were selected—from health clinics serving older people and from other health-care institutions—because they were undergoing a transition that affected their independence or were viewed as being vulnerable to such a transition. The interviews focused on everyday life, with an emphasis on perceptions of life disruptions, major as well as minor. Most often, the disruptions were linked to decreased physical function. For example, changes in physical function sometimes resulted in forced moves, which precipitated a disruptive transition, although the majority of persons lived at home at the time of the first interview.

5. *The Ethnic Minorities Study* (Cultural Responses to Illness in the Minority Aged). The ongoing ethnic minorities study, with Yewoubdar Beyene, Edwina Newsom, and Denise Rodgers, examines cultural responses to illness of 240 women and men age fifty and older. It draws on several ethnic minority groups (African Americans, Latinos,[60] Filipino Americans, and Cambodian Americans). I include only data from the first twenty-four African Americans because these data had just begun to be collected at the time I was writing this book. The research focuses on the onset or worsening of chronic illness and on people's views of their illness and its effects on their daily lives. We recruit the persons in this study from home care services, from health clinics for low-income people, and

from community contacts. We interview the participants in-depth three times at six-month intervals about their experience of illness, their religious beliefs, their health practices, their identity, their family relationships, and their access to health care. Most have multiple chronic illnesses that interfere with daily life. Incomes vary for the people in this study, but most live at or just above the poverty line. Recent changes in the health-care system, as well as changes in social services and health-care coverage for low-income populations, pose a particular problem for the people in this research, who have few economic resources and many health problems.

The five studies share several methodological commonalities: (1) they are all based primarily on in-depth interviewing, (2) they are all longitudinal with at least six months elapsing between interviews, and (3) the data from all the studies were analyzed qualitatively by means of one basic process.

As different as their ostensible topics are, these studies share a common conceptual focus: the disruption of personal meaning and the consequent destruction of a sense of continuity. Taken together, they encompass an array of age groups, health problems, classes, and ethnicities. Using examples from all the studies makes it possible to consider a range of concerns.

These samples represent different age groups.[61] For example, the age range in the infertility study was twenty-eight to seventy-one with a mean age of thirty-eight, and the age range in the stroke study was forty-eight to one hundred five with a mean age of seventy-two. Not only were the daily concerns of persons in these samples different, but, depending on the nature of the disruption, their lives were informed by historical differences and by social, cultural, and economic changes. For example, most respondents in the stroke study were born before the Great Depression. All had lived through World War II, and some had been born before World War I. Some were refugees from Eastern Europe, while others were the children, grandchildren, or great-grandchildren of slaves or immigrants. Those born in the United States were often from rural areas.

The work ethic and an ethos of "rugged individualism" characterized the values of this sample, which was primarily working class and lower middle class. Most had no formal education beyond some high school.

In contrast, most of those in the infertility study were born after World War II. The economy was robust during their formative years, and the wars fought during that time had different social impacts. These people often came from families with ethnic and class characteristics similar to those in the stroke study, but the majority of respondents in the infertility study were middle class and affluent, predominantly college educated, and employed in white-collar and professional jobs. Although the work ethic, autonomy, goals for the future, and control over the environment were also valued by the people in this group, they were valued differently. Thus there were considerable variations, for example, in ideas about the use of the health-care system, about the role of women, and about the place of work in everyday life.

While people's responses to disruption varied by age, ethnicity, gender, class, and health, there were similarities in how discontinuities and efforts to create continuity were portrayed metaphorically. These similarities suggest that the narrator's experiences elicited cultural meanings of a highly specific nature. That the responses have in common the use of similar metaphors to make sense of disruption, limbo, and efforts to create continuity suggests that core constructs in U.S. life persist despite generational change. This multifaceted approach to change and continuity, initiated by respondents and developed in their narratives, suggests that continuity is embedded in the cultural ethos of North American society.

Educational background and socioeconomic status often affected the selection of specific metaphors: for example, upper-middle-class women and men often used science metaphors. However, lower socioeconomic status did not preclude the use of metaphor or the ability to be articulate. Indeed, some of the most articulate narrators in this book have modest educational backgrounds.[62]

I selected narratives for this book on the basis of several criteria. (See the appendix for more details of the selection process.) First, I tried to select narratives to reflect diversity, to demonstrate a range of experience across gender, age, ethnicity, education, and class background. To some extent my ability to do so has been limited by the nature of the studies; for example, four-fifths of the persons in the infertility study were white/non-Latino and middle class, and from the ethnic minorities study I have drawn on data collected with African Americans only. Second, I tried to select cases that reflected frequently mentioned topics such as the process of trying to recover from an illness. For example, people invariably talked about disruption to their lives and feelings of being in limbo. In all cases, I chose narratives in which the general content, if not the particulars, was representative of the data as a whole.

The people whose voices are heard in this book are all struggling to make sense of their lives after a disruption. The disruptions conflict with their assumptions about the world. These people are questioning and trying to make peace with particular cultural ideas. Although culture is an abstraction, it becomes much more concrete when people experience disruption; they may "see" culture as they identify those cultural norms that pose problems for them. As they step outside themselves and try to look dispassionately at the cultural norms that cause them distress, they become anthropologists. They raise questions about what is meaningful. This book may therefore be seen as a collection of people's dialogues with culture and its constructs through both body and narrative.

2 Narratives as Cultural Documents

In this book, narrative is the primary path for examining disruption and continuity.[1] I have chosen this path because I want to record the profound nature of life disruptions in people's own voices. Narratives, the stories that people tell about themselves, reflect people's experience, as they see it and as they wish to have others see it. Some have suggested that narratives are a way to articulate and resolve core, universal problems and a way to avoid or heal biographical discontinuities. Through stories people organize, display, and work through their experiences.[2] Narrative can be a potent force in mediating disruption, whether the disruption is caused by illness or personal misfortune.[3] As I suggested in chapter 1, narratives are performative and, thus, empowering. They represent action and, thus, agency.[4] Experience is reshaped in the narrative process, and narratives are subject to change with subsequent experiences. As an analytic tool, narrative enables us to understand how coherence is created and maintained over time.[5] Viewed as the practice of everyday life, narratives can provide us with important insights about people's experiences and their perspectives on them.[6]

Narrative is a means for giving voice to bodily experience, to embodied despair. While I rely considerably on text in this book, I try to demonstrate the deep connection between embodied experience and its enactment through narrative. Although narrative is not necessarily primary in many cultures where other senses are very powerful,[7] narrative does enact the experience of disruption in U.S. society. Indeed, I would argue that in the United States, where sensation and bodily expression are undervalued, narrative is our primary means of accessing the world of bodily experience and is essential to our understanding of that experience.

In order to make full use of narrative as a tool in understanding culture, we must develop ways of linking narrative to culture so that both individual and culture-level phenomena are captured.[8] Narratives of disruption, especially those that unfold in repeated interviews over time, capture the temporal and phenomenological dimensions of disruption in the cultural life course. As noted in chapter 1, the very notion of a life course is cultural in nature and represents a powerful collective symbol. Yet Western thought has been concerned with development throughout life as an individual process rather than one that is culturally shaped. By examining an interrelated set of topics that emerge in personal accounts of disruption, one can identify the cultural contents of those accounts and see how they reflect broadly construed cultural concerns.

The narrative process enables the narrator to develop creative ways of interpreting disruption and to draw together disparate aspects of the disruption into a cohesive whole. Narrative is a way of expressing development over time.[9] Paul Ricoeur notes that the corpus of our individual histories is brought together by a work of imagination that, in articulating the various points of connection, transforms it into a coherent story. He maintains that in the midst of experience it is not possible to know the meaning of one's actions—that only with time do certain aspects of what is meaningful emerge.[10]

As mentioned in chapter 1, narratives carry the moral authority of the narrator; stories are not ideologically neutral.[11] For example, Keith Basso finds that the landscape is an omnipresent moral force in Apache stories, and Hayden White, a historian, has portrayed one of the functions of narrative as providing conclusive endings that contain moralizing messages. Moral authority is not an absolute, however. Narratives can have contradictory and multiple interpretations.[12]

Specific elements of narrative theory are central to the analysis of narratives of disruption. The stories all have a common plot: a disruption to life is followed by efforts to restore life to normal. Plot forms give stories coherence and order. Events are defined not in terms of their singularity but in terms of the contribution they make to the unfolding of the story or history in question; that is, they contribute to the development of a plot and a story line. Plot has the capacity to model our experience.[13]

Plot provides the underlying structure of a story; emplotment is the process that draws a configuration out of a simple succession. Emplotment brings together heterogeneous factors such as agents, goals, means, interactions, and unexpected results and renders the story's contents intelligible.[14] Emplotment can be viewed as a crucial imaginative task of people who face sudden illness.[15] Emplotment can readily be seen in the narratives of disruption in this book, where it is used as a tool to mediate disruption and promote self-healing. Emplotment is thus rendered political by the fact that people choose how to plot their narratives.[16]

Conceptions of time are cultural. How people emplot their stories can therefore inform our understanding of cultural notions of time. Edward Bruner suggests that "Life consists of retellings," thereby calling attention to the importance of time and process in narrative.[17] Emplotment is the process that unifies the chronological with the nonchronological: "reading the end in the beginning and the beginning in the end, we also learn to read time itself backward."[18] This conception of narrative time draws on Heidegger's notion of being-in-time (or within-timeness) and is not reducible to the portrayal of linear time.[19] A biography tends to reorder the significance of a life, reading that life backward and using past events as explanations for the current state of affairs.[20]

The narratives of disruption in this book are embedded in lengthy interviews, but interestingly, they have been lifted out of the interviews intact most of the time. That is, these stories of disruption form stories within stories and illustrate the active component of emplotment in reshaping events and memories. These emplotted narratives address the ways in which disruption is portrayed, the changes women and men undergo in response to disruption, and the ways in which disruption is reframed over time.

The stories in this book all have a beginning, a middle, and an end, although in many cases the imagined or hoped-for end is not yet in sight. That is, many of these stories do not have an end that is satisfactory to the storyteller. Sometimes the storyteller presents several possible scenarios from which he or she is attempting to engineer the desired end. This phenomenon is referred to as the subjunctivizing element in narratives, which engages in human possibilities rather than in certainties. Stories have subjunctivizing elements when narrators are in the midst of the stories they are telling.[21]

Many stories are partial, and people have their reasons for not telling everything there is to tell. This selectiveness does not invalidate what they do tell, however. I assume my interviewees have edited their stories as I have edited mine, to lend their stories a greater coherence and a sense of wholeness, which, in turn, lends one a greater sense of self-consistency. I believe the editing process is itself cultural in nature, so that the narrative as it is presented is, at once, a personal and cultural account of disruption. I am otherwise at a loss to explain why, in collecting hundreds of narratives of disruption, I have observed the same topics emerge over and over again. These topics are central to U.S. society.

Narratives analyzed in this book come from previous studies undertaken with different goals. I reexamine them here with a focus on the experience of disruption. In revisiting these narratives I did not search for themes, but they often emerged when I examined stories to see what people viewed as meaningful in their lives. In analyzing data, I emphasized the story level of a given narrative. I do not consider my analysis to be a thematic one in the usual sense.[22]

In the chapters that follow, themes will emerge from the narratives, and some of these themes will surface again and again. The thematic portrayal of experience is apparently highly selective and is subject to change depending on the context and the temporal nature of experience. I view the selective portrayal of themes as part of the overall task of emplotment in categorizing and structuring experience in both the short and long term. Some themes may remain dominant. Others recede into the background only to reemerge in the foreground with the advent of new experiences, such as a disruption to life.[23]

Themes can be viewed as cultural resources that people draw on to make sense of their experience. However, the cultural resources people draw on change with time and circumstance; that is, in subsequent interviews people may take up different topics that reflect more recent experiences. "No interpretation can be final, as all are contrived in view of the various potentialities inherent in a life while it is being lived."[24] Themes that represent what is meaningful must therefore be regarded as fluid and, sometimes, as transitory.

Although phenomenological approaches are by no means new to anthropology, there has been a growing emphasis on bodily distress.[25] Scrutinizing narratives for clues to that distress has been a goal of my research, and I carried those techniques into this work and embellished on them. I studied all references to the body and bodily distress, and I examined all reports of health problems or medical interventions, as well as all expressions of intense emotion, for their relationship to bodily concerns. I also scrutinized narratives for linkages between expressions of embodied distress and discussions of cultural expectations. I followed the same analytic strategy for each of the studies described in chapter 1. (See the appendix for more details of the process of data analysis.)

EMBODIMENT IN NARRATIVE

When people experience illnesses and health conditions requiring considerable medical intervention, they monitor and discuss their bodies. How they talk about their bodies tells us much about the nature of embodiment and about how gender, age, and ethnicity influence the way they experience embodiment. How they talk also tells us much about the *portrayal* of bodily experience; that is, the connection between how people talk about their bodies and how they experience them. Bodily experience and bodily concerns are deeply embedded in the various elements of narrative, such as time, plot, emplotment, subjunctivity, themes, and coherence. In the example that follows, all of these elements in the narrative revolve around the body as it is experienced.

The story of Nadine, whom I interviewed for the infertility study, illustrates a theme that will be echoed repeatedly in this book: when disruption occurs, the temporary or permanent destruction of people's sense of "fit" with society calls into question their personhood, their sense of identity, and their sense of normalcy. Nadine's effort to achieve this sense of normalcy is an enduring focus of her narrative. In addition, her story epitomizes the moral authority embedded in the narratives in this book. As we will see, the moral force of normalizing ideologies deeply affects Nadine's struggles to attain a sense of normalcy.

Nadine is a forty-two-year-old, single, Anglo woman who is trying to have a child. She works as a clerk and lives in an apartment near her workplace. Unlike most of the people I interviewed in the infertility study, for whom the difficulty of having a child came as a surprise, Nadine was not surprised by her infertility. She has ovarian dysfunction, a chronic condition that has affected her since puberty. This condition overshadows her gender identity, her sexuality, her reproductive potential, and her life plans. For many years, most of her energy and income have been given to dealing with this problem. She lives an isolated existence, as her condition has inhibited her friendships with both women and men.

Nadine's one pregnancy, achieved through donor insemination, ended in a miscarriage. Nevertheless, her pregnancy was the high point of her life: it made her feel normal.

> I think that being pregnant was about the best experience that's ever happened to me. Very fulfilling, very rewarding. Outside of those complications, and I did have a few serious ones that caused me a lot of pain and suffering and were really hard to live with. But the joy and the psychological feelings overshadowed all the negative things. I was just so happy. I mean, I just had that glow on my face. And I made friends with people at work that I hardly ever talked to before. Because they had kids

and they'd come up and say, "Well, when I was this way, I would do this and that." And you kind of form a bond with other people. Not that you would be friends with them. It's as if you had that one thing in common. Your child. And women who didn't talk too much at all would come up and . . . not give me advice but discuss things with me. Like, "Are you taking vitamins?" and things like that or give me some of their stories. And it was very nice. You feel normal you're having kids. You just feel normal. And I felt normal. I hadn't felt that way about myself before. I felt normal for the first time in my life.

I interjected, "In your whole life?"

Well, yeah. Pretty much my whole life. Because I knew when I was about thirteen or fourteen, somewhere along then, fifteen, see, I had problems even going back then. I was late in starting my cycle, my period, and then when it started, it was irregular and I didn't get medical care and when I did, the doctor didn't know. I went to a regular ob-gyn. And he just said, "Well it takes time for your system to adjust and by the time you're twenty-one, everything will be okay." And of course it wasn't. And I knew then, when I was in my teens—I knew when I was in the tenth grade, age fifteen to sixteen, that my cycles were different from my friends and from all the other girls. I knew mine was irregular, and I knew that wasn't right. And so I knew there was something wrong with me, and it made me feel very abnormal, even at that point in time.

In this narrative we see the interplay of two facets of normalcy: normalcy as an existential state and as part of the cultural discourse on womanhood. At the core of Nadine's story is the question of what constitutes "normal" for a woman. The cultural ideal of the normal woman emerges as Nadine examines the various facets of the cultural discourse on womanhood and attempts to reconcile her own experience with that discourse. The disparity between her experience and the cultural discourse has seriously affected her gender identity.

Normalcy is defined differently by different social groups. Nadine first felt a sense of abnormality when she identified herself as different from her teenage peers because her menstrual cycles were irregular. Nadine's view of herself as abnormal evolved throughout her years as a teenager, and deeply troubling symptoms further undermined her sense of normalcy.

I knew my cycle wasn't up to par with the other girls'. Because girls talk. You know? You went through that in school. In every other way I developed normally, but not enough. I knew there was something wrong. And then I think I started late because back then the girls will take the one that starts early is doing the best, type of thing. It's a contest. Really, there's a lot of peer pressure on you, and your status, as a woman, is kind of tied into that. To a degree. And I started a little bit later than most did. I think I would have felt all right about myself if my cycles had been regular. And normal. And when they weren't, that really messed me up. It really messed me up good.

And that's even before I knew I had polycystic ovaries. That's before I had all the hirsutism [male-pattern hair growth] and the acne and all the other stuff; before the weight gain and the oily scalp.

Nadine attests to the power of the peer group in this statement. Her status as a woman depends on her successful navigation of this ritual along with her peers. It is cultural rite of passage for the initiation into womanhood around the world, and there is competition involved. Her inability to participate fully in this ritual is compounded by the many other symptoms that appeared over time, symptoms that affected her physical appearance, undermined her sense of attractiveness, and further triggered her sense of disruption.

And then when all this hirsutism came up, I just didn't know what was happening to me. That was the summer between my sophomore-junior year, so I was sixteen. I started to grow hair on my face. Right here [pointing to her face] and on the side. Mostly on the right side. It was more predominant on the right side, and I think that's because—I think the cyst is larger on the right ovary than on the left. At least that's the way I understand it. Because there's a considerable, heavier growth of hair on the right side than the left. And then, also at the same time, well, I always had the acne. Teenagers have acne but I had a lot of it. Like on my neck and on my back. Then I had my first case of insomnia, my first bout with that when I was only seventeen. Within a month or two after this. I woke up in the middle of the night, between three and four, and I just couldn't go back to sleep. And I don't know how I got to school the next day. I just don't. And then I was okay after that, but then my sleeping was always rather shallow. And then, finally I found out about the sleep disorder. I was in my thirties when I found out about it. A long time later.

With the development of male characteristics, Nadine's efforts to fit the cultural model of the normal woman seemed hopeless. The symptoms that Nadine experienced are manifestations of embodied distress. Although she tries to be matter-of-fact, she acknowledges that something is very wrong: in some ways she is like a man, the wrong gender. Her health problems have underscored her sense of abnormality by striking at every aspect of her life, from her identity as a woman to her ability to get a good night's sleep. The plot continues to revolve around her body, as her symptoms become more unmanageable over time. Although the assignment of her symptoms to a specific medical condition, hirsutism, legitimized them, it also reinforced her sense of difference from other women.

From Nadine's perspective, her pregnancy symbolizes normalcy, it represents natural order. It is what women "do," what gives them a common ground. However, pregnancy was an almost unattainable goal for Nadine. The pregnancy she eventually did conceive, even though it was short-lived, made her feel like everyone else; it was the "proof" that she was a normal woman.

> I was four and a half months pregnant when I had the miscarriage. My bubble burst. It went right down the toilet, literally. Because I got up in the middle of the night to go to the bathroom and my mucus plug came out and I saw it and I didn't know what it was. And I was going to pick it up and take it into my doctor's office because I didn't know what it was. Before I could do anything, my whole water came out of my bag. All the amniotic fluid just went down the toilet. Because you can't stop it. And I tried to stop it and I couldn't stop it. And I thought I was going to have a miscarriage then. And I was just devastated by it.
>
> He [her physician] told me the prognosis, and I was just devastated. At four and a half months, my umbilical cord fell out of me, and I went to the emergency room and they said she was dead. I wouldn't wish it on anyone. It was a horrible experience. But I'm really happy I had her because I got to know her for four and a half months. And that's very important to me. That was the most precious time of my life and I cherish them. I have the ultrasound pictures of the footprints and everything, you know. That's very important to me.

As Nadine tells the story of this loss, it becomes clear that much more has been lost than the fetus. Motherhood itself, which would have proven her to be a normal woman, has been lost, possibly forever. In the absence of the child, however, the ultrasound pictures of footprints become proof that she is a normal woman.

> I went through a lot of hell but sometimes when I think how bad it is and how sorry I feel for myself, I say, "I'm bad, but I'm not as bad as that woman who's out there, infertile, and has never been able to conceive." I'm one step above her because I know something and have had something that she has never had. I'm very thankful for that. And that kind of gets me out of my pity pot!
>
> I'm really thankful because I deal not only with infertility but I also deal with this loss. And most women, you get one or the other. But you don't get both thrown at you. But on the other hand, I'm luckier than those women. It's just literally tearing them apart.
>
> I was just lucky that I got that experience for four and a half months, you know. I'm forever thankful. It gives me a lot of peace of mind and a lot of serenity just to have had that. Because I was halfway to term. You know, I got halfway there. And some people don't get anywhere. It could have been worse. It could have been worse.

Nadine draws attention to the many aspects of this experience that give her life meaning. Through her pregnancy she metaphorically claimed womanhood. Life was created from her body. For Nadine, as for many women who have miscarried, the fetus was a child she came to know during the pregnancy. New technologies facilitate the creation of this emotional connection with the fetus: ultrasound provides pictures of the fetus, complete with footprints, and allows gender identification. Nadine engages the question of when life begins when she views herself as a woman whose child died rather than as a woman who miscarried a fetus.

Nadine's efforts to take charge of this long series of disasters and view her experience in a new light reflect emplotment. She emplots her bodily experience, reframes it, so that she can see and experience her body as a mother's body, as a woman's body. Emplotment can be seen as a form of therapeutic work.[26] It helps her to heal this profound disruption and place it in perspective in her life.

Nadine's story also includes subjunctivizing elements. In spite of the odds against her, she has not stopped trying to have children. For her, the end of this story remains in doubt, and this fact influences her view of the current situation. She is thankful for the experience, distressing though it was, and in spite of her deep sense of loss, she feels lucky when she compares herself with other women. Her four and a half months of pregnancy give her peace of mind and serenity because she has proved to herself not only that she is like other women but also that she has embodied normalcy. She *lived* normalcy for four months, through every physical and emotional nuance of her pregnancy.

Although the outcome of this ordeal was tragic, Nadine has been able to find meaning in it that gives her a sense of normalcy. However, she has not been completely successful in her efforts to become a different person—a woman with a child. In addition, she still must rely on cosmetic solutions to cover up her hirsutism: depilatories and artful haircuts hide the effects of the illness she feels so deeply. She continues to try to bolster her gender identity after a lifetime of assault. Being a mother for four and a half months negates, to some extent, her lifelong feelings of abnormality. Nevertheless, her pregnancy is still only a memory, albeit a cherished one.

Nadine's unfolding narrative has been shaped by biomedical discourses on normalcy. This process has occurred in two stages. In the first stage, the diagnosis of hirsutism, and the gradual tying together of the signs and symptoms that were part of this medical complex, reinforced her sense of difference from others, but it also gave her an explanation for why she felt different from others. It is impossible to tell whether the biomedical diagnosis made her assessment of her situation worse, but the diagnosis does appear to have made concrete something that was previously indeterminate. In the second stage, biomedicine helped Nadine to pursue a goal, pregnancy and motherhood, that, in her view, would enable her to return to normal. Biomedical discourse affirmed her conviction that becoming pregnant is what "normal" woman do. Although it ended in miscarriage, the pregnancy she achieved with the help of biomedicine did make her feel normal again, thus partially undoing the negative effects of her previous encounter with biomedicine.

As we have seen, Nadine's story also has been shaped by the societal discourse on womanhood to which she has responded by trying to become a mother. Moreover, her decision to attempt to become a mother can be seen as a political one, one that has social consequences regardless of the outcome. Nadine makes this decision even though she is a single woman with limited resources because she believes that motherhood will put her on a par with other women. She believes that motherhood will facilitate her entry into the social group, that it will put an end to her long-term sense of social isolation, and that it will resolve the moral dilemma posed by her ambiguous status as a woman.

3 Order and Chaos

It's like a bad dream. I keep thinking I will wake up

from it and everything will be all right. But I never do.

seventy-five-year-old woman,
after a stroke

When their health is suddenly disrupted, people are thrown into chaos. Illness challenges one's knowledge of one's body. It defies orderliness. People experience the time before their illness and its aftermath as two separate realities. This perception of a dual reality—of the known world (the recent past) and the "bad dream" (the present)—constitutes chaos. Living a nightmare that never ends raises the question, What is real?

Cultural notions of order provide anthropologists with many clues to the workings and worldview of a given society. Order is at the foundation of structures of meaning in human life, and it permeates social life.[1] Notions of order are culturally organized; that is, people not only have clear ideas about what constitutes order in a wide variety of contexts, but they also create order in specific ways. In Western societies, three is a culturally significant number. A range of examples attests to this culturally informed organization: the Holy Trinity in Catholicism, plays in

three acts, rituals in three parts. Narrative structure also reflects this tri-
partite structure, which is often echoed in stories of disruption. People
expect stories to have a beginning, a middle, and an end; and, in the
telling, stories, even when incomplete, anticipate subsequent phases.
People expect the event that precipitated a sense of chaos to be followed
by a gradual resumption of normalcy. Normalcy may be preceded by a
third state, a liminal or limbo-like state, which is informed by the hope
of eventual resolution of the problem and a return to normalcy. Thus,
there are similarities between the disruption process and the structure of
narrative.[2]

Their organization of the world along such cultural lines enables
people to believe that order prevails. When a sense of order has been lost,
following their particular cultural template of order enables people to
believe that order will be regained. As we have already seen, the narratives in this book are organized around the view of order that is characteristic of Western culture.

All the stories in this chapter address issues of life and death. Death is
the ultimate disruption; and, thus, the moral force of normalizing ideologies in any society surrounds death especially. The strength of these ideologies is apparent not only in rituals surrounding death itself but also
in the interactions people facing death have with others. The narrators in
this chapter speak with the moral authority of those who must meet
head-on the imminent possibility of their own death. They speak plaintively, with uncertainty as well as with authority, to the moral dilemmas
illness presents for them. They express, sometimes emotionally, their
sense of loss and describe actions taken in response to their illness experiences. In all cases they emplot their stories to highlight the moral authority of their narratives, and their doing so reveals the cultural foundations of narrative and metaphor with respect to views in the United
States of the body, health, illness, death, and dying.

FACING CHAOS

The onset of a chronic health condition disorders a person's knowledge
and experience of the body, thereby disrupting not only a sense of the

integrity of the body but also understandings of specific body parts and systems.[3] Suffering arises not only from the experience of bodily disruption but also from the difficulty of articulating that disruption.[4] There is a temporal dimension to illness that affects people's responses to their bodily changes. Both past experiences—including illnesses, life transitions, and other major events—and expectations for the future inform current experiences of health and illness. People experience illness and impairment from a perspective determined by their historically situated and contextually informed bodies.

According to Laurence Kirmayer, two orders are affected by people's experience of illness—the order of the body and the order of the text, or narrative.[5] Inescapable circularity exists between the two: expectations about the order of the body are expressed in the order of the text. When this circular process is interrupted, that is, when people are unable to reconcile disorder of the body by creating order in their narratives, intolerable dissonance is created. The cultural ordering of meaning and narrative apparently emerges out of this circular and, as we will see, complicated process.

An illness is a major disruption to one's biography.[6] When the body is assaulted by a serious illness, one's sense of wholeness, on which a sense of order rides, disintegrates. One must reconstitute that sense of wholeness in order to regain a sense of continuity. The experiential calamity caused by such a disruption is illustrated by the story of Kirk, an Anglo businessman who participated in the infertility study. I had arrived at his apartment expecting to interview him about the infertility treatment he and his wife had undertaken. Instead, I listened as he talked about a sudden and recent threat to his health and well-being, the possibility of cancer of the kidney.[7] Two hours later, as he walked me to the door, he apologized for what he perceived as his incoherence in telling me the story of this sudden illness.

> I hope I've been reasonably coherent tonight. It doesn't feel coherent inside my brain. If I am being articulate and clear, it seems like an artifact as opposed to a reflection of how it really feels inside. It's such a odd thing because there are times when I feel so profoundly present. You know, more so than I've ever been. And other times I just fly away.

If an illness comes on or is discovered suddenly, people's sense of continuity may completely unravel. Illness necessitates the surrender of the cherished assumption of personal indestructibility.[8] Kirk, at forty years old, has always been healthy. He articulates his sense of chaos brought on by this assault to his body as he knows it.

> We've been having a really rough time . . . with *my* health, unfortunately. I passed my kidney stone, but they took some X-rays and discovered a little mass in my kidney that they're worried about. It looks like I'm probably going to have surgery on it, and probably have the kidney removed. And it may be cancer, so . . . it's been hellacious.

Kirk had been going on with everyday life when he was suddenly plunged into uncertainty about his health and life itself. He depicts living with the threat of cancer as like being in hell. The likelihood of a diagnosis of cancer was increased in his mind when he had to undergo painful diagnostic medical procedures.

> They did a CT scan, and that revealed some things they didn't like. Some things that were slightly cancerlike. So we started seeking second opinions. My doctor was still hoping to save the kidney. So we did a needle aspiration of the kidneys, which was horribly painful. He [physician] just called me today with the result, which was although they didn't find cancer, they found . . . something conducive to growth in this cyst, something that was worrisome. He said he would probably be recommending surgery. And he said, "Don't be alarmed." But the longer we wait, if it is cancer, the more likely it is that it might spread. One doctor says, "During surgery, if they did the biopsy, there's a chance of the cancer spreading, and why take that chance as you will be perfectly fine with one kidney?"
>
> One of the questions I will ask the doctors is, "What will life be like [with only one kidney]?" Some people are apparently born with one kidney. Many others lose a kidney during the course of their life and live on. So it looks like I'm going to be joining that rank. That's always worrisome. You know, you always feel like if you got two of anything, you were meant to have two of that something and not reduce it. But, at the same time, cancer is such a scary word.

Kirk juxtaposes his emotional pain and the disruption to his embodied knowledge of himself against the rational decision-making process invoked by his physicians. His sense of vulnerability is further affected by having his nose broken in a soccer match in the midst of this experience. He shifts back and forth between discussing his fears and reporting on the ins and outs of medical diagnostics and his efforts to understand them. Moreover, Kirk attempts to integrate medical thinking—that he will be fine with one kidney—with the potential loss of a body part.

In addressing the possible loss of his kidney, Kirk addresses the natural order of the body. He adds a rationale for tampering with this natural order, however, when he acknowledges the metaphoric connection between cancer and death. Kirk identifies the crux of the matter when he says,

> I've been in a lot of emotional turmoil. The broken nose—that was painful. I'm usually incredibly healthy. It was sort of like, "I'm paying my dues now." And then this came up, which seems excessive to me. It seems unfair. The extra worry of possibly having cancer. I think I've had a lifelong denial of my mortality, and I've always assumed that I was just going to go on and on and on. I never contemplated my death—how it might affect me and how I look on my life. This has been a major dose of reality that I have really thought about . . . that you can die anytime. And that's been the terrifying part.

The idea that "you can die anytime" is at the center of this disruption; it has dislodged, perhaps for all time, Kirk's sense of complacency about living a long life.

> Two weeks ago I was shattered. He [the physician] called me up and told me he didn't like the results of the last CT scan, that he was worried about it. I was still denying that there was anything to worry about it. It wasn't until we actually met with the doctor, that was . . . unfortunately, that was the day that they rebroke my nose, so it was a hard day. It was all happening at the same time. And that's when it really came home— you know, what I was facing and that I might die. . . . This life of mine, which I was expecting to live until I was eighty or ninety at the least, may end sooner. That was terrifying.

The threat of cancer remains somewhat remote because of the intangibility of the diagnostic tests; it is the coincidental broken nose, painful and highly visible, that Kirk uses as a symbol for unpredictable disorder.

The added insult of the broken nose compounds the emotional turmoil caused by his confrontation with his own mortality and drives this new emotional reality home. He is in constant discomfort, and his exercise schedule, an intrinsic part of his everyday life, has been completely curtailed. As a result, he is continuously reminded that his life has changed. But the injury to his nose becomes less significant as he describes his fear of the surgery that lies ahead.

> Now I'm getting afraid of the surgery. I have a pretty good tolerance of pain. I know I'm healthy and fit. But it's very major surgery.

Trying to deal with the sudden onslaught of so many health problems, Kirk tries to exert control over the situation.

> I was really depressed and feeling bad about my nose, that it hurt, and I just sort of tried to get used to this new fear that I was facing. So I started calling doctors and making appointments and trying to learn what I could about this, and that made me feel better, you know, like I had some control.

In trying to exert some control over his health problems, Kirk attempts to reengage with cultural expectations of order. Control over the environment is a key value in the United States.[9] Ironically, acquiring biomedical information may undermine efforts to regain control because such information is often presented in terms of probability and metaphors of gambling.

> So I started feeling more up. And then we started getting better from a 40 percent of it being cancer. The other doctors were placing it at a lower percentage, you know, from 10 to 20 percent to 5 to 15 percent, and that all sounded better. And talking to our doctor, he said it was more like 10 to 20, although that's not what we heard the first day with him, which was people with a cyst like mine have about a 40 percent chance of cancer, and that makes it sound sort of like 50/50. You flip a coin, well, now you have it, and that sounded horrible. So things started to sound better to us. Things sounded more hopeful. More like we probably didn't have cancer. So things were getting better until today, when he called to say they found some cells that weren't good, but not cancer. It could be an infection, but it sounded like it was most likely cancer.

Kirk's recitation of "the odds" illustrate how ineffective biomedical information is at providing control to patients. In fact, he find this welter of conflicting conjectures so frightening that he adopts the plural pronoun, subliminally drawing his wife into sharing his diagnosis.

One of Kirk's underlying fears is that the surgery and all this worry may be for nothing, that the doctors will find that nothing is wrong.

> Now I am faced with what is almost a certainty, which is surgery, and making a decision about keeping the kidney or not. Let's just remove it [the kidney], and if they find that it doesn't have cancer, I mean, I really hope that they can use it as a donor organ. And then I'll feel better about this. But it scares the heebie-jeebies out of me. I feel like if my kidney can make another person live better, that will feel a little better.

He tries to reconcile the possibly needless removal of his kidney by thinking of it as a donor organ. His doing so reflects his effort to lend some order to this situation.

As he deals with these issues, Kirk struggles to keep his perspective.

> So here we are trying to get pregnant. When this first . . . the cancer, the kidney cancer—when it first came out—one of the really touching parts was that Jill really wanted to try to still have my child and that felt so warm and wonderful. That if I was to die, it was important to her to have a part of me around. But we sort of tabled that, you know? I sort of talked her out of it.

When Kirk experiments with saying "the kidney cancer," he is trying the words on, placing them in the context of what came first: trying to conceive. This crisis has forced Kirk to examine issues of life and death not just for himself but also for his loved ones. It raises questions of generation and regeneration of the self, questions which he has not yet resolved. The possibility of extending himself through another person beyond his death is a form of continuity. He puts the infertility he and his wife have experienced into perspective.

> But this whole thing makes infertility seem trivial. And it's funny. But it really puts infertility in a whole different light. When you're facing a life and death sort of question.

Several months later I went back to see him, feeling remorse that I had not checked up on his health. When I asked about his health, both he and his wife looked nonplussed, and he responded,

> Oh that! They decided it was nothing to worry about. They're not even planning check-ups. We're going on with our lives.

One year later he reported he was trying to reconcile living with long-term uncertainty.

> They can't tell me if it will ever turn into anything.

In undergoing this biomedically induced rehearsal for death, Kirk was thrust into chaos, and he spent an extended period confronting life and death issues. He experienced a series of reactions typical for a person given a life-threatening diagnosis, beginning with a newly found awareness of his body. He describes undergoing a sudden shift in perception, from taking his body for granted, to becoming self-consciously aware of having a body, a fallible one. He refers to the breaking apart of embodied knowledge of himself as whole, healthy. In many statements, Kirk demonstrates the great extent to which embodied knowledge is entwined with expectations about the course of life. The disruption of bodily knowledge necessitates reworking these expectations, but doing so presents a major challenge, as the future is fraught with uncertainty. The uncertainty of his future underlies everything he says and frames his illness in a culture-specific way: the future-orientation of U.S. society shapes both the way the diagnosis is presented to Kirk and the way he deals with it.

Kirk's responses are also typical of what happens when cultural expectations about order are destroyed by the onset of an apparently life-threatening illness. He grasps for metaphors and uses narrative to help him deal with his profound sense of disorder and impending loss. His broken nose serves simultaneously as a body metaphor for chaos and as a sign of the possibility for resumption of order: his nose has been broken, but it will heal. The possible loss of his kidney is another matter, however. The ever present possibility of cancer, a metaphor for death, hangs over this discussion and remains unresolved, and Kirk struggles with chronic uncertainty.

Kirk's story is one example among many in this book that illustrate how narrative is a culture-specific response to disruption. Specifically, we see the role of narrative in Kirk's efforts to restore bodily knowledge and reconstruct biography following a disruption, his attempts to create a sense of continuity. We see how he emplots his story, placing infertility, the ostensible topic of my visit to him, in perspective. We also see the presence of subjunctivizing elements when, for example, Kirk experiments with scenarios ranging from not having cancer but losing a kidney, to having cancer and being given only a short time to live. As he experiments with the words "the kidney cancer," we see the profound effort he is making to come to terms with this new life situation at both the level of the body and the level of his future life. Talking about what has been happening to him is clearly an effort to heal the breach in his life story and begin to create a new sense of continuity, one that encompasses this disruption.

Kirk's story illustrates not only how people's sense of order is disrupted by the diagnosis of a life-threatening illness and how being-in-the-world is disturbed but also how biomedical treatment may wreak havoc with people's lives and with their notions of order and control. Through Kirk's eyes we see how physicians, in giving bad news, attempt to alter the reality of dying of cancer by presenting Kirk with their reassurances and with the statistical odds of survival. We see an example of the careful scripting of hope into the dialogues between physicians and patients about the treatment of cancer.[10] Kirk does make a concerted effort to accept their reassurances in order to take control over the situation and restore a semblance of order to his life, but ultimately he abandons this effort; the complacency associated with the taken-for-granted body has dissolved and cannot be restored.

When a chronic or life-threatening illness is diagnosed, the cultural discourse on health is engaged. In the United States, personal responsibility for health is paramount, and people feel a keen sense of responsibility for regaining their health when they become ill. The question of what caused the illness raises a moral question for the ill person: Is he or she responsible for the illness? Regardless of the answer to this, the person is seen as responsible for restoring normalcy. This discourse on personal responsibility has been articulated in Talcott Parsons's theory of the sick role—that people get sick, remain sick for a while, then become well again. Although Parsons's theory has been challenged, especially with respect to chronic illness,[11] the ideas that underpin this theory remain dominant today in popular thought. People with a chronic, potentially life-threatening illness are thus required to assert the moral authority of their stance as the unsuspecting-person-turned-patient in response to the moral force of normalizing ideologies about health.

One aspect of Kirk's story indicates that cultural notions of normalcy can be contested. That Kirk's physicians paint a picture of a good outcome (his remaining healthy with only one kidney) suggests that cultural notions of normalcy are being challenged and redefined by biomedicine. Although Kirk rejects the proffered biomedical version of normalcy, had his kidney been removed, it is likely that he would ultimately have accepted this version of normalcy because doing so would have helped to restore a sense of normalcy and order and, thus, strengthened his efforts to create a sense of continuity.

BETWEEN LIFE AND DEATH

The threat of death temporarily, and sometimes permanently, destroys people's sense of order. People who experience the sudden onset of a chronic illness face the destruction of life itself, the destruction of the habituated, embodied self, as well as uncertainty about whether they have time left to create themselves anew. They are immersed simultaneously in addressing the possible end of their lives and learning how they will manage in daily life if they live.

A cataclysmic series of events profoundly altered the life of Mr. Lucas Post, a sixty-six-year-old African American in the ethnic minorities study. Mr. Post was typical of many of the African Americans in the study in the way he dealt with his illness with equanimity in the face of ongoing uncertainty. A retired merchant marine, Mr. Post had had a series of heart problems and strokes. When he was first interviewed a year after his most recent hospitalization, he continued to ruminate about these events and their impact on his life.

> I wasn't sick. I just went to pick up some medicine and got in an argument, and I guess I blowed my top and hit the bin, and I fell dead in the medicine line! Since I was in the hospital I got lucky, and they had that code blue and they had everything there that bring me back to life. Then they put me upstairs, intensive ward, and I died again. They brought me back again, and then they were trying to do something [surgery] and they asked my baby daughter, that we might have to do it again [They asked whether or not they should resuscitate him, should the situation arise again]. She said, "Yeah. I want my daddy to live." My older daughter said, "No." I think they were trying to clean my arteries out or something, and I think a piece of that stuff must of went into . . . you see it goes through your neck and the neck gets a little fine, that's what they tell me, and it probably couldn't get through and got blocked.
>
> Then my oldest daughter spent about two days with her two sons in the hospital. She used to work there many years ago. Sixteen years. And she was sitting there and noticed I hadn't moved. Then she told them, "My daddy hasn't moved. There's something wrong with my daddy." Then they said, "There ain't nothing wrong with him." That's what she told me. So she went upstairs and got the doctor, and they found out I was getting a blood clot. It was coming in really slow 'cause I was in bad shape but not, *you know.* I was happy at that. My baby daughter said, "Well, Daddy, if the Father [God] would've wanted you to die, you would've died downstairs." So I stayed there 'til they sent me to rehabilitation.

Mr. Post captures the immediacy of the disruption: "I fell dead in the medicine line!" But his heart attack is only the beginning of the disruption. The threat of death becomes chronic: "They put me upstairs . . . and I died again." He drives home his point—that this abrupt experience did not resolve itself—by raising a host of other issues, one of which is the issue of resuscitation. That his younger daughter wanted him to be resuscitated while his older daughter did not raises a thorny question: Does one daughter value his life more than the other does? That the daughter who did not want resuscitation subsequently saved his life adds more layers of complexity to a situation already fraught with emotion. He concludes this portrait of repeated near-death experiences by calling attention to his daughter's remark that it was not time for him to die. Through a religious allusion, his daughter provides an explanation for why he is still alive, an explanation that is meaningful because it is tied to their religious beliefs.

Near-death experiences heighten awareness of the fallibility of the body, and they initiate or reawaken an awareness of mortality, an awareness that death is near. Such experiences may be unfathomable; they generate a perplexing kaleidoscope of emotions. From this welter of thoughts, feelings, and bodily responses emerges a need to make such experiences meaningful. Biographical schemes cannot avoid the problem of death, and they attempt to solve the problem by linking existence to something that transcends it.[12] This "something" is what is meaningful in life. As he tries to pick up the pieces of his life, Mr. Post illustrates this effort to make sense of what happened to him.

> When I left there [the hospital], I went to my daughter's house. I stayed with her until I got this place here. Then I had another stroke, that was the March stroke. They said that I was all right, and so I don't know what this is.

Because he needed help from others when he first left the hospital, he had to move from his own home to his daughter's home and then to congregate housing, and these moves created another disruption. Just when Mr. Post began to feel that he had weathered this episode of illness, he became ill again, and the resulting long-term uncertainty and ambiguity have not been resolved.

He reflects on how his health problems began and on the ways that his illness has disrupted his daily life.

> What gets me is that I wish I knew what I know now as a youngster. I don't understand it neither, 'cause I used to work out and box a lot. Stay in shape. Then I started going to sea as a merchant seaman. I started eating and couldn't work all that off. You had three courses a meal, everyday. I think that's what did it with my cholesterol.
>
> Now I eat different. I eat beans and rice, no fried foods, no eggs, low-fat milk, no cheese at all. No fried chicken. No nothing. Now according

to that book, I can't even eat greens. You know, they're crazy, losing their minds. They [the physicians] took everything. No fried chicken. When I got that book I almost cried, then. See, I used to cook and bake myself. Ask [his friend]. She'll tell you. I used to cook for her when her and I were just courting. I started when I went to sea. Baking, I learned that when I was in the navy. Sometimes when I was out there, I used to make a lot of pies. I'd like to cheat sometimes. I'm just tired.

Mr. Post describes the erosion of meaning in his daily life that results from not being able to eat what he wants: "They took everything." The effort to live with his limited diet is a major preoccupation. It is not easy for him to keep from backsliding into his old eating habits.

But I mean, these old ladies around here, you walk down the hall and you sniff, sniff like it is going through the wall. Then I put my nose up and smack my lips together. Smells like bacon out there. Fried chicken. I could just smell what the neighbors cook, and I'd be tasting it. That's why I say they should never have put me here [in congregate housing]. But I got will power. It's dangerous, and I have a hard time.

When the interviewer asks, "So do you think your illness has really affected your daily life?" Mr. Post's response indicates how much of his former daily life revolved around food and community activities.

Oh yeah! I'd be working. I'm used to working. Especially I like a big kitchen. I used to cook a whole lot on Thanksgiving. All the kids you know, all the grandkids and my step-daughter's kids now, they come in here. But I look at that small kitchen and I just . . . I can't even get a table in there. When I make pies, where am I going to put the pies? In my other house, I had everything. The kitchen was bigger than my bedroom, and I had extra tables there and I just put everything there and I used to cook for the whole building. Pies and things.

Yeah. But now I'm lost. Nowadays I got to go see a watchacallit [therapist]. They think I'm too depressed. So I go to see her. The same day I go see my regular doctor.

It becomes clear that food is an active ingredient in Mr. Post's efforts to create meaning in his life. The activity of preparing food for everyone else was apparently more important than preparing food for himself, as it connected him to many people in a social system based on reciprocity and sharing. Deprived of this activity by his illness and his unwanted move to a smaller apartment, he now finds little meaningful in daily life and has difficulty filling his days.

Mr. Post's role in life, that of a cook for family and friends, is not the only thing that changed. At the time of his hospitalization, Mr. Post was planning to marry a woman who was considerably younger than him. These plans have been completely altered by his illness.

> Me and my girlfriend were going to get married, but we changed our minds 'cause me sexually—I'm not working for her. Besides, I don't want to hold her life up, you know. 'Cause I know she wants to get out and have some fun, some sex and things like that. I told her I just don't have no nature. You know, I can't do anything. You know, this medicine I'm taking.
>
> Boy, I'll tell you when things get all right. That was the trouble I had before, and I tried to tell them I still think it's the medicine, but since I'm so diseased in here I got to have that medicine. So I just said the devil with it.

Mr. Post faces a dilemma: he can reduce his medication so that his sexual function, his "nature," is not diminished, but if he does, he risks death. He has made the choice, but has thereby given up his relationship with his girlfriend. He contrasts himself as he is now with who he was.

> My friends, they couldn't beat me up. I was way bigger, and now I come out and they said, "Oh crippled man." I tried to catch them. It makes me mad. They say, "I'm just playing with you." I say, "I don't play games like that. I wish I was well." But it gets me mad, though, because I can't do what I used to do.
>
> I've been through a lot. I just hang in there.

Mr. Post is beginning to establish a new routine after a long period of disruption. Almost everything in his life has changed, including key aspects of his habituated, embodied self. He looks physically different both to himself and to others. Although he now weighs about 150 pounds, he was once much bigger and stronger. Now people poke fun at him. He tries to catch them and can't because he walks slowly with a cane. But more has changed than his physical appearance and ability to get around:

he has lost his "nature." His body can no longer perform functions he once took for granted, and consequently he has become very depressed.

Not only are his bodily functions dramatically changed, but his ability to nurture his body with the food he likes is also gone. His relationship to food is embodied; that is, food is an extension of who he is. Moreover, food signifies reciprocity and family relationships, and, most of all, activities surrounding food make him instrumental to his family and friends. For him, food signifies personhood. It connects him through his body to others. The embodied knowledge represented by food is now lost because food and its sources of meaning are now inaccessible to him.

Mr. Post presents the dilemma created for him by his physicians: if he experiences his embodied self through food and sex, he will die. But he questions whether living without food, sex, an intimate relationship, his home, and his avocation—cooking—is worthwhile. Depressed to the point that his physician has sent him to a therapist, he is trying to identify reasons to go on with life.

Mr. Post's story illustrates how embodied knowledge is tied to the essentials of life and how embodiment can be destroyed or constrained by the removal of those essentials. Not only does illness wreak havoc with embodiment, but the antidotes for illness may effectively stymie life reorganization when people are trying to recover. Although biomedical interventions restored Mr. Post's life, they also dramatically altered it.

Mr. Post, feeling disconnected from his former self and from his former life, clings to willpower as a means of negotiating his way through the dangers of temptation. The emphasis in the United States on will, on the belief that hope and determination can will a change in the course of an illness, reflects efforts to control and order illness through rational determinism.[13] Efforts to control a chronic condition are rooted in two ideas: that people can control their environment and that people should take responsibility for their health.[14] The notion that chronic illness can be controlled is common in U.S. medical practice, whereas discussions of the limits of control are uncommon. Often couched in terms of illness management in both the medical and social science literature, control over the condition reflects interpretations of Western Cartesian philosophy, which, in contemporary thought, has been interpreted as mind over matter.[15] The responsibility people feel for controlling their chronic illnesses and the efforts they make to overcome the constraints such control places on everyday life affect self-perceptions that alter as the illness waxes and wanes.[16]

We see in Mr. Post's story how embodied knowledge is assaulted by the ethos of rational determinism. Mr. Post has embraced this ethos. However, biomedical ideologies about health compete with Mr. Post's embodied knowledge. As he relinquishes these bodily connections to personhood as he defines it, he tries to establish mind over body. Prescriptions for care of the body can result in increased emphasis on mental over bodily activities and bodily knowledge may consequently be eroded. Mr. Post's story thus illustrates the paradox of illness management: that although it is intended to empower people, it may also be a burden, one that interferes with embodied experience.

The moral force of normalizing ideologies, seen through medical prescriptions for health, may interfere with embodied experience. In Mr. Post's case, habituated bodily activities were swept away in the interest of complying with these ideologies, and Mr. Post was left in chaos. The imposition of another type of order left Mr. Post without meaning in his life. The close relationship between embodied knowledge and meaning is thus relegated to a subsidiary position, while control over the body becomes preeminent.

STROKE AS A METAPHOR FOR DEATH

Metaphor is central to embodied experience.[17] Michael Jackson maintains that all metaphor is embodied, that it reveals unities—"this is that"—and that metaphor reflects the "interdependency of mind and body, self and world."[18] George Lakoff's thesis that metaphor is grounded in the body and emerges from it, creating categories of thought and experience, has been given increasing attention recently in anthropological discussions of embodied metaphors.[19] Studies of disruption bear out the embodied nature of metaphor and the unity not only of mind and body but also of individuals and the world.

When a chronic condition disrupts the body and renders the sufferer helpless, the situation may be labeled as hopeless, and this labeling may affect people's efforts to recover. In the United States, this situation occurs when people are unable to live up to cultural norms about productivity. Notions of productivity—which are informed by the value placed on activity, work, and progress—are directly related to attitudes about health. People in the United States anticipate and value sustained productivity throughout life. When people are no longer seen as productive, they may be viewed by others, and by themselves, as useless.[20]

Cultural meanings associated with hope and productivity in U.S. society are embedded in Western constructions of how individual development occurs. These meanings lead to the question of whether metaphors associated with hopelessness and death help people make sense of suffering. If so, how? Susan Sontag argues there should be no metaphors that represent illness,[21] but metaphor has an explanatory power and emotional valence that may help to make sense of suffering. Although cultural meanings cannot be reduced to metaphors,[22] metaphors may serve to explain feelings and express bodily suffering as people attempt to understand disruption and reestablish a sense of order.

An examination of stroke allows us to reformulate meanings associated with impairment, especially those impairments that occur in old age, and to explore how impairment foreshadows death. Stroke lends itself to this exploration because of its potentially devastating effect on people's bodies and their lives. While stroke may appear, initially, to be a nihilistic, uncomfortable focus of study, one that addresses stereotypical issues of aging such as physical and cognitive decline, mobility loss, and paralysis, it is precisely because such images assault us that an examination of stroke is relevant.

Emergency treatment of a stroke is often dramatic. Whether conscious or unconscious, patients are placed in a hospital's acute care unit until their physical condition is stable. Awareness that something is wrong dawns soon after they begin to respond to their surroundings. The following example is typical of the initial response to a stroke and illustrates the sudden, profound nature of the changes that people experience.

Mrs. Laura Leonardi, a sixty-one-year-old Italian American, came onto the rehabilitation unit nine hours after having been admitted to the hospital with the diagnosis of a severe left hemisphere stroke. When an occupational therapist who had been feeding Mrs. Leonardi returned to the room and pointed out that Mrs. Leonardi was "pocketing" her un-chewed food in her cheek, Mrs. Leonardi looked stunned. She was un-aware that she had not been eating properly. She was silent for a few moments and then said slowly, "Oh my God, this is what a stroke is." She began to cry. The awareness that she had had a stroke marked the first phase in a process of life reorganization that went on unabated for over a year.

A stroke embodies death. Stroke so profoundly affected the lives of the women and men I studied that they spoke of it as if it was a death. Life, at least as they had known it before the stroke, was over. They won-dered what the stroke meant; they wondered why they were still alive.

One month after her stroke, Mrs. Leonardi had not recovered as she had initially anticipated. She voiced her sense of hopelessness and doom when, crying, she blurted out,

God killed me when I had the stroke. Why didn't he let me die?

For several months thereafter she often talked about committing suicide. At other times she said,

I want to die—put that in your book.

or

I'm going to lay down and die.

Edith Smith, a seventy-six-year-old African American woman, echoed Mrs. Leonardi in reporting how she could no longer maintain her daily routine, said with finality,

The stroke killed me.

Edna Brown, a seventy-four-year-old Anglo woman who had a stroke during knee surgery, said plaintively,

I thought I was doing right, getting a brand new pair of knees, and now they won't work. The operation was a success, but the patient died.

Trying to describe how the stroke had affected her body and her daily life, she gave up in anguish and concluded,

It's like being dead inside and dead outside.

A stroke was often seen as the first indication of impending death, a warning that a person might not have long to live. For example, Jacob Steiner, a sixty-two-year-old Jewish man, reported that his physician had told him he was at high risk for additional strokes, and he concluded sadly,

As I grow older, it may get worse. I don't know how much longer I have to live. So in a sense it is dying with your boots on.

In verbalizing his fear that he might die prematurely, before it was "time" to die, he anticipated his own mortality and the disruption of being "off time" for the final transition in life.[23] He began to reorganize his experience in anticipation of the possibility of death, thus lending a sense of order and continuity to life while, at the same time, resisting death's approach.

The imagery of death also surrounded individual body parts that no longer functioned as they should. The "death" of body parts not only anticipates death itself but also affected the ability to carry out meaningful activities of daily life, as Edna Brown's comment illustrates:

My hand—this is the awful part. I try to work with it every day but it's awfully difficult. One thing has killed me, broke my heart—that I can't play the piano anymore. I loved it better than anything.

Confronting the changed body became the first task of recovery after a stroke. Mrs. Brown said,

I didn't know anything about my body becoming so distorted. I've become the Hunchback of Notre Dame. I told them [members of her support group], I said, "Well, a lot of you have this problem, a withered left hand, if your left side is totally done away with, like mine. I figure I'm going to have to carry this thing around with me the rest of my life." So later I was searching back in my reading, and I thought, "What can I call this?" So I was thinking of the Hunchback of Notre Dame—he was such a grotesque thing and this is so grotesque. Maybe I'm not quite that bad, but when I try to get up in the morning I think I cannot survive because it's every bone in my body. See, when the stroke hit the left side, it just took everything with it. It blew out the sockets of my shoulder and it just took everything all the way down. Then you have constant pain. That is no exaggeration. When [my husband] gets my feet on the ground and stands me up in the morning, we have our little dance to do [transferring her from the bed to a wheelchair]. This leg, I cannot let it get out from under me or the whole thing will just crack.

Mrs. Brown combines several metaphors in her effort to capture the effects of the stroke on her body and her life. She addresses her sense of distortion and her efforts to reconcile herself to feeling "grotesque" through the hunchback metaphor. She talks about having to carry her "withered" left hand around and about how the left side of her body that has been "done away with." She also uses an explosion metaphor when she alludes to the stroke as blowing out the sockets of her shoulders. When she refers to the move from bed to wheelchair as "our little dance," she conveys an image of brittle instability: if she loses her balance and lets her leg get out from under her, she will fall and break apart. Mrs. Brown tried to make sense out of the stroke's profound effect on different parts of her body. She summarizes,

> A stroke doesn't just hit one part of your body. You can't just say, "This happened" and "that happened." My left leg is paralyzed and my left arm is paralyzed and my shoulder. But that is not all because it seems my whole torso—my trunk—is just totally messed up by the stroke. It's like being dead inside and dead outside. That's exactly what it is.

A stroke destroys the fabric of predictable, everyday life and disrupts health and wholeness, which are viewed as part of the intrinsic order of daily life. Women and men described their stroke as a cataclysmic disaster that gave them a sense of unreality. Mrs. Mary Jordan, eighty years old, described what this initial period after the stroke was like.

I was just laying there in the hospital, crying half the time because I just didn't know what was going to happen to me. I thought, "Would I ever come home again? How would I manage this and how would I manage that?" Now I've had a taste of what can happen to someone who is in the stream of life. It's just unbelievable that it happened to me. I was so active, so busy all the time. Then I was laid low, and all of a sudden I was trapped. I'm always thinking I will make this plan or that plan, but I am laying here now, and I didn't make any plans for anything and I don't know what is going to happen to me.

Mrs. Jordan's former reality, her view of herself as "someone who is in the stream of life," has been replaced by a reality in which she is "laid low" and "trapped." The journey of her life has been interrupted midstream.

Starting when she was in the hospital, Mrs. Jordan struggled to place the stroke in her life. Although she, unlike many people in the study,[24] ultimately resisted viewing the situation caused by the stroke as hopeless, she wavered back and forth between hope and hopelessness when the stroke first occurred:

From the very first they said, "We can see that you are pretty motivated." I said, "Well, I want to get better." You know, I was just laying there. It was a terrible shock, really just terrible. I was crying half the time because I didn't know what was going to happen to me. This thing knocked me flat and scared the pants off me.

In addition to processing their emotions, people in this study were simultaneously addressing the possible end of their lives and learning about how they would manage in daily life if they did continue living. They were facing the destruction of the habituated, embodied self as well as their uncertainty about whether they had time left to create new selves. They were forced to deal with fundamental reformulations of self and daily routines that lead to life reorganization.[25] For many, however, this work of linking past, present, and future was beyond their cognitive and expressive abilities.

As women and men became aware of the magnitude of their impairments, they addressed issues of normalcy and productivity through multiple metaphors, which sometimes imparted conflicting messages. If they felt hopeful, they demonstrated renewed determination to regain their productivity. For example, Mrs. Brown said,

> The hardest thing of all is realizing there can be a light at the end of the tunnel. I want to be as normal as I can but I'm not normal. But when you have been put in that position, you have to make the best of it. Like bathing. I'm determined to go in there and bathe myself. The aide would say, "Oh, no, you can't do that." I said, "The hell I can't. I can't be a vegetable, you know."

Metaphors that characterize bodily phenomena reflect embodied knowledge and shifting understandings of the body. Mrs. Brown's poignant statement situates the self with respect to what is real and fathomable and what is not. Mrs. Brown reaffirms cultural beliefs about what is rational and knowable that underlie her sense of continuity; she refutes the unthinkable—being a vegetable. The effort to fulfill cultural ideals such as perseverance, determination, and self-reliance gives meaning to the daily struggle to go on with life. But in order to persevere, people who have had a stroke need to maintain a glimmer of hope in the face of a hard reality.

In these narratives we can clearly see how the moral force of normalizing ideologies shapes meanings about stroke. Cultural meanings attached to a stroke are part of a cultural discourse on old age in which serious illness is seen as leading to decrepitude and death. The narrators in this study reflect this discourse when they portray stroke as conveying uncertainty, loss of hope, and the anticipation of death.

4 Metaphors as Mediators in Disrupted Lives

Nora, an attorney whom I interviewed for the midlife study, was fifty when she reached a crossroads in her career. At the time I first interviewed her, she had just learned of changes in her employer's law firm that would force her to decide whether to leave law and try something new or open her own law practice.

> If I were thirty I would be out there with my lance, trying to change things, like Don Quixote. But I don't care that much. I think the whole legal system is archaic. And I'm too old. I'm tired of tilting. I have tried to do it in my life. But it's not my time of life to do it.

In metaphorically linking herself to Don Quixote, Nora puts the difficult decision she faces into the framework of the cultural life course. She acknowledges cultural notions about age: she addresses the metaphorical journey of life and the possible futility of certain undertakings at her stage of that journey. These cultural considerations frame her decision about which direction to take: she is influenced by the idea that middle age is not the time to tilt.

Metaphors such as the Don Quixote metaphor used by Nora are cultural resources that people draw upon as mediators of disruption; they enable people to recreate a sense of continuity, to reconnect themselves to the social order after a disruption. Metaphors, and by extension tropes, equate one conventional point of reference with another, or substitute one for another. A metaphor may be extended into a broader frame of cultural relevance that leads to a larger metaphor; the metaphor in Nora's comment has been extended in this way.[1] This extension of metaphors results in the constant recreation of cultural meanings.

The narratives in this chapter illustrate how people work with metaphor as they grapple with disruption to life. When life must be reorganized, metaphors can provide a transforming bridge between the image of the old life and the new one. Because metaphors frame and structure meaning,[2] they may be highly significant in the process of attempting to reconstitute sense of self after a disruption. Metaphor can be seen as a "split reference"; that is, it opens up new possibilities for referring to the literal and the conventional, as well as to a fundamentally new view of reality.[3] Metaphor lies at the intersection of what has been and what can be; the use of metaphor thus represents a critical moment in which the known field of reference is suspended and a new, more comprehensive picture is invented. This invention is twofold, reflecting the discovery of what was implicit in the past, as well as creation of a new reality.[4] Metaphor thus represents an intrinsic synthesis of interpretation and creation, in which previous interpretations yield to new, more complete ones.[5]

This process of synthesis has practical implications for reorganizing life when a major disruption occurs.[6] Metaphors not only help people to make sense of disruptions in life and mediate efforts to create continuity in the face of change but also enable people to change their view of cultural phenomena that impede resolution of disruption.[7] Metaphor has the ability to bind the past and future together and the ability to give the impression of coherence or "return to the whole" when exploration of the metaphor is fulfilled.[8]

THE DISRUPTION OF "NATURAL" ORDER

I first began to understand how metaphors help people to grapple with and frame disorder as I analyzed narratives of disruption in my research on infertility.[9] In analyzing this data, I realized that I had stumbled onto a pervasive cultural discourse in United States society, one that suggests life is an ordered, continuous whole.[10] This cultural life course and its root metaphors provided the context for women and men who underwent medical treatment for infertility. Although the word *continuity* was seldom used by respondents, their statements clearly reflected the belief that their lives should follow predictable, coherent, linear paths. Their ideas about what course their lives should take were based on cultural values about productivity, the construction of goals for the future, and control over the environment. Until the discovery of infertility, they had taken for granted the order and predictability in their lives. In the face of sudden chaos, they sought to return to the predictable sameness of daily life.

The problem of unwanted childlessness grew in the 1980s as a consequence of delayed childbearing. As people increasingly sought medical treatment,[11] unwanted childlessness came to be seen as a medical problem rather than a social one.[12] Although infertility is not a disease, it is treated like one in biomedical systems.[13] Medical evaluation for infertility identifies physical "defects" that cause infertility. The presence of these "defects" in otherwise healthy people, these deviations from the medically defined norm, accentuates people's sense of disruption.[14]

The diagnosis of infertility triggered a complex set of responses: attempts to undo the diagnosis, to rectify the sense of abnormality, and to "fix" the infertility.[15] Women and men anticipated a prompt solution to their childlessness and were unprepared for a lengthy and often complex series of medical procedures in which they gradually became immersed if they had the financial resources. This long, drawn-out treatment process sometimes accentuated respondents' sense of disruption and undermined their sense of life as a continuous whole.

The theme of continuity in these stories of disruption was underlined by the use of metaphor in narratives to call attention to the significance of disruption and loss, to recreate a sense of continuity in life, and to portray conflicts related to disruption that were difficult to resolve. Moreover, the narrators cited cultural values as central to their assumptions and embedded them in metaphoric statements of struggles to maintain continuity. Metaphors of disruption and continuity reflect the processual nature of response to a disruption such as infertility. These metaphors addressed discontinuity at several levels: body, identity, and personhood in relation to the social order. Metaphors were used to address a sense of disruption to body and personal world and to address limbo in the face of uncertainty.

When I began to examine the notion of order in the different studies of disruption I conducted, I found that the nature of the disruption dictates the cultural images of order that are invoked. Infertility, for example, brings women and men face to face with a cultural assumption: that biological reproduction is an automatically occurring event, one that is part of the natural order of life. The preoccupation with blood ties and biological connections is a key element of the cultural ideology about the family in the United States. Failure to fulfill this cultural expectation is disruptive to women's and men's lives and to their sense of their place in U.S. society.

In describing what has been disrupted, respondents articulated this cultural discourse on natural order. The story of Julia, a middle-class, college-educated Jewish woman, illustrates many aspects of disruption caused by infertility. Married for ten years, Julia had been trying to conceive for seven years. After two years, her frequent absences from work for medical appointments were being questioned by her employers; and she and her husband, a businessman, decided she should quit her job in order to pursue infertility treatment. (Although women in the study typically found combining work and medical treatment for infertility to be a source of tension, few quit their jobs.) During the ensuing five years, Julia underwent many medical procedures and had one miscarriage. After a subsequent pregnancy was terminated by a therapeutic abortion because the fetus was malformed, Julia described how her sense of order in the universe was destroyed.

Right before the abortion I drove into the driveway and ran over a kitten from next door, [one of] a bunch of wild cats that the neighbors feed, and it was like a metaphor. It was as though I were being given a test: if you can stand this experience, see this squashed kitten in your driveway, maybe you can stand what you're going to have to do later in the week. I was hysterical, I couldn't stop crying.

Julia felt she had no choice but to have an abortion: the fetus was malformed. She nevertheless lived with a heavy sense of responsibility. The kitten metaphor—the destruction of an innocent creature and the necessity of living with that experience—haunted her. The squashing of the kitten represented disorder.

Julia articulated through metaphor the chaos she perceived.

The world is not an ordered place. It is a chaotic place, and random events occur in this chaotic world all the time. We fool ourselves into thinking that the world is an ordered place. That's how we get up in the morning and how we go to bed at night, because we are ordering the world in some fashion, and it is just an illusion, an illusion that keeps us going. If we didn't pretend that that's the way it is, we wouldn't be able to function. We created a nice little world that we work in; we sleep from night to morning and we eat three meals a day. We know about gravity, and we know about the elements, but in fact we don't know anything. The world is just a massive pile of molecules zipping around, knocking into each other. At any time one of these random events can occur. Earthquakes and floods and other acts of God, being symbols of that, that all our houses with all of their roofs can be blown off, airplanes could crash into apartment buildings, babies can be taken away from their mothers. A baby that you've waited six years to conceive can go completely wrong inside. It's very, very difficult to go back to an ordered, normal life after this because my illusion of order has been shattered.

By juxtaposing images of order and chaos, Julia was able to place the inexplicable loss of her baby in a new framework of understanding: a disordered world in which chaos reigned. This new framework provided an explanation for why the fetus was malformed: random events could not be predicted. She invoked all forms of explanation available to her—a physical science model as well as "acts of God." She concluded:

I think what I'm experiencing is the loss of my illusion of a normal
world.

Her new view of the world as chaotic gave her a way to comprehend the
loss of her child.

Identifying normalcy as an illusion compelled her to view this experience in its magnitude.

You need to have a life cycle. She was dead before she could even
breathe. That puts it into another realm of tragedy that I can't . . . that I
find it really hard to accept.

Death *before* life was another manifestation of chaos. Julia makes it clear
how central the notion of a life cycle was to her view of continuity: the
death of her child before the cycle could begin created a tragedy beyond
comprehension.

Julia was able to articulate what she had lost: hope.

I was expecting a baby, just the words themselves . . . it's the expectation of a lifetime, it's the expectation of a family, it's the expectation
of a dream coming true after all these years. It's extraordinary to think
about. It is the essence of hope. It's what the world is all about. It's what
makes man and woman need to procreate, this sense of hope and belief
in the future.

In this statement, the baby becomes a metaphor for hope—hope for the
future and the continuity of life—and a metaphor for the future-oriented
life that is the ideal of U.S. society. In the metaphor, the baby is distilled
into "the essence of hope," and having a baby gives meaning and order
to life. Julia continued,

It's a very strange feeling. I feel as though the baby took part of me with
her on the way out, and I'll never ever be the same. That's more scary. I
feel she took all hope with her.

Here the baby metaphor is inverted: the baby becomes a metaphor for
death and loss of hope, both Julia's and the baby's.

In her impassioned statements, Julia demonstrates an important quality of metaphor: the emotional valence of metaphor helps to enact change.
"Metaphors move us."[16] Although cultural meanings cannot be reduced
to metaphors,[17] metaphors may be seen as idioms of distress. That is, they
may provide a means of explaining feelings and expressing bodily distress in people's efforts to understand disruption and reestablish a sense
of order in life. The use of metaphor thus helps people to make sense of
suffering. Through metaphor people are able to reframe the inexplicable
and reorganize their lives.

Metaphors themselves do not reorganize thinking, but they provide
one way of locating new meanings, which, in turn, may facilitate efforts
to reorganize life. The use of metaphor is one way in which people impart elasticity to their personal frameworks of meaning. In altering these
frameworks, people use components of cultural discourses in creative
ways to create the most culturally relevant fit for their life experiences.
Individual constructions of cultural discourses apparently encompass
contradictions. For example, people combine different explanatory systems through metaphor: acts of God and scientific models of causality.
By reworking their understandings of self and world, they remain within
the bounds of a cultural discourse, yet the meanings they attach to many
of the parameters of a cultural discourse gradually change. Metaphor
mediates this process.

Efforts to understand and reconcile disorder lead people to grapple
with all-encompassing concepts such as good and evil and their cultural
meanings. Steven, a forty-two-year-old Jewish man in the infertility
study, juxtaposes metaphors of order and chaos, good and evil, to indicate how inexplicable he finds his infertility.

> I always assumed there is a natural order, even when things happen that
> are bad. All of my family was lost in the Holocaust except for my folks,
> so I've had to rationalize evil and all kinds of things. I don't even know
> when it all started, but the sum of it is that I've always believed in some
> sort of natural order, and that evil is maybe part of that, or bad things are
> part of that. I've always tried to figure it out or rationalized it that way.
> But then I come to this shit, and I'm stumped. It just seems like it's more
> than I can make sense of. This has thrown me for a loop.

In this statement, Steven illustrates how the cultural discourse on natural order is at the core of his explanatory system and how the explosion of cultural expectations through the diagnosis of his infertility disrupts the entire system. "Evil" and "bad things" are part of the cultural discourse on natural order; they are necessary to explain the Holocaust. However, in spite of his belief in a natural order that encompasses evil, infertility leaves him "stumped." That traditional explanatory systems may fail to provide answers when people are dealing with complex issues of order and chaos may explain why people tend to seek new or composite explanations that draw on models from the biological and physical sciences in efforts to resolve disorder.

Metaphor facilitates the expression of emotion by channeling words to convey the power of emotions and cultural ideas in creative ways. The "black hole" metaphor serves as an example. The term "black hole," a relatively recent addition to the language of astronomy, has penetrated everyday speech. This metaphor was used by respondents in the infertility study to convey the disruption to life and the consequent obliteration of meaning. Sam, a forty-five-year-old man, and his partner, both college-educated, had met and, after a brief courtship, married several years earlier. It was the first marriage for both of them. Because his wife was thirty-five years old when they married, she wanted to start a family immediately, so they began trying to conceive. Sam describes the erosion of well-being in his marriage.

> It [infertility] became a black hole for both of us. I was happy when I was
> getting married, and life, to me, was consistently getting better. And she
> was continuously depressed. Everything was meaningless because
> she couldn't have a baby. And so it was a tremendous black hole, it was
> a real bummer. I mean, in the broadest, deepest sense of the term. It was
> very upsetting to me because it was like no matter what . . . it seemed like
> every time . . . I was, like, taking off and feeling good, and she was drag-
> ging me down. And it wasn't always that she was dragging me down,
> but she was dragging herself down. It was contrary to the overwhelming
> evidence of our lives, and it was very disturbing, to the point where I
> said to her that it was not tolerable anymore. And she went to a psychia-
> trist. She wanted to improve because she couldn't get out of it. I mean,
> she could not get out of it, and the Prozac [that was prescribed] made it
> worse. But it broke that cycle of depression, and she got out of it. But that

was terrible. It ruined our sex life. It was just like everything was going down the black hole.

I interjected, "There's something about the symbolism of that . . . " and he responded,

> The notion of the black hole is that it's this magnet—this negative magnet in space through which all matter is irretrievably drawn—that was the image that I had of it. It was just sucking everything down out of our lives. Down this negative hole. It was bad.

Sam depicts the black hole as a constricting force, the opposite of the life spiral, a negative force that was preventing him and his wife from experiencing the productivity and growth that U.S. culture associates with the early stages of marriage. The black hole, which stands for infertility and its all-encompassing effects, sucks the life out of their relationship. Instead of the image of building that is frequently applied to early marriage and family life, he conveyed an image of dismantling: various parts of the relationship were being swept away as his wife's inexorable depression took hold of their lives.

In descriptions of being plunged into chaos, both Sam and Julia used metaphors from physics. In doing so, they capture their sense of loss and void, the opposite of growth and fulfillment. Such metaphors may lead us towards an understanding of a particular worldview.[18] These statements exemplify the filtering of science-based metaphors into everyday explanatory systems among the general public.

These narratives reveal the cultural foundations behind metaphor: they reveal the dominant U.S. notions of life as orderly and predictable. They tease apart cultural notions of what is good, orderly, and hopeful through metaphors for evil, chaos, and hopelessness. Moreover, all these narrators ask metaphorically, Why me? In doing so, they establish their moral authority as innocent participants in a cultural world. Even though they were following cultural norms in trying to have children, they were nevertheless faced with obstacles beyond their control. Behind these expressions of outrage, frustration, and despair lies the moral force of normalizing ideologies.

GUIDING METAPHORS IN STORIES OF DISRUPTION

When their lives go awry because of a disruption related to family life, people must rethink the way in which they understand the family. Although the family is a primary conduit of culture and continuity, the cultural significance of the family is often overlooked. Sometimes the family fails to fulfill its expected role in the nurturance of family members, and people feel abandoned by the family. When they attempt to start a family of their own, the previous experience of abandonment re-emerges and becomes a "guiding metaphor," that is, a central motif in a story.[19] A guiding metaphor may help in the reinterpretation of the life story and may serve a clarifying function.[20] Metaphors are tools for working with experience and embody the situational knowledge that constitutes culture.[21]

We will explore aspects of abandonment in two narratives that follow in order to understand how life experiences may stand in direct contradiction to the U.S. cultural discourse on the family and, moreover, why metaphors of abandonment are so compelling in U.S. culture. Many people in the United States feel excluded by social norms for family; that is, they feel betrayed because their families don't live up to the normative family. The meaning of such abandonment has become a central theme in the U.S. psychology literature in the last fifteen years, and an influential book by psychoanalyst Alice Miller, *The Drama of the Gifted Child* — which dealt with psychological abandonment in the context of family life in Western societies—triggered the subsequent focus on abandonment in the popular psychology/self-help literature, especially in the United States.[22] Psychological perspectives on emotional abandonment provide much-needed cultural explanations in U.S. society, where the moral force of this normative view of family life creates a profound sense of difference for those whose experience differs from this view.

In the story of Ray, a fifty-year-old Anglo businessman in the infertility study, abandonment is a guiding metaphor. After Ray was abandoned by his mother and father, he was adopted by extended family members. Nothing about his life has been straightforward. For Ray, mending broken connections has been a lifelong preoccupation. In his story, he continually differentiates his experience from what is considered normal. The metaphor of abandonment is mediated and transformed by another guiding metaphor, a fight metaphor that enables Ray to see himself as having transcended his original story.

> I usually try to fight. I use my legal mother's old adage that "If you can't hide it, flaunt it." . . . And that's basically my philosophy towards all of this stuff. I never felt a connection with any of my parents. And so, you know, the lack of connection is . . . not an issue with me. That's normal, okay? I detested my birth mother. I've known her. I've lived with her since I was age three or four. She was just the kind of person that turned me off. She married an alcoholic, schizophrenic carpenter for a second husband who had no great love for her.
>
> Then I lived with my birth father and his second wife for four years, from ages eight to twelve. And it was nice. But there was never anybody home. I can't remember having one conversation with them at the end of four years. I was, more or less, on my own. I was a fairly accomplished storyteller at that age. I talked my way out of that one [that living situation], and then I went back to live with my aunt and uncle, who were too intrusive as far as I was concerned. I had been abused in my earlier years, from the age of about four to eight. Gotten fairly badly beat up periodically. My stepfather had a bad temper. So as far as I was concerned, they were all a pain in the ass. My concern was, "Go away and leave me alone. I can fight on my own—don't give me any help."

If people experience one disruption to life after another, they may begin to experience disruption as the rule rather than the exception. When this is the case, disruption may, to some extent, become normalized, as it has for Ray. As he tells his story of childhood abuse and being shuffled from one set of apparently uncaring adults to another, several themes emerge: (1) people are unreliable, (2) life is unpredictable, and (3) life is a struggle to be fought alone. His statement "If you can't hide it, flaunt it" reflects his effort to embrace the marginalized self. His philosophy of self-reliance reflects U.S. cultural values of independence. He explains his perspective further.

> It's the assumptions you make in life. My wife always complains that her mother was never there for her. She expected her mother to be there.

I never expected people to be there for me, so it was not an issue. I tried to avoid the disruption in my life that my various parents' turmoil inflicted on me. That probably represents a very big difference between my wife and I. She did live in a fairly stable home most of her life and had some sense that the world is stable and can be planned for. I have sort of the reverse view, which is that planning is a useful activity. However, I don't take it too seriously because I've never expected to come out with it. You sort of have to play the balls as you find them. I don't get so upset when something isn't quite the way I originally thought it was going to be. I just more or less say, "Okay, I have it. What am I going to do with it?"

According to Ray, life is a game or a gamble, and this view reflects his philosophy of not taking anything too seriously in order to protect himself from hurt and has enabled him to mediate disruption and make sense of his life.

I had parents that were just elsewhere. If I had interaction, it was because somehow I had violated something I shouldn't have done and that was overreacted to, so I'm not going to take that person seriously. To take a one-hour beating with a hair brush, you don't have the mental set to take the perpetrator very seriously or anything else they're going to ask you to do. The trick is to avoid getting beaten rather than try and follow some prescribed behavior. Most people feel they have a duty to emulate some prescribed behavior. I guess I never had a prescribed behavior in all of youth, so I don't.

People's multidimensional life stories reflect the complex interaction of cultural discourses and metaphors that need to make sense, above all, to the narrator, who, in giving their stories coherence, also communicates that sense of coherence to others. Ray's philosophy of life has emerged out of a deep sense of alienation, and he dismisses cultural ideologies of the family, claiming he ignores them. He appears to be unconcerned with conforming to cultural notions of normalcy. His experience is apparently too far afield of normalizing ideologies of the family for him to derive any comfort from them.

Ray's story is a metaphor for abandonment. As he recounts a horrific childhood experience of being passed from one set of family members to another, it becomes clear that abandonment is the underlying theme. This history of abuse and apathy reminds us that the family can be fragile, fragmented, and fragmenting. Ray's experience is juxtaposed with the cultural ideology of the family as enduring, encompassing, and a source of continuity.

In telling his story, Ray maintained an air of amused detachment. He smiled and shrugged his shoulders often. Indeed, this detachment can be seen as part of the fight metaphor: rather than allow himself to appear emotionally touched by his story, he embodied the fight metaphor in his demeanor and his whole approach to his distressing story.

Despite his childhood experience, Ray has pursued a successful career and developed a solid relationship with his wife. He doesn't expect order or stability to prevail in life, but he does subscribe to other cultural ideologies. While Ray appears to pay little more than lip service to "prescribed rules of behavior," he nevertheless adheres closely, in his use of the fight metaphor, to the cultural ethos of self-determination, which serves him as an alternative code of behavior. The use of metaphor helps him to create linkages that make sense of disruptions to his life.

MENDING SENSE OF SELF THROUGH METAPHOR

Although abandonment and its amelioration have been exhaustively analyzed from a psychological perspective, the underlying cultural reasons for viewing certain kinds of actions in families as abandonment have received virtually no anthropological attention. The theme of emotional abandonment has recurred again and again in my fieldwork, whenever people have addressed issues about the family. This topic recurred in the infertility study, in which people were engaged in trying to resolve old family disruptions in preparation for becoming parents. Abandonment, whether emotional or physical, signifies the antithesis of what constitutes normalcy in U.S. family life. It lies outside of the cultural ideology promulgated about the family.

Cultural notions of the ideal family have such strength that the effort to enact them in the face of disruption may become part of a lifelong search for coherence. In the United States, kinship is culturally defined by biology first: "blood" is ranked higher than "love."[23] The emphasis on biological connections to establish a family is unusual in comparison with other societies, where the notion of having surrogate kin is better developed.[24]

In people's efforts to mend sense of self when families are disrupted, metaphor serves as a critical mediator of disruption. In the following story, Andrea, a thirty-eight-year-old Anglo woman in the infertility study who was adopted at birth, struggles to bring a sense of coherence and continuity to her life. She addresses cultural meanings of kinship through the use of various metaphors. In Western society, adoption encompasses abandonment because in order for a child to be adopted, that child must first be given up.[25] Andrea's adoption has been a lifelong preoccupation because her life with her adoptive parents did not go well. She has struggled to make sense of being adopted. From Andrea's perspective, the lack of coherence she experienced stemmed from the way her adoptive mother told the story of her adoption.

> I was raised knowing I was adopted, and I remember her [adoptive mother] telling me this chosen baby story, that they went to the agency, they couldn't have children, and they saw me and I smiled at them, and they said, "I have to have that one," and then they picked me up, and I remember asking if they paid for me because I had this image in my mind of this supermarket, like with babies lined up, and they went shopping for one and for some reason, because of the way I smiled at them, they decided to choose me, and they carried me to the register and paid for me. This is the image that I had in my head. Because of the way she told the story.

The metaphor of a purchase affected the way in which Andrea saw herself and her adoptive parents. Was she just an object? What if she— the person behind the smile—didn't live up to their expectations? Would she be discarded if she didn't? She became concerned with the possible tenuousness of her relationship to her parents.

> And then as I got older, I asked again, and then she told me the real story. Well, with whatever information she had—very limited—and

we didn't really talk about it very much. But when I got into my teens
I started asking more questions, and she didn't have very much information other than age, and I was told she [birth mother] couldn't take care
of me and she really loved me and this is why she did this. But I could
tell my mother [adoptive mother] seemed very threatened when I asked
the questions, and so I didn't ask too many questions.

Andrea had a deep desire to know more about her origins, partly because she felt abandoned by her adoptive family.

My first attempt at searching was when I was fifteen. I knew where I was
born and I wrote the hospital, and of course they said, "You can't have
any information. You're too young." . . . I really wanted to know. I went
to boarding school when I was ten. I was sent to boarding school, and I
felt really abandoned by my mother, and so I thought, "I'm going to find
this good mother I have." My mother became the bad mother, and I had
these fantasies, these elaborate fantasies of sort of a chubby mom, house-
wife type, with lots of kids, middle class, you know. I was adopted into
a wealthy family, and I just wanted to be normal. You know, it's like, I
didn't fit into this family. Everybody was showy and extroverted, and
I was and still am very introverted and quiet and shy, and it didn't fit.

Andrea's statements illustrate how she believed she did not fit into the
cultural notion of the normal family or into the cultural discourse on
normalcy. They also illustrate how she attempted to create coherence for
herself: she felt that she did not belong there; but she believed that she
did belong somewhere, and belonging was just a matter of finding the
family she came from. Meanwhile, her troubles with her adoptive family,
and growing up, intervened.

So I tried at fifteen and got nowhere, and then I didn't really think about
it very much in my later teens. I got into a lot of trouble with drugs, and
I did a lot of drugs when I was a teenager and ran away from home. I left
home at seventeen, got married at nineteen, got divorced at twenty-two.
I had a, um, not too happy a life. And then I was in college, and I saw
something about ALMA, the Adoptees Liberty Movement Association,
and search groups forming and Adoptees Right to Know. This is when
this started to gain publicity, and so I thought, "I'm going to try again."
So I wrote the agency and I got nonidentifying information, and I con-

tacted the hospital again and got the name of my birth mother. And then, I kind of ran up against a brick wall. I didn't know what else to do. I wasn't part of these organizations. It didn't even occur to me to actually join one. I was still doing drugs so . . . I wasn't all together a part of the world, and it got put on hold.

Andrea's back and forth progress toward finding her birth mother is underscored by her comment that she had "not too happy a life." Struggling with getting through daily life, she was poorly equipped to take decisive action. Stymied in her efforts, she uses the metaphor of the brick wall to characterize the impasse she faced.

Then finally I started working at it, and I found her. It was amazing. That was a peak experience for me. It was just . . . you get obsessed, you really start . . . it's just an obsession. You get obsessed, and to finally have . . . there are so many hurdles in your way, and then to finally reach your goal is something.

But when I phoned her, I could tell over the phone that I didn't like her, which was very disappointing. But we made arrangements to meet, and I drove to meet her—I was adopted in another part of the country, but it turns out she lives nearby—and I took her out to lunch and spent the day with her. There was certainly a resemblance in our looks, but I didn't like her at all. I thought that she was really kind of infantile almost—childish and inappropriate laughter—no sense of boundaries. She's all over the place.

Finding her birth mother was one of the first, and certainly the biggest, goals Andrea had ever set for herself and undertaken, and she achieved it, although it had taken all her energy and had finally become an obsession. Success was new to her. But when her birth mother did not live up to her expectations, she became angry. She had given so much energy to this effort, only to find that the woman she had dreamed about, with whom she expected to share so much, did not exist.

I asked about my birth father at that meeting, and she couldn't tell me much, but she was clearly still in love with him, which I don't get after I heard the story from him, which is another story. She said, "I hope you find him because maybe he and I can get back together." I mean, this is like, "Wow, wait a minute, she's not all here." And then she kept writing and eventually asked me for money, and then when I turned her down, she got furious with me. Somehow she felt like because she had given me this life, that I owed her. So that was the end of that, and I haven't had any contact with her for ten years.

Disappointed by her birth mother, Andrea began trying to find her birth father.

I tried off and on for six years. I knew his name, but I didn't have a date of birth, and it is really hard when you don't have a date of birth. But finally I found him. And he came across the country to meet me. He was just totally, unconditionally, accepting of me, which was . . . made me . . . I mean, it was like, "I don't get this. I'm not used to this." He is a nice simple man. He sort of fits the fantasy of my birth mother. He's just a real simple, down-to-earth, nice man, and it's very interesting, the range of similarities we have from, like, we eat the same cereal. Our diets are the same. We have the same interests, the same hobbies, we both run, we both love the outdoors, we both have an attitude that your job is not your life, and that you work to enjoy life and not the other way around. Where do you get these kinds of values? Because *nobody* in my family had that value. A really outdoors person. He used to bake bread, and I used to bake bread. And . . . it's just amazing the similarities. So we keep in contact.

Using her similarities to her birth father as the foundation, Andrea began to build a sense of coherence about herself and her life. She couches the search for her birth parents as a necessary key to discovering who she is. Having told the whole story, Andrea then offered her own analysis of what happened.

I'm oversimplifying, but I think adopted kids either identify with being chosen or being given away, and adoptive parents were told in those days, "Emphasize the fact that your child was chosen," and of course they didn't think about the implications of that: "We chose you; you better live up to our expectations."
I have always identified with, "I was given away." Therefore, there must have been something wrong with me. I took it personally, I took it on, it's my fault, and then my mother sends me away to boarding school at ten, when she remarried, and her husband had a daughter, so the stepsister came to live with us, and she stayed and I left. I have never

forgotten that because that was when the relationship started to go. Because I will never and can't forgive my mother for doing such a stupid thing.

Cultural notions about the self and their relation to the cultural discourse on the family recur often in Andrea's story. Andrea dichotomizes the adoption story: one is either chosen or given away. Both alternatives can be viewed negatively; adoptees are in a double bind. Not only did Andrea see herself as given away, but also she felt she couldn't live up to the expectations of the family that chose her.[26]

The adoption story is followed in Andrea's narrative by a story that resembles the first, unhappy part of the Cinderella story: her mother remarries and sends her away to boarding school; she is "replaced" by a stepsister who comes to live with her mother. Andrea views this as being given away again. These events fulfill her worst fears: she was given away because she did not live up to family expectations. These fears hinge on the idea of personal responsibility: she feels that she is somehow responsible for this apparent rejection.

At the point where the two stories converge, the adoption story and the remarriage-abandonment story, Andrea is able to articulate why she was haunted by an ongoing sense of disruption. Her search has been for continuity because in her early life she experienced so little. Her sense of disruption arose from her earliest memories of the adoption story and was exacerbated by subsequent events in her family life.

> I think all my life I've really suffered from abandonment. But finding my parents, working on finding them, and learning about birth parents, it just changed my whole understanding of what had happened. These women were in such pain over having relinquished years and years later, and then I really understood that this wasn't the giving away process, that it was a political thing. You know, these women would have kept their children if they had had social support, family support, financial support, and that helped me to deal with the adoption abandonment. I can see this stuff, it's still alive, very much alive.

With this statement, Andrea identifies the sociopolitical nature of the situation into which she has been thrust. Her sense of personal failure with respect to her birth mother is ameliorated by her identification of the sociocultural context in which adoption occurs. Andrea sees her search for her birth parents as a way to assuage her sense of abandonment, as a way to seek threads of continuity. Doing so ultimately enables her to understand adoption and contextualize it as a social, cultural, and economic process, one in which she is innocently caught. She now recognizes that it is not her fault that things have gone awry in her family, that there were societal forces bigger than her and her family. This new knowledge of a broader context contributes to her growing sense of coherence in her life story. The search itself has become the means of establishing a sense of coherence.

In analyzing what went so wrong for her as an adoptive child, Andrea has been working with the cultural discourse on the ideal family, deconstructing it as she analyzes the social, cultural, and political forces at work. Yet deconstructing the cultural discourse on the ideal family does not allow her to discount it. Her search for continuity is not resolved and perhaps never will be. Now facing a new disruption in her life—infertility—Andrea says,

> Anything about loss or dependent children or animals, especially animals, it just kills me, to see children or animals abused or anything like that. This movie, "Gorillas in the Mist," there's a scene in there of when the baby gorilla was separated from his mother. It took everything for me not to sob.
>
> As an adoptee, I'm denied my past heritage, and as an infertile person I'm denied the future. And because of the nature of my family, I hoped that I would be able to create my own and that would really ground me and I would have something and I would look at my child and see myself and see a resemblance and feel like I belonged somewhere.
>
> And now, for that not to happen, is really difficult. . . . Even though finding my birth parents grounded me, I don't feel grounded. I don't know if I ever will.

Andrea's experience of the disruption of infertility keeps her sense of disruption actively alive and unresolved. Following on the disruption of her childhood, not being able to bear children leaves Andrea feeling unrooted in profound ways that most people never experience. The baby gorilla is a metaphor for the lost baby, Andrea, as well as for the baby she is unable to have.

This story demonstrates how work with metaphors is part of the process of creating a sense of continuity. Andrea's story is not simply about the cultural discourse on the ideal family, it is itself a metaphor for abandonment. Andrea's own infertility blocks any resolution of the disruption of being "given away." Yet Andrea's story portrays the creation of a new structure, in which an old, static view gives way to a new one that incorporates both past and future. Hence, the baby gorilla metaphor is key to Andrea's effort to bridge past and future; it incorporates simultaneously her overwhelming sense of loss and her transition into a woman who lives with the knowledge of her losses but has a life ahead of her. The baby gorilla metaphor also incorporates her emotions about this sense of loss. In U.S. society, where profound expressions of emotion are usually taboo, expressing emotion toward baby animals is permissible. Andrea imagines the baby gorilla's loss as she experiences her own.

The primary thrust of this narrative, the significance of blood ties, pervades Andrea's story. "I would look at my child and see myself and see a resemblance and feel like I belonged somewhere" captures this cultural ideal. Andrea could not consider adoption as a solution to her dilemma because her own adoption did not give her a sense of belonging. A cultural emphasis on generational continuity through biological ties reinforces Andrea's sense of being adrift. The very lack of cultural tools with which to work around the complex problem of infertility results, for Andrea, in a sense of rootlessness. Yet, ironically, Andrea's efforts to ameliorate her sense of rootlessness, a lifelong preoccupation, have given her life a sense of coherence.

Abandonment, so poignantly portrayed in this story, is a metaphor for loss, and it is a metaphor that is imbued with moral authority. Human agency is implicit in the notion of abandonment: someone else did the abandoning, and therefore the abandoned person is innocent of responsibility. It is therefore not surprising that, as an explanation for family-related distress, the abandonment metaphor has helped people to make sense of disruption.

Various discourses are continually being disavowed completely, reworked and subsequently embraced in their new form, or replaced by other discourses that hold greater meaning. We see these kinds of shifts occurring in Ray's and Andrea's stories. Ray completely disavows the discourse on the normal family yet embraces the discourse on rugged individualism. Andrea is unable to completely disavow the discourse on blood ties because it provides her with a way to make sense of her experience and embues her story with moral authority.

5 The Disordered Body

Martina clasped her hands together as she talked. She sat surrounded by her artwork—huge canvases of bodies in motion. Gradually, she compressed herself into a very small shape on the sofa. She had come to the most painful part of her story of infertility.

> I felt something was wrong with me. It was showing up in very unovert ways. Broke my finger. Broke my toe. Fell between the subway train and the platform. I hurt my knee. That's permanent damage. I felt like I was dying. Or that I wanted to. I was very depressed. I sunk to a very deep level. I realized the last thing I did was break my toe by just stubbing it on things in my studio. I was getting the art work ready for something. For what? For me being gone. I wanted to kill myself.

Disorder that pervades the body plunges people into chaos and may signify for them the approach of death. Martina recounts how her body became engulfed by chaos. Her sense of disorder obscured her bodily knowledge: she fell off platforms and walked into things. She lost bodily awareness and became increasingly immobilized as she became more depressed. As her depression deepened, she began to prepare for death. She was drowning in depression: "I sank to a very deep level."

Martina's story illustrates how bodily experience is given voice through narrative. There are other means of expressing bodily distress, such as Martina's canvases of bodies in motion. As I listened to people's stories, I repeatedly witnessed the enactment of bodily expression, through narratives as well as through emotions expressed in bodily movements, tears, gestures, silences, smiles, and explosions of grief and rage.

Prior to a disruption, people move through their everyday routines without attention to their bodies as bodies.[1] A disruption cuts through this routinization of bodily experience. The immediacy of being-in-the-world is ruptured by incapacity.[2] In *The Body Silent,* Robert Murphy graphically portrays the disarray he experienced when he became progressively paralyzed by a tumor. His paralysis gradually led him to "reside in the brain." He expresses the profound disjunction that an interruption in bodily response brings: "the quadriplegic's body can no longer speak a 'silent language' in the expression of emotions or concepts too elusive for ordinary speech . . . proximity, gesture, and body-set have been muted, and the body's ability to articulate thought has been stilled." Murphy demonstrates that the body is a crucial connection to oneself and to the world.[3] And even if a disruption is not primarily physical, the disrupted body may reflect distress.

The examples given throughout this book attest to the immediacy of bodily disruption. In this chapter, I turn to an examination of narratives that specifically address bodily distress. I do so in order to demonstrate the holistic basis of such expressions and the effects of challenges to bodily knowledge on people's lives.

CHALLENGES TO BODILY KNOWLEDGE

The known, experienced body is altered profoundly when the flow of bodily experiences in daily life is disrupted. The body becomes an unknown terrain that must be relearned; flawed and distorted, it becomes the focus of identity, the shaky ground on which a new order—if there is to be order—must be built. The undermining of routines of everyday life and the assumptions that sustain them severs a sense of connection with an array of personal meanings and leaves a void.[4] To fill the void, people must redraw relationships between self, body, environment, and daily life.

Martina's narrative illustrates the unity of mind and body: she did not become separated from her body. Instead, the distress and confusion she experienced permeated her whole being. One way to tap embodied experience is to examine what happens when distress blurs bodily knowledge. Martina was somehow able to rouse herself long enough to take action.

> I finally decided to call a therapist. Only this year did I feel like I had a breakthrough. To let go of it. Let go of this dark issue of guilt for infertility.

As she comes out of her depression over infertility, Martina reports she has identified the source of her distress, her guilt over her infertility. Making sense of the disruption restores a sense of order and coherence to her life.

Several years after this series of events, Martina, once again fully engaged with life and art, looks back on that time and tries to make sense of it.

> My parents had six kids. Many of our relatives had fourteen. Half of the family two generations back died of starvation in Poland before reaching adulthood. I guess the instinct [to have children] came in handy back then. If half of them died off, then you just have more. You can see where those instincts come from. This is something to be reckoned with.
>
> I submerged this strong undercurrent of the "If you don't have a child, there's something wrong with you" mentality or "You're a witch, you're bad, there's something you did and are being punished for." I have these primitive things underneath, thinking that way. We are very Catholic. My parents are very religious people. The church was very important in our lives, and I went to Catholic school. We grew up in a very ethnic Polish neighborhood.
>
> Going through the train and the platform . . . whenever I think of

people—the jumpers or something—I say, "Well, maybe they didn't jump." Well, that's my feeling. Maybe it was just an accident. If that happened to me. But consciously I was depressed. It was causing me to want to hurt myself. I needed to be punished for not having children and not being fertile. But I don't feel like that now, but I understand where that came from. It is the stigma of infertility that had me going. Like I had done something wrong or I was being punished somehow for something I did or didn't do.

In trying to reconcile this frightening period of her life, Martina draws on the cultural discourse on continuity that has biological reproduction as its base and examines the effect of this discourse on her. The moral force of normalizing ideologies is readily apparent in her comments about the nonconformity of not bearing children and everything that engenders: you are a "witch" (not human), you are "bad" (as opposed to "good"), "there's something wrong with you" (you are not normal), you did something that you "are being punished for." In other words, she sees herself as deviant because she has not lived up to cultural expectations. She attributes her sense of responsibility for reproduction partly to the hardships endured by her family in Poland, to her Catholic, Polish upbringing. Thus, normalizing ideologies emanate, for Martina, from several realms: the cultural imperative to reproduce, the family, and religious beliefs.

The depth of the dislocation she experienced as a result of not conceiving suggests how embodied knowledge and the order of the body may be seriously threatened when it is not possible to live out such cultural expectations. Martina's story, and those that follow, illustrate the critical connection between representation and bodily experience. When people cannot live out ideal representations of the body and the normalizing ideologies that are reflected in them, their bodily distress may be profound.

EMBODIED METAPHORS AND THE GENDERED BODY

How the body is represented may be a critical factor in shaping the nature of embodied distress. Gendered representations of the body in the dominant cultural discourses on masculinity and femininity may cause women and men to feel inadequate. Both women and men in the infertility study expressed the gendered nature of embodied knowledge as they described how infertility unraveled their basic understandings of themselves.

Women in the infertility study equated fertility with the ability to nurture. The ability to nurture others, and by extension their fertility, were central to their sense of who they were. Nurturance is associated with womanhood across cultures.[5] In the West, such associations span millennia, going back to the Greek myth of Demeter, goddess of the earth and soil, and to Sarah in the Book of Genesis.[6] The ability to nurture others is an integral part of the socialization of women in the United States.[7] Because fertility is a basic and embodied expectation for most women, infertility assaults embodied knowledge and the core sense of self. It causes the collapse of the assumptions around which women and men have structured their lives and renders bodies unpredictable.

The body, from which experience and categories of thought emanate, is metaphor's ground.[8] Body metaphors provide a way to communicate bodily sensation, as well as social, cultural, and political meaning.[9] Metaphors are one of the major means by which cultural models are elaborated and developed.[10] For example, pregnancy is both an embodied metaphor for and a cultural symbol of the discourse on womanhood. In the infertility study, pregnancy affirmed that a woman was "normal," that she was a woman, that nothing was wrong with her, that her body functioned as it should. In the United States the discourse on pregnancy emphasizes its ideal state: getting pregnant is easy, and, once pregnant, women are filled with well-being and satisfaction. Moreover, a pregnancy is expected to progress without difficulty. The women in the infertility study were able to articulate this cultural ideal of pregnancy without hesitation. They idealized pregnancy, overlooking the realities of morning sickness in the early stages, complications, or physical discomfort in the later stages.

Michelle's story takes up this theme of motherhood as a natural event. Michelle had expected motherhood to occur in a planned, timely, and predictable way. When it did not, her life was disrupted, and she and her husband underwent increasingly invasive medical treatment over several years. When at last she did conceive, her pregnancy did not follow the cultural ideal. She developed gestational diabetes, and then preterm labor forced her to stay in bed for five months of her pregnancy. When she finally went into labor, both her life and the life of her child were endangered, and surgery was necessary. Although Michelle gave birth to a healthy child, her view of herself and her life was seriously altered.

> I went to a parenting group, but nobody had a story like mine. They don't have groups for women who have gone through high-risk infertility pregnancies. These women didn't relate to me, and I didn't relate to them. They acted like pregnancy is a piece of cake, and meanwhile, here I was planning to try to go through it again!

Michelle's view of herself as deviating from the cultural ideal throws that ideal into relief, so that it can be clearly seen as an ideal, one that is cherished through women's stories. Michelle was forced to address the ideal of the natural mother because her experience repeatedly differed from it.

> I've been taking breastfeeding classes and everything having to do with breastfeeding. It ended up being one more failure of mine, and I was very much prepared before that not to breastfeed. But then I tried it and I was able to do it some . . . not enough to satisfy her, but I can do it. You've got women spilling milk down to the floor, and you're the one who pumps and you get this little bit of milk out and you feel like, "I'm not able to enrich my child. Now I have to go to the grocery store." When other women's bodies respond to motherhood and yours doesn't, and that's very irrational, but we all connect that with being a woman, you know? Being able to have your body do these things—I couldn't get pregnant naturally, I couldn't deliver a baby naturally, I couldn't feed my baby naturally. So it's very hard. I try to remind myself that this is not really important, but I am jealous of women that can breastfeed their babies exclusively, you know? I had that option taken away from me.

Michelle's story illustrates the idea that pregnancy is not only a cultural ideal but also an embodied metaphor for womanhood; that is, pregnancy stands for a body that is nurturant, natural, and healthy, and these qualities represent womanhood. Michelle draws the link between embodied distress and her failure to live up to the cultural ideal of mother-hood. She articulates the cultural ideal of the natural mother, one who nourishes her child with the riches of her body. She does not have to resort to grocery stores and infant formula, as Michelle does. The grocery store becomes a metaphor for failure, the failure to become a "natural" mother. Michelle also makes the linkage between the cultural ideal of motherhood and ideas about the womanly body. She has had to face *not* following the cultural ideal of natural motherhood.

For men in the infertility study, the news that they were infertile caused profound embodied distress because embodied representations of masculinity were undermined. The ability to father a child is central to the idea of masculinity. It is seldom questioned. Representations of the male body are central to this cultural attitude. In the West, from antiquity to the eighteenth century, women's bodies were viewed as inferior and in-verted versions of the male body.[11] In some societies, women are viewed as having sole responsibility for fertility, and a man can claim infertility as grounds for divorcing a woman.[12] Patriarchal notions of male domi-nance—the superiority and rights of men over women—further rein-force such beliefs. Cultural ideals of men in the West emphasize sexual prowess, and these expectations are linked to expectations about male fertility.

The literature on male infertility suggests that men are usually shocked to learn of their infertility and that male infertility is highly distressing.[13] Kenneth, a thirty-five-year-old Anglo man, describes how he felt upon learning the news that he was infertile.

I was worried that everybody would think that I was gay. Because I felt embarrassed. Because it is sort of a macho thing. Even though I try not to think of myself as worrying about that kind of thing. People would say some incredibly stupid things, like somebody came up to me once and said, "Why don't you just go out and knock some woman up if that is what you need to do?" It is great—everybody else can do it. I thought, "Here is some stupid idiot with the brains of a pea, and any chipmunk can hop into bed, and I can't." And I felt like I couldn't do what every-body else could do, and it made me mad. And it made me feel real stu-pid, and it made me feel really impotent. I felt like I wasn't a real man.

The equation of virility with potency further affects the views men hold about their fertility.[14] Their use of metaphor illustrates the difficulty men had in separating their virility from their ability to procreate. They used images of emasculation to describe the results of their semen analyses. For example, one thirty-five-year-old man said in anger,

> What all these doctors are saying to me is, "Let's face it—you're a eunuch."

This metaphoric statement highlights confusion over perceptions of sexual adequacy. When men's sperm were described as deviating from a medical "norm," sexuality and masculinity, as embodied aspects of core male identity, were experienced as being under attack. Kenneth expressed his confusion.

> Sometimes I get real mad and sometimes I am read sad and most of the time I am just real confused. I want to come to grips with it, but I can't seem to get a handle on it.

When they mistook potency for virility, men who were diagnosed as infertile addressed their bodily link to the social order through metaphor. Jackson, a forty-three-year-old African-American man reported,

> I had one semen analysis and I came in the world class. Then I did it again, and it was in no class, no class.

Lack of "class" was the antithesis of this successful businessman's view of himself. This statement reflects not only the interaction between embodied distress and the social order but the ability of medical treatment to disrupt sense of self. Steven's story of learning about his low sperm count echoes this theme.

> The doctor was blunt. He does not mince words. He did an analysis, and he came back and said, "This is devastatingly poor." I didn't expect to hear that. It never had occurred to me. It was such a shock to my sense of self and to all these preconceptions of my manliness and virility and all of that. That was a very, very devastating moment and I was dumbfounded. I was just shocked. I had to work that afternoon. It takes an

hour to get there. I was just in a dream state and a shock state the whole drive. I got to work and I was immobilized. I couldn't accept it. So that was my initial reaction. In that moment it totally changed the way that I thought of myself.

After much reflection, men sometimes realized that they had fallen into stereotypic ways of viewing themselves. In sorting out their embodied distress from those of others, they used metaphor, as Steven did.

In all the ways that society sort of paints an infertile male or those stereotypes—that's the corner that I painted myself into. Equating it with impotence and with failure. There was no explanation, so there was really no hope.

Here Steven used the painting metaphor as an analogy for stereotyping, then applied the paint himself by painting himself into a corner, one that was a dead end because it provided no explanation.

In these examples of women and men facing infertility, we see how embodied knowledge was disrupted and how metaphor was used to understand lack of fertility. Both women and men viewed infertility as a failure of their body that was their responsibility. This gendered knowledge of the body was expressed among both women and men, who experienced themselves in relation to cultural representations of gendered bodies. Weaving metaphor into their narratives helped them to reestablish embodied knowledge.

THE WEAKENED BODY

Negative representations of old age affect embodied knowledge in later life. Visible markers of functional limitations, such as canes, walkers, and wheelchairs, are associated with advanced age and the end of life. These markers complete a picture of a person as unproductive or useless, reinforcing an assumption that loss of function is normal in advanced age.[15] Senescence is associated with an accelerating loss of control or ownership of the personal body and with a series of losses and is viewed as a prelude to death.[16] Although a life-stage view with biological markers is common across cultures and is often marked by rituals to demarcate various phases, the culturally specific U.S. emphasis on values of individualism and productivity provides a particular context for how the process of growing older and the aging body are viewed.

With few exceptions, the notion of bodiliness has not been applied to those who are old; yet the concept of bodily experience has great relevance for aged, infirm persons because it addresses the gap between how individuals see themselves and how others see them.[17] In old age, embodied knowledge represents the accumulation of a lifetime of self-understanding. Embodied knowledge encompasses peoples' historical experience of their bodies. "The experience of present-day impairment is infused with a sense of being seamlessly connected to past, present, and future experiences and identities, both actual and idealized or expected".[18] Persons in the late-life transitions study were engaged in creating these connections through narrative reconstruction, attempting to repair and reconstitute ruptures between body, self, and world through biography.[19] Their efforts reflect the fluidity of the embodied self in old age: individuals simultaneously experienced conflicting realities of inner strength, strong identities, and physical infirmities.

Embodied knowledge among older people in this study was of a healthy body that had sustained them for most of their life. While they understood that their infirmities presented challenges to their autonomy, they saw these challenges as obstacles to be worked around. Their understanding of their impairments depended on whether they experienced the impairments as gradual, incremental physical changes or as abrupt disruptions to daily life, and on whether their health stabilized or continued to deteriorate. Illness is only part of life. Illness and physical limitations were absorbed into daily life. Life went on as usual, even for those who were seriously impaired, unless illness had occurred suddenly and had dramatically altered everyday life.

Persons who had experienced a reduction in their social activities and routines of daily life were more preoccupied with their bodies and their efforts to maintain their current level of independence than those few who continued to take their bodies for granted as they went through the daily round. When Soledad Lopez was first interviewed, she was ninety-one and was recovering from a mild stroke. Three years later, one and a half years after a fall, Mrs. Lopez reported (in Spanish),

> I feel a little better. I have had three falls. It's not sickness I have. It's the falls that I've had, and because of that I hurt, but now I feel better.
>
> Now I feel the body watery [*aguado*]. I don't feel my body solid [*macizo*]. I feel the body weak. . . . I was a solid woman. Very strong. And now I feel bad because I feel weak. . . . It [the weakness] took away my hunger, and I got very skinny. Now I have an appetite. I worked all the time. Now I miss work. I lack something to do. And I can't. My hands, they . . . are numb.

Mrs. Lopez, in using a water metaphor to describe her body, conveys how her body shifted from "solid" to fluid. She links her varied experience of her body, past and present, with action in the world: she used to work, but now she has nothing to do.

Despite her sense of loss of substance, Mrs. Lopez compares herself favorably to others. Her opinion about her age and longevity is based on her father's longevity.

> Well, I don't feel very old [laughs]. No, I don't feel very old. Well, for ninety-four. I've seen other people, people younger than me, they're incapacitated, crippled, and I'm not. I want to do things. My mind I still have. It's only the eyes that suddenly get cloudy. I've seen those younger than I who are more ruined/decrepit [*arruinada*]. Their mind already doesn't function. Like the neighbor. And he says he is younger than me. He's ninety years old. I descend from people—my father died at one hundred years—I come from people that have lasted many years. That's why I'm like this. And my father was upright. He wasn't old [*viejito*]. For one hundred years, he didn't look old. I believe that's why I am also that way. I am very healthy, very healthy. I arrived here alone [from Mexico]. I suppose that this is independence. I have always been this way.

Mrs. Lopez, it emerges, has always had expectations of living a long life because her father lived to one hundred years old "upright." She reflects a phenomenon I found among people in her age group: if their parents lived to be very old, women and men had the same expectation for themselves, and that expectation shaped their experience of their bodies in old age. Mrs. Lopez sees herself as "very healthy." She also portrays herself as very independent.

A year and a half later, Mrs. Lopez, now ninety-five, reported,

> I'm not sick with anything. I have fallen. Five times I have fallen. Because my body [makes a shaking motion with her hands] and I fall. But illnesses I don't have. I have finished with the blood and all [menstruation], and I don't have anything.

Mrs. Lopez does not view the falls she has had as signs of illness. Instead, they have been a sign to her of the weakening body. Although the major falls did create a crisis for Mrs. Lopez and her family because they involved hospitalizations and surgery for a broken hip, she recovered, unlike most people her age for whom a fall can lead to fatal complications. Because she recovered, she no longer regards the falls as crises. They have been absorbed into her life and affect her attitude about maintaining her mobility. Asked if the effects of the falls still bothered her, she responded,

> Not now, because it has been some time since I fell. And the years, too. The years dominate one. I'm ninety-five years old. And this I believe— the years dominate one. It takes your strength [*fuerza*], and it's not the same as when you're young. Age takes away your strength. You don't feel the power to do something. Everything tires you, even your own body. Although it's not sick, it tires.

In explaining how she now feels about the falls she has had, Mrs. Lopez uses old age as a metaphor for the removal of strength. She differentiates between being sick and being tired and draws the body into this equation.

As she went through the daily round, Mrs. Lopez focused on being careful. She identified falling as the one ongoing risk.

> If I stand, I feel like I want to fall. I'm afraid of falls. With so many falls that I've had. I'm afraid. If I stand . . .

Her fear of falling affected the way she spent her days. Mrs. Lopez said,

> I get up, I bathe, and I breakfast. And now I can't do anything more. Because my body . . . the body feels weak. I feel my body weak. I'm seated

all day. When I walk is when I fall. Sitting I don't feel it so much. I stand and walk and that makes me wobbly.

Mrs. Lopez was frustrated by her inability to be active.

> When one is young one works. I worked all my life, I worked until I couldn't, anymore. Now I don't do anything because I can't. Even my fingers hurt me. My fingers do this [curling up her fingers].

When asked, "Is it arthritis?" she responded,

> Yes, this finger curls up like this. I have to raise them up and massage it. And I'm deaf. And my eyes, half cloudy. My eyes, I see half cloudy. A little, not much. It's the years already. Illnesses I have none. Thanks to God for the years I have. Even my doctor says to me, "I would like to get to your age and be as healthy as you are." My doctor told me, "You are healthy for the age you have." And it's the truth.

Further enumerating her bodily changes, Mrs. Lopez continues to differentiate between age-related changes—fingers curling up, being deaf, having eyes "half cloudy"—and illness. She differentiates between the tasks of youth—working—and the inactivity of old age. In Mrs. Lopez's story, we have seen how embodied knowledge is integrated with the ongoing assessment of the body and personhood in everyday life. During periods of physical stability, people who are disabled apparently experience their bodies as whole,[20] as Mrs. Lopez did, although they acknowledge the everyday ups and downs they experience.

In the next two examples, we will see how people mediate the moral force of normalizing ideologies in old age, in which embodied knowledge takes precedence over differing kinds of social pressure. Mr. O'Donnell, an eighty-five-year-old Anglo, is a retired longshoreman who has had asthma for many years. He describes a typical day, one that involves the continuous monitoring of his body.

> The first thing I do is to take my pills. I got to get jump-started because the asthma sometimes gets so bad that I find that it is better to keep the pills near the bed along with water. So the first thing I do before I get out of bed is knock them pills off. That gives me a little head start. Then I head to that coffee pot for a stimulant to get going, and then after that I

find my way around the house, get dressed, look at the day, see what the hell we got out there. Sometimes I make up a schedule of what has to be done that day because it's a form of discipline. Then I try to go for a walk if I can possibly do it because I know it helps me. It helps the lungs and it helps the system. I take about a mile walk. Sometimes it takes me longer as I get older and older. Sometimes I don't know if I'm going to make it or not. First, I am reluctant and it's a hell of a lot of hustle. But the other part of me says, "Well, if you want to do it tomorrow, you better do it today." So I get out of the car and begrudgingly make the walk. I start coming back and I feel I have accomplished something. So now I feel good, although a little exhausted.

Mr. O'Donnell's embodied knowledge of his ever changing ability to breathe well is completely integrated with his daily routine. He uses the metaphor of starting a car with a dead battery. As he goes through the motions of his morning, he describes how he convinces himself to take a walk—how he balances the "hustle" of taking the walk and the potential to go on walking. He places the need to exercise in the context of his future orientation, and notes the ever present uncertainty about his body continuing to function adequately. The walk itself is an accomplishment with a mixed result.

Mr. O'Donnell relies on his body and forgoes the oxygen tank that is recommended for people who have severe asthma.

I take the oxygen tank in the car to keep it there. I try to avoid it if I can because it's something you don't want to get into a habit with. It's like a pill.

For a man, getting old is a macho business, anyway. You could be half dead laying on the floor and somebody will call, "How ya feelin'?" "Oh, I feel okay." Ha Ha. As you're crawling along the floor and can't get up.

The notion that getting old is a "macho business" for a man means that embodied understandings of oneself may be overlooked or ignored in the effort to perform socially. Mr. O'Donnell is acknowledging the moral force of normalizing ideologies, in this case the notion that men must be strong regardless of age or illness. His statement is a reminder that, in U.S. society, it is less acceptable for men to acknowledge their bodies or to defer to them than it is for women.

The story of Mrs. Locetti, an eighty-three-year-old Italian-American woman who lives with a full-time attendant and runs her household from her telephone, has a different theme. She resists the moral force of normalizing ideologies. Her choice to stay at home is one way to both protect the body and promote a sense of autonomy when mobility is limited.

> I like my house. I walk up and down, every once in a while I get up and walk up and down the room just to get a little exercise [with a walker]. I just go around the house. I don't even want to go up and down the stairs. I don't want to go out. I get mad because I used to take care of this house. I'd clean the stairs and do all the work around here, garden. Now nothing. I have to have everything done now, and it's been nuts. But what the heck, I'm eighty-three years old. The hell with it! I've earned the right to sit down.

Although her family continuously encouraged her to let them take her out, she adamantly refused. Her wish to stay at home first became a family joke, and ultimately became part of her identity.

> My family, my grandson, they want to take me out. For eighty-three years I've had good legs. Why should I abuse them? I respect my legs. Right? They've carried me around long enough. I tell this friend whose feet hurt, "They've been carrying you around eighty-three years. We used to dance the tango together, don't you remember? Remember those days, don't think about today."
>
> I'm too damn independent. I just don't want anyone to carry me. I want to go on my own power, and if I can't, I'm not going to go. A stubborn dago.

In asserting her right to view her autonomy on her own terms, Mrs. Locetti presents a strong message of identity and self-determination. In doing so, she weaves in memories of herself as she once was and reminds the listener that she is the same person. As a strong-minded person, she actively resists her family's efforts to take care of her. In reaction to their efforts to take her out, she presents an alternative narrative of what is normal—"respect" for the memory of when her legs could do anything. Now constrained by immobility, she rejects the indignity of being carried

and, thus, the potential for being seen as dependent and infirm. Her solution—staying at home—is thus a refusal to engage in normalizing ideologies about old age and dependency and reflects a common response
found in this study, in which people attempted to ignore societal discourses about age-appropriate behavior and carry on with their lives according to their ideas about who they had always felt themselves to be.

In the late-life transitions study, those who were newly impaired
puzzled over the issue of impairment and looked at their lives and themselves anew, having recognized their reduced ability to function fully in
daily life. A fall or the onset of a chronic illness often triggered this
awareness of a change in their body's ability to perform at its fullest. Nevertheless, as long as bodily changes were gradual, women and men expressed a sense of continuity.

People who had previously recognized their infirmities were sometimes forced to deal with the progression of disability. Mr. George Grieg,
an eighty-five-year-old Latvian-American man who had had a series of
small strokes and had other health problems as well, had made a major
decision several years previously to stay in his apartment rather than live
with his son in another state or go to a nursing home. Doing so necessitated finding a part-time, paid caregiver to run errands and take him out.

> It became a problem to get along. But I phoned a man who comes over
> each week. We both go to Safeway [supermarket], I give a list and he
> buys, then we come back home. I pay for him. But that is the way I'm
> getting along. That has really helped. Very lucky, in fact, that I got that
> man. He has a car. Without him I would really be in trouble. Really, it's a
> bad thing what can happen if you go to a nursing home. He took me
> once to the hospital. I phone him if I need him to help me. That's how I
> am living. Otherwise, I am completely alone.

As new symptoms appear and multiply, people rethink their impairments in terms of their daily life: they consider how much additional
time they must allow to accomplish daily routines, what further concessions they must make, and what special precautions they need to follow. Mobility changes especially require this kind of attention. For example, Mrs. Lydia Johnson, an eighty-four-year-old African-American
woman, said,

I don't think I'm doing too bad. I have good days and bad days. I haven't been really feeling my actual best since I had the stroke. Now I'm short-winded. But my breathing is much better than it has been because it was so bad I couldn't walk too far [because of the recent onset of asthma]. And then I get tired. I have to use a cane to balance myself. If I don't be careful, I'll fall.

Mobility is a major marker of independence; its loss signals loss of independence and may be viewed as a sign of impending death. In a follow-up visit one year after he was first visited, Mr. Andreas Pappas, an eighty-four-year-old Greek-American man, reported he was losing his ability to walk. One year earlier, he had reported that he rode his exercycle daily and walked one-half to one mile daily.

I've been doing well except that lately, in the past two or three weeks, I don't have control of my legs. If I walk a hundred yards, I can't walk anymore. I don't know what the hell it is. I told my doctor about it. So it's a process of wearing out. That's the only way I can describe it.

Preoccupied by his mobility problems, he volunteered his trouble walking later in the same interview.

Like I say, my ability to walk is declining. I don't know what it's going to feel like a year from now, if I'm alive. I just may give up for all it's worth. I just don't have any control over it. The legs just give out, that's all there is to it. My legs become very, very heavy. I become tired and I have to stop. But they haven't given up in the sense that I have fallen down. I stand still and they hurt.

Monitoring the body is an incessant process in old age. When impairment threatens to disrupt daily life, as difficulty walking does, people contemplate what these changes might mean: decreased autonomy or death. Anticipatory grief, an awareness of an impending loss,[21] was observed when people faced the loss of mobility because immobility symbolized loss of autonomy. In later life, awareness of bodily changes raises the question of impending decline and death.

In old age, the disparity may be great between a person's embodied knowledge and others' observations of that person's physical capacity.

For example, Mrs. Lida James, an eighty-five-year-old African-American widow, had lived in senior housing until she was forced to move to a long-term care institution because of her inability to walk or care for herself. She was unhappy there, and because she was judged to be competent by staff, she was given a seventy-two-hour pass to go home to visit her still intact apartment. The visit had disastrous results: it was subsequently noted in her chart, "At home she enjoyed herself but yesterday she fell into the toilet and was unable to extricate herself and called 911. She's not happy to be back." When asked later how she felt about that incident and the subsequent dismantling of her apartment, she replied,

> I just want to live a free life until I die . . . As long as I can make two steps. If I can get somebody to help me, I will move out [of the institution] but if I don't, I'll be gone.

In other words, if she cannot leave the institution she wishes to die. When old people are faced with dependency, it is not unusual for them to express a wish to die.[22]

Mrs. James summed up the dilemma of encroaching impairment as she reaffirmed her identity and at the same time voiced her frustration over her loss of autonomy.

> I feel just like I did when I was sixteen. I do, except the crippled part. I'm fine just sitting here.

In this statement of who she is, she omits "the crippled part" from her sense of self. Her embodied experience of being "fine just sitting here" affirms her sense of autonomy, yet illustrates how her autonomy-in-the-world has shrunk to the boundaries of her body.

The exploration of human vulnerability underscores the key values and beliefs that define a particular culture.[23] In U.S. society, loss of function may be especially feared because of the cultural emphasis on autonomy. The social consequences of vulnerability and dependence challenge U.S. ideologies about the role of the individual in society.[24] In old age, people may be powerless in the face of the moral force of normalizing ideologies. As a social institution in U.S. life, biomedicine reinforces and reshapes moral discourses about normalcy and makes judgments about what is normal and what is not. Whereas younger people may be more autonomous and may be able to develop an expanded view of what is normal, Mrs. James was redefined by biomedical practitioners as not able to care for herself and thus as not "normal." This redefinition by others resulted in her loss of the right to make a personal decision about where to live. Thus, the redefinition of what is normal becomes part of the moral discourse on normalcy. Through the clinical gaze, discourses on, and redefinitions of, normalcy may become measures of surveillance.[25] The case of Mrs. James raises questions about what happens when technological limits are reached and biomedical sanctions assert themselves by defining normalcy in a restrictive sense, with the result that people lose control over their lives.

In the analysis of this example, the invisible presence of other discourses on normalcy is felt. Mrs. James is a poor African-American woman who lived in subsidized housing before she was moved to a public institution. The discourse on entitlement, though invisible, is nevertheless present in the reconfiguration of normalcy. This discourse is part of normalizing ideologies and thus informs the actions of those who assume the roles of moral arbiters in making decisions for others.

Although it has been suggested that attitudes about old age will change as the baby boom generation ages,[26] there is little indication that these changes will occur soon. When they do occur, it is likely that negative attitudes will continue with respect to those over eighty and those who live with chronic illnesses. Their embodied knowledge may be given little credence by others.

6 Personal Responsibility for Continuity

As I analyzed narratives for this book, I observed that a preponderance of the narratives expressed concern about the effects of disruption on people's sense of self. This came as no surprise. What was surprising, however, was that in describing the effects of disruption, people psychologized and internalized the struggle to deal with disruption. That is, people felt responsible for disruptions that were essentially beyond their control and for righting these disruptions, both at the social level and at the personal level. Although people's narratives reflected an ongoing tension between personal experience and social expectations, they almost invariably culminated in the acknowledgment of personal responsibility for managing the disruption. My findings are in keeping with the observation that, in the United States, the ideology of individualism is concerned with continuity of the self rather than with cultural continuity.[1] It is not society but, instead, the person who is seen as responsible for creating continuity and permanence.

I also observed that this struggle to deal with disruption created embodied distress, as attested to by the examples in the previous chapter. The disruptions people experienced to their sense of self were lived out at the bodily level. When the burden of their sense of responsibility for creating continuity became intense, people experienced that conflict through their bodies. They sometimes described themselves as feeling like they were literally being torn apart by the conflict they experienced. As they discussed the profound bodily response they were feeling, many people expressed a renewed awareness of their bodies and the strength of their emotions. Some people rethought past bodily experience, such as physical abuse or illness, and its long-term effects on them, including its effect on the way they experienced the present disruption. As I observed this intense process of rethinking in person after person, I saw the totality of people's engagement in their struggles with disruption and the futility of academic attempts to separate body, self, and emotion from each other. In daily life, they are inextricably tied to one another.

In addition, although self-definition was strongly shaped by family dynamics and expectations, and by broader social and cultural issues, the narrators gave comparatively little emphasis to social and cultural causes of disruption and instead focused on dialogues of individual responsibility. The family—which was, in most cases, the locus of disruption and reflected broader social problems as well—was relegated to a salient but nevertheless subsidiary position compared to issues of personhood in people's narratives. Although, as I selected narratives for this chapter, I recognized anew the great extent to which the family is a salient force in self-concerns, I did not initially notice how the narratives I selected were so closely concerned with family disruption, or the threat of family disruption, and with social and economic causes of disruption. This work has attuned me, once again, to an imbalance in the United States: the propensity, in determining the causes of disruptions to a family, to view the person as all-important and to diminish the role of cultural ideologies and social and economic conditions. The study of disruption reveals the critical links between the family and society in formulating personhood.

In the analysis of narratives of disruption, it emerged that not only people's analysis of their own state of affairs but also their view of themselves at the personal level is inherently cultural. In the United States, working conceptions of the person are shaped by a psychologistic concern with the self.[2] When people tell their narratives of disruption, they not only focus on the meaning and significance of events for their lives but also interpret their actions and those of others through the lens of a cultural construct of the self. This construct is increasingly the focus of people's explanations, queries, and ways of making sense of the world, and is borne out in a cultural discourse on the self.

There is an ongoing debate, influenced by postmodernism, in anthropology about the extent to which the self is culturally determined, that is, the extent to which the person acts as an agent in his or her social milieu.[3] A related debate questions whether there is a stable, cohesive self or whether such a portrayal is simplistic.[4] Katherine Ewing suggests people continuously reconstitute their identities in response to internal and external stimuli, that they create an ever changing "string of selves" in which they may overlook inconsistencies and experience wholeness and continuity. This perspective is supported by recent work on the narrative structure of life stories and borne out in the narratives in this book.[5]

In this chapter we will explore people's efforts to create continuity with respect to cultural discourses on both the self and the family and examine the moral force of normalizing ideologies on people's lives. By doing so, we are able to view the family as a potential mediator of disruption and to see how, when disruption to the family occurs, the cultural discourse on the family intervenes in people's efforts at mediation.

"WHO AM I?" IN CULTURAL CONTEXT

People are likely to question who they are when they are confronting a disruption to life. When their taken-for-granted world is changing, they are forced out of predictable routines and ways of seeing their lives to handle the contingencies with which they are faced. Their identity may change, and they may see themselves anew. Although people may be preoccupied with sense of self, that very preoccupation is cultural in nature.

The story of Grace, a forty-year-old African-American woman in the midlife study, illustrates how life disruptions can trigger such intense self-examination, a process during which Who am I? may become the central question. We will see how cultural ideologies influence Grace's story.

At the time of this interview, Grace was going through a series of major changes in her life. Feeling vulnerable and unsure of herself, she had left her job of over ten years in order to resume her education and was trying to start a business of her own. I asked Grace the usual initial question I had developed for that study: "Tell me about the changes you have been going through. You can start anywhere you want." I had intentionally designed the question to be vague and open-ended in order to fit a multitude of life circumstances. Also, I did not want to impose my own ideas about continuity and change on the men and women I was interviewing. To my surprise, Grace started over ten years earlier, at the beginning of another period of change.

> I guess it started in the late 1970s. I started feeling "Something's not right—my life just doesn't feel right." I was at a cocktail party one night. My social thing was very important to me—my social friends, being with the right people. We were all talking, and I guess I kept saying, "John says this, John says that," and this woman said to me, "Well, I'm really damn sick and tired of what John says. What about *Grace?* What does *Grace* say? What does *Grace* think?" This is a woman I had known since I was eighteen.
>
> That really haunted me. Because at that moment I realized that I was this assortment of people that I knew, and that I really had no substance that I could find.

Catapulted by a friend's comment into a concerted effort to discover herself, Grace viewed that time of her life as the beginning of an extended period of disruption. Not having an identifiable core that she felt she could call her self threw her into a tailspin.

> I didn't know who I was. And I don't know that I know it now. However, I feel that what I'm doing, and what I have been doing since then, is shedding all of these other people that I picked up and incorporated into myself since I was a child.

We immediately learn several things about the cultural discourse on the self. First, when Grace describes her anguish over her sense that she did not know who she was, she delineates a central tenet of the cultural discourse on the self: people are supposed to know who they are. Second, we learn that people are apparently supposed to identify only one core self. Grace's metaphorical statement that she is "shedding all of these other people" that she has acquired during her life provides the clue. Third, the tension between the notion of the person as a social being and the person as an autonomous individual emerges when Grace reports her memory of another woman asking her about her own opinions. That Grace has a notion of who she *should* be fits the social science notion that there is a "normative" self. Commonly held ideas about the self have apparently shaped social science notions to reflect the cultural discourse.

In the midst of the career changes Grace was experiencing, her daughter, who was about to graduate from college and was on the verge of beginning a career herself, announced that she was pregnant and planning to raise her child without marrying her partner. Grace, concerned not only with her daughter's future but also with what others would think, was adamantly opposed to this plan. She and her daughter, who had always been close, became immersed in a conflict that both found agonizing.

Grace reported that at first she had alternated between hysteria and anger, asking her daughter repeatedly, "How could you do this to me?" After an angry stand-off, her daughter proceeded with plans to move out of Grace's house and live with her partner. Grace became more and more distraught. She believed that all her plans for her daughter, whom she had raised alone since her divorce ten years earlier, had been destroyed. Moreover, she felt that through her daughter's actions, she, Grace, was being destroyed. Grace described her family as one that had been concerned for generations with being respectable members of the African-American middle class. She was afraid of her family's being labeled by a cultural stereotype that portrays African Americans as ignorant and uneducated, as people who have children young without benefit of legal marriage. Grace felt herself to be a victim of this stereotype. She felt that the world she had worked so hard to build for her children was collapsing, and at the same time, the image she had always projected, of a controlled, competent businesswoman, was also crumbling. She felt that she was trapped in an unacceptable situation, one from which there was no escape.

Although Grace portrayed the conflict between her and her daughter as intrapsychic and interpersonal, it assaulted Grace's interpretation of normalizing ideologies of the family. She had struggled to adhere to specific ideals of family for many years despite her divorce, and now she saw them slipping completely from her grasp. She was angry not only with her daughter but also with herself, angry that she could not tolerate her daughter's decision. In an effort to make sense of this crisis, she started reviewing her family's emphasis on social status.

> My mother used to say to me, "You have a friend and you pick up their mannerisms, you pick up their speaking pattern. Why don't you be yourself?" Yet with the same breath, she would say, "Why don't you be like so-and-so? Why can't you be so-and-so?" And then she would go on to say, "So-and-so is like this, like that. You're just nothing." Then when I would try to emulate these people that she thought highly of, she would get very angry.
>
> I was never allowed to pick anything—friends—I was not allowed to pick them. If she liked them, if I was lucky enough that she liked who I picked, then I got to keep them as a friend. But if she didn't, they didn't get to be friends with me. She picked my clothes, she picked the classes I took in school. Everything. The church I went to. They [parents] didn't go to church. But I had to go, and I had to go to the church of her choice. Everything I did.

Making the connection between how her mother had run her life and how she wanted to run her daughter's life, she realized that her anger was at her mother, not at her daughter. She suddenly sat bolt upright, her eyes opening wide.

> Oh, I get it! I'm being very angry. I'm expressing anger not so much at my daughter for what she told me, but that what she told me was the catalyst to open the door for my anger and my rage at everybody in my whole life. Yeah, that's where I am. I'm feeling all these emotions inside. It's like I'm on some kind of roller coaster. My daughter said to me,

"You're spewing all this hate and anger." and I said, "No, I'm not." And I just realized, "Yes, I am." I just realized it at this moment. I am spewing a lot of hate and anger. It's like the other night [fight with daughter] opened the door. It's suddenly safe enough for me to feel all the hate and all the anger that I've ever held inside of myself.

When she identified other family members, especially her mother, as the source of her anger, she identified the problem as the disparity between normalizing ideologies and her view of herself. Crying, she said,

There *is* a me there, and I really do know who it is. I don't want . . . I'm so *afraid* of what other people are going to think about me or say to me or do to me or not do, until I don't want to have anything to *do* with who I am.

Suddenly, Grace was overwhelmed by the pain she felt. Rocking back and forth, she said emphatically,

I hate it! I want it to be easier. I want to get through this. My whole life has been such a struggle. I want to get through it easy. And it's not happening. I know it's a process of constant improvement. A never ending cycle. And now that I accept that, I can't say, "Well, when will it end?" anymore. I just have to say, "I'm not going to be attached to the outcome. I've just got to be willing." I know that I made a choice. I can choose to deal with my stuff now, or I can put it off till later. But I always choose to do things now. It's hard. There has got to be something past this pain.

I had this period where I was really happy. Life wasn't quite the struggle it had always been. And then, all of a sudden, you get to a plateau. And then you start all over again with the struggle.

In her anguish, Grace further embellishes on the cultural discourse in which the self is seen as autonomous and self-actualizing. She has personalized and taken responsibility for the tension between participating in social relationships while simultaneously living up to dominant cultural notions of the self. The invisible protagonist in this struggle is the cultural discourse on normalcy, which is played out in Grace's efforts to be likable and accepted by others. Grace assumes it is up to her to fulfill this goal, and that she must change in order to do so.

Trying to maintain a sense of coherence in the midst of a tumultuous period, Grace frames her identity issues metaphorically, portraying change as a cycle with plateaus of stability and her search for herself as work, a struggle for "constant improvement." In doing so, she is attempting to create a framework for viewing her life that gives her a sense of consistency in the midst of change.

Grace expresses the bodily disruption that goes hand in hand with the disruption she experiences to her sense of self:

> This is a volcano erupting. This is it! You see me holding myself? I literally feel split inside. It's like . . . I don't quite know how to explain it. On the one hand I'm feeling really calm, and really outside myself. Like I'm the observer. And on the other hand, I'm being totally off balance, totally in the red, totally . . . angry and full of rage. I feel myself striking out on an emotional level. It's really icky.

The volcano is a body metaphor for all the emotions Grace cannot articulate. In likening herself to a volcano, Grace gives expression to a jumble of feelings—volcanic feelings of being "off balance . . . in the red . . . striking out." She describes her sense that there is a split within her: part of her experiences her emotions while the rest of her calmly looks on, as if part of her is a stranger looking at her. This bifurcation in her view opens her up.

What is hardest for Grace is experiencing a loss of control. Control, a core cultural value, has been her way of dealing with uncertainty.

> I feel out of control. It's not like me. I'm always in control. As a matter of fact, I'm so in control of my anger at all times that it never comes out. It's never even felt in my body. And now I'm feeling it, and I'm owning it. And I don't mind owning it. It seems like it's okay to feel this way, but nevertheless it's scary. It feels very out of control. When you came through the door, I felt like a volcano about to erupt. Gee, all this stuff! It's like I've owned it and I've acknowledged it and I've made peace with it through this conversation. And I feel better inside. I'm not feeling like there are sparks flying every which way.

In returning to the metaphor of the volcano, Grace indicates that the explosion is over. During the explosion, however, she experiences a reawakening of embodied knowledge: she now feels her anger in her body but finds that to be okay, if "scary." In taking on the body metaphor and letting go of control, Grace reestablishes embodied knowledge. Here again we see the transformative power of metaphor.

Grace's story illustrates how efforts to create a personal sense of coherence are shaped by cultural processes that are mediated by the family. Specifically, we see that the dynamic interplay between individual-level processes and cultural-level normalizing ideologies is mediated by Grace's interpretations of her family's expectations. She describes two levels of conflict that pose an ongoing source of concern: the conflict between her experience and, on the one hand, the cultural discourse on the normal family and, on the other hand, the cultural discourse on normalcy, as interpreted by her family. Her extreme anguish is triggered by her feeling that she has failed to fulfill cultural expectations promulgated by her family. She believes her tenuous hold on respectability, as dictated by the discourse on the normal family, has been undermined by her daughter's decision. In the case of the cultural discourse on normalcy, she does not know what *is* normal, but she assumes that she is *not* normal. Because she is unsure about what are normal social expectations, she tries overly hard to please others.

Families may both aggravate disruption and create continuity. As she relates intergenerational conflict, first between her and her daughter, then between her and her mother, Grace engages a form of generational continuity. That conflict revolves, in each case, around the choice between socially conformist behavior and independent thinking and action. In the end, Grace opts for the latter; she prepares to live with her daughter's decision. In doing so, however, she must forego a sense of generational continuity that she might have experienced by following in her mother's footsteps, that is, in dictating her daughter's behavior. By not taking this path, Grace is opening herself up to a form of discontinuity, deviation from tradition. As she decides to break with family traditions that would preserve the past, albeit with undesirable emotional consequences, she fashions a new sense of continuity. By acknowledging her daughter's analysis of her anger as accurate, Grace not only makes a break with the past but also begins to reshape her life story to maintain a sense of coherence.

As she moves back and forth between stories of events as she remembers them and agonizing questions about locating a self she views as hidden, Grace begins to bring closure to the disruption in her life. Part of this process is her effort to make peace with her own sense of deviation from cultural notions of self, family, and normalcy as they were portrayed within her family. She begins to weave the disruptions she has experienced into the story of her life. This back-and-forth, in-and-out process not only helps her identify an emerging sense of herself as a person but also enables her to refine her overall story. This process gives her a sense of continuity in the face of a lifelong series of disruptions.[6]

Grace's story is embedded in a specific cultural context, the African-American middle-class family. Her family strongly values respectability and social status, as well as self-determination, autonomy, mastery, and individual responsibility, and Grace has internalized these core cultural values. Cultural notions of the normal family and of normalcy had specific overtones as interpreted by her and her family. Her daughter's pregnancy and subsequent decision not to marry her partner catalyzed the breaking apart of Grace's particular vision of the family, leaving her with a profound sense of disruption as well as a crippling sense of responsibility for restoring normalcy to the family and to everyday life.

In the United States, such a scenario is not unusual but, indeed, quite typical when pregnancy occurs out of wedlock, despite the frequency with which this happens among teens and young adults. When events conflict with cultural ideologies, cultural buffers to help people counter the effects of disruption may be unavailable. The family could not serve as a buffer in Grace's case because the construct of the normal family was contested. Moreover, because questions about Grace's fit with the cultural discourse on normalcy were also triggered, her sense of responsibility for resolving the dilemma was exacerbated. This story thus exemplifies a key predicament in U.S. society: when a disruption calls cultural notions of the self into question, people engage in agonizing self-examination until they can reconcile how they see themselves with the cultural discourse, but if the disruption calls into question the discourse on the family, a primary buffer in mediating cultural processes, the family may become problematized and unavailable as a resource for grappling with disruption. The cultural emphasis on individual responsibility for the resolution of problems leaves people without adequate cultural supports to help weather crisis. In this cultural quicksand, identity is challenged, and dilemmas that are essentially cultural in nature are interpreted as personal failure.

REWORKING MEANING THROUGH VALUES

In analyzing narratives for this book, I found that values are the ground on which cultural discourses are developed. Values give unifying meaning to the events in people's lives and are a primary means through which individuals interpret and explain reality.[7] Values facilitate the connection between the mundane events of everyday life and the macrosocial, historical, political, and economic context in which lives are lived and cultural constructs are shaped. Not only are values integral to cultural-specific guidance and direction, they become the basis for common-sense constructions of the world and may lead to the creation and perpetuation of ideologies as well.[8]

As we see throughout this book, values are entrenched in people's lives. People in chaos cling to their values as a source of order. Values inform cultural discourses, which often encompass several related values. Values may be linked to memories of significant life experiences to form an individual belief system, to life experiences and goals for action, or to the ways in which dominant social ideologies are connected to experience.[9]

Mary Ann, a thirty-nine-year-old Anglo respondent in the infertility study, ruminates about the extent to which family values played an important role in her unsuccessful efforts to have children.

> The message that I got from my family is that children are a pain in the neck. I got that pretty strong from my mother. I think it's interesting that we have this pattern in the family, so it makes me wonder how I would do [as a parent]. Our family did not communicate at all that you've got to have kids and that having kids is part of being married. We never got that attitude. But I have this book by a Christian physician, and there's a quote in there that says having children is as innate a need as eating and

breathing. I read that, and I thought, "That's just another sexist, Christian man who is trying to keep all women barefoot and pregnant." But I can't shake that. I was raised in the church. It was the whole center of our social life.

In this statement Mary Ann contrasts her family's attitudes about children with the cultural expectations about motherhood espoused by a Protestant fundamentalist religious leader. Although she interjects her feminist view into the discussion, she acknowledges her difficulty in "shaking" the cultural beliefs that were part of her upbringing. Despite the absence of overt statements by her parents about the importance of children, her early socialization through her religion, by means of which values about women's roles in bearing children were strongly inculcated in her, affected her gender identity.

The ideologies of individualism and rational determinism are underlying themes in the United States.[10] Precepts of these ideologies were ingrained in Mary Ann, and, in relinquishing motherhood for herself, she falls back on these well-entrenched ideologies:

> I find that I can't assign meaning to infertility—I can't find meaning in it. But I guess I'm very much of the American philosophy of whatever that happens—bad or good things happen for a reason, and if a bad thing happens like that, I can say, "Well, this will help me to reach out to other people and help them through something like this," or "This will help me build character." People tell me that a lot, and I'll agree, it is building character in me, but that's not meaningful enough for me to understand why I'm going through it. So it's not an answer, but it's given me a framework to kind of grasp this experience and to understand why I can't seem to get past it.

Mary Ann articulates the ethos of rational determinism as she searches for answers to her dilemma: things happen for a reason, so if bad things happen (such as her unwanted childlessness), they can be rationalized as character building. As she searches for ways of assigning meaning to infertility, she herself draws the link between the cultural ethos and frameworks of understanding. Her frameworks of understanding do not encompass the notion that she might be unable to have children, however; hence her statement that she cannot find meaning in infertility. Searching through her repertoire of values, she finds none that can adequately explain this conundrum. That it will build character is as close as she can get to an explanation for why she has had to endure this disruption to her life.

Mary Ann goes on to delineate other values that articulate with the cultural ethos.

> The main thing for my family, I think, is the value of an education—my Puritan work ethic in positive ways. If you do a good job, you get results, and I feel like I have. We've worked hard, and we have a nice house, and you know, good things happen to people who work hard. Maybe there's too much of a work ethic in there. But the value of an education and to just be honest and about lying. And so those are things that were really upheld in my family.

In espousing the Protestant work ethic, Mary Ann identifies the cultural notion associated with it: "good things happen to people who work hard." She connects this cultural tenet to her family's values about honesty and hard work. In this narrative, we see how Mary Ann wrestles with the moral force of normalizing ideologies as she tries to place her experience of childlessness within a dominant cultural framework that emphasizes children as essential to a meaningful life. She is driven to examining dominant cultural ideologies in relation to her philosophy of life. Doing so enables her to find meaningful explanations for her life that she can use as she relinquishes her efforts to have children. She substitutes the normalizing ideologies about the importance of hard work for those of having children: she prepares to pour renewed energy into her career. In doing so, she ties the work ethic to personhood and family values, thereby restoring a sense of order to her life.

MEDIATING CULTURAL NOTIONS OF THE NORMAL FAMILY

As we examine linkages between cultural discourses on self, family, and normalcy in narratives of disruption, we see the depth of the disruption that people experience when any one of these discourses is questioned. Moreover, the invisible tenets that guide ensuing efforts to create a sense of coherence become more readily apparent. Charles, a thirty-year-old African-American man in the infertility study, highlights disruptions caused by family conflicts in early life. Charles was unemployed when he was first interviewed. He had a high school education and some trade school experience. He and his wife of five years had been trying to conceive for several years. As he planned to start his own family, he revisited his own childhood and its disruptions. His parents had separated when he was a child, and his father subsequently gained custody of him.

> In living with my stepmother and my father, it was first just my dad, and that was great because I really didn't see him that often [when the parents were together]. And the way it happened, he came by and picked me up, and for some reason I remember my mother being present. And I remember looking at her and being happy and not having a lot of tears, or crying, but I do remember the expression on her face. It wasn't one of joy, and so I had a look of happiness and wonderment because I was wondering why she was so sad, I guess. Because I didn't know that I was never coming back.
>
> When we did move in with my dad, I remember it was the fall. Because he bought a brand new car. Those were beautiful cars. I see them every now and then today, and I remember the fresh leather and playing, sitting in the back seat, just touching it. And looking at my daddy being all proud and being happy that I was with him. And being oblivious, not really knowing what was going on. Spending the night, and a consecutive amount of days and finally asking, "Daddy, when are we going home?" And then he broke it to me. "You are not, this is your new home." And I think from that point on things kinds of changed for me. Because I never . . . here is a man that I knew was my father, but I really didn't know him. I don't think my father ever held me as a baby.

Although this initial disruption to the family occurred when he was a small child, he continues to reflect on it and to address the loss of being taken from his mother. While he was still mourning this loss, his father remarried. There were many tensions below the surface of daily life once his stepmother joined the family. Periodically, these tensions erupted into conflict.

One day my father came to us [him and sister] and I must say this, she was the sweetest woman before she got married, she was the sweetest woman, you know. She was *so* sweet, but after they married she became a tyrant. That's how it seems to me today, seriously. Because there was a lot of covert abuse.

When I was sixteen, I left my dad's house because I couldn't take the pain and the abuse. I couldn't deal with it anymore. I had smoked weed and put this in my journal, in my autobiography. That time my dad and stepmother had just come in from shopping, buying groceries. I recognized those footsteps, I knew who it was, the message telling me that she is angry. I thought, "Just go see if you can be of help," so I went to the kitchen and asked, "You want me to help you with anything?" She says, "Don't say anything to me, you are just like your damned daddy." She picks up a black cast-iron skillet and she swings it at my head because I pissed her off. I went to protect my head, and she sent me across the floor. I said, "You ain't never going to have to worry about hitting me again. Never, because I am out of here." And I went to my father who was on the porch. I didn't cry in front of her, but as I approached him I was crying, and I said, "Daddy, I love you, I love you very much, but I can't stay here no more." I just told him like that and I left. I left home and walked to my mother's house, and I didn't look back when I walked away. I am sure my father had some pain around that. Now, when I am around my dad, that elephant is on the floor, we don't ever talk about that.

After I left everything fell apart. It was like I was the one holding things together. Because I was a scapegoat. Everybody could take their anger and aggression out on me. And when I left, the whole structure just deteriorated and crumbled.

This fight disrupted Charles's family. His father and stepmother divorced, and his siblings went to live with other relatives. These events occurred at a critical juncture in his adolescence. He began a long period of wandering from place to place and from one job to another. Almost fifteen years later, he is still sorting out these chaotic events, trying to make sense of them in order to lend his life a sense of coherence. He sees himself as a scapegoat who held the family together by serving as a catalyst for conflict, and his analysis of family dynamics relieves him of the heavy responsibility for his disrupted family. In a state of extreme despair and alienation after this incident ripped apart the fabric of his life, Charles became addicted to drugs and alcohol. He is now in another period of transition as he recovers from his addictions and attempts to create a new life.

This narrative is about the cultural discourse on the normal family. Implicit in Charles's story is the idea that his experience does not adhere to cultural notions of the normal family. We learn what he views as normal from his explication of events that he views as not normal, or right. First, he is taken from his mother without being told. Second, his stepmother is not simply unloving but also abusive. Third, his father appears to take his stepmother's side in family conflicts. In teasing apart what is normal, Charles engages the cultural discourse on normalcy, of which the cultural discourse on the normal family is a part. Only by identifying what is normal can he see his own experience as abnormal. Doing so has enabled him to view these disruptions as not his responsibility or fault.

Charles attempts to integrate these family disasters through metaphor. Having analyzed the dynamics underlying these disruptive experiences, he attempts to weave them into his life story in a coherent way by using an elephant as a metaphor for the tensions in family relations that remain unspoken almost fifteen years later. The elephant metaphor creates a sense of continuity with the past. The elephant—the unspoken history of conflict in his family—remains with him and is taking its place in his life, both past and present. Embodying a long and messy series of conflicts in the figure of an elephant is also a way of tidying them up into a single package, which perhaps allows one to regard them as more manageable though still large. With the passage of time, these conflicts have been smoothed over but not forgotten. The elephant metaphor that Charles uses fulfills the task of metaphor: to return to the whole and thereby create coherence.

Despite these several disruptions to his family, cultural notions of the normal family remains an ideal Charles hopes to experience. As he prepares to become a parent, he continues to emulate cultural expectations about the normal family. His grandparents fit the model he aspires to.

> I want children, I want a family because that is one thing that I missed.
> The fact that my grandparents were in Tennessee, when they were here

there was some structure in my life, and when they left, all the structure disappeared, so I want that. My grandparents have been married forever—at least thirty-two years, and I think that is beautiful. So that is what I want. Because it is very important to me to have family structure. To have family and to build, because with a large family you can start to work on a community, and you can build a community, and you can have structure in the community. And it is directly related to our community [the African-American community]. It empowers our community.

Charles's narrative is emplotted to bring his identity as an African American to the fore in his efforts to reconcile the disruptions in his life. Charles analyzes what has been missing in his life: he identifies structure and sense of community as key elements he wants in his life. They are extensions of cultural expectations about the normal family, and they provide potential linkages to others. Charles thus identifies some of the key components of the cultural discourse on the normal family, as he sees it: children, long marriage, and structure. These are also the links to community, which stand for the cultural discourse on normalcy.

Charles embellishes further on the cultural discourse on normalcy by calling attention to the link between the African-American family and the African-American community and, beyond that, by calling attention to the goal of empowerment of that community. His vision of the community springs from the cultural base he believes the family should afford. Charles has drawn on cultural meanings of being African American to create a sense of coherence that sustains him through adversity. His strong emphasis on community and its connection to cultural discourses on both the family and normalcy suggests that there may be a formulation of cultural discourses about self, family, and normalcy specific to African Americans: the community becomes the repository of those discourses on family and normalcy. This view is supported by literature on the lives of African Americans and borne out in work on the meanings of identity.[11]

Charles's gender identity is also central to his story.

What type of man am I? An honest man. One that is willing to grow and change. I am a man becoming a man. I think that is a continual process. The reason I say I am becoming a man is that there are some things I need to change within myself before I can truly say I am a man. These character flaws take away from true manhood, like lack of self-confidence and self-esteem, like not wanting to be responsible when I become overwhelmed and delegating that responsibility to my wife. That is not being a man. But I am doing something about those things today. I am taking charge. Being a man is being solid in your judgment. So that is what kind of man I am.

A strong sense of personhood is critical, in Charles's view, to the actualization of his plans. In examining cultural expectations about the self, Charles identifies the cultural discourse on manhood. In his description of himself, Charles articulates core American values such as responsibility with respect to his gender identity: men take responsibility; they exercise their judgment. He observes of himself,

I have to be self-reliant; I can't depend on anybody. If I want something, I have to do it for myself.

His comments call attention not only to how the North American ideology of individualism is tempered by gender but also to how gender identity shapes emplotment in narratives.

The contrast between Charles's view of himself and his current unemployment threatens his sense of continuity. Consequently, he expresses uncertainty about himself and his future.

I see my life unfolding in so many beautiful ways. I am going back to school. I want to do something positive. In whatever community I am in I want to be a positive asset to that community. I have heard so many positive things about [city he is planning to move to]. I don't want to go without having something to offer. But I have lost my drive to hustle. I don't have that hunger, that drive. That bothers me.

I don't want to do nothing. I am a very creative person. I have a lot of ideas. But I am finding that the older I get, the less I am using my imagination because I am doing mundane stuff. I am starting to lose my life, basically. I feel like this is where my life is, up here [tapping head], it ain't got nothing to do with my heart. My life is in my mind, and that life is creativity, my ability to be creative and create things. When I start to stop dreaming and stop being creative and stop wanting to go explore, I might just as well wait it out and die because all I am doing is existing. I don't want to exist, I want to live.

Being creative gives life meaning for Charles. He uses the metaphor "lose my life" to underline his fears of losing opportunities to be creative, and hence, being unable to assign meaning to his activities. Not using his imagination represents a form of dying; mere existence represents the death of the mind.

Charles is at a crossroads. While he is frustrated because of his unemployment, he looks to the future as he sets new life plans into motion, plans that reflect U.S. values of achievement and participation in community. Although he is plagued by self-doubt, having plans enables him to create a bridge between his old life and his new one and lends him a sense of continuity.

His view of himself as a man is directly related to the role he sees for himself in the family he is trying to establish.

> I believe you have to have some politics in the family. There has to be a hierarchy in the family. There has to be some one person running things, and if there ain't, it all falls apart. Because if there is no somebody running something and keeping the order, then you get what we have here today. Children are running amok. And there must be a tribal elder to keep it simple. I look forward to being a tribal elder, I really do.

In Charles's story we see how the cultural discourse on the normal family informs people's understanding of what their lives should be. These cultural elements are ascribed to the family. Charles identifies these elements as order, structure, and the opportunity to build a community. He expresses a sense of community and views the family as the key to actualizing his vision of that community. Personhood, so well articulated in his statement of who a man is, facilitates his sense of coherence and is strongly tied to his vision of the family. He anticipates his role as a "tribal elder," thus linking himself in an instrumental way to positive, future action.

Charles's narrative illustrates both the continuities and discontinuities in family life. His relationships with his father and his grandparents have proven to be enduring continuities in his life. Charles equates order with having an intact family. Order is thus part of the cultural discourse on the normal family. He extends his own experience into a broader social domain: the current state of affairs in African-American families, as he sees it. His intent, to become a tribal elder, is part of his effort to restore order that he views as missing and his wish to adhere to cultural expectations about the normal family. Although he acknowledges that there are deviations from the dominant cultural view of the normal family, he nevertheless continues to strive to fit this ideal. For Charles, it is the solution to a lifetime of discontinuities.

7 Living in Limbo

Following a disruption, people experience a period of limbo before they can begin to restore a sense of order to their lives. Although the concept of liminality has been applied to disabled persons and persons experiencing difference from a physical norm, it has not been applied to studies of disruption more generally.[1] In his classic work *The Rites of Passage*, Arnold van Gennep identified three stages in life crisis and other rites of passage: separation, merger or transition, and reincorporation.[2] During transition, a person enters as "one kind of person" and emerges altered in some essential way. Victor Turner, who developed the notions of liminality and being "in between" in his work on ritual, observed that liminal people are suspended in social space.[3] Liminal people are at a threshold outside the boundaries of society: they have "been declassified but are not yet reclassified: they have died in their old status and are not yet reborn in a new one."[4]

I have found that a period of limbo inevitably follows a life disruption like infertility. When people discovered that they were infertile, their sense of order was disrupted, and life lost its meaning. Their hopes for the future had been the ground for their sense of continuity, and because they could not foresee the future, they consequently felt unable to proceed to the next phase of life. Their culturally derived sense of being propelled through time had stopped. They felt trapped in the present. The need to envision a future for themselves became the pivot on which all of life turned. The limbo metaphor enabled women and men to begin the slow and painful process of reestablishing a sense of future and a sense of order. By understanding this period of disorder and disaffection as temporary, by placing boundaries around it, they were able to better endure their sense of disruption. The limbo metaphor enabled them to separate a time of limbo from a future time when life would return to "normal." This period of limbo continued for the majority of the sample who remained childless for several years. During that time they laid the groundwork for reordering experience.

Carrie, a forty-year-old, middle-class, college-educated Anglo businesswoman, had been married for fifteen years but had not attempted to conceive until she was in her early thirties. Like others in this study, Carrie had expected that her life would form a continuous whole. The disruption and fragmentation caused by unexpected infertility and several miscarriages forced her to address constructs of wholeness and continuity. She was wrestling with the cultural meanings of discontinuity and trying to create continuity. When asked an open-ended question about how infertility had affected her work and her view of her career, she talked with great emotion about her feelings of being in limbo.

> This was what our year of therapy was about. One of the major factors of our therapy. I have had my life on hold for so many years now, thinking that "I'll be pregnant and then I'll do that" for years and years and years and years. "I'm not going to start this because I'm going to stop that." Intellectually, it is almost inconceivable to me how you can contain or put your life on hold like that for so long and not go bananas, but I've done it, I've lived it for over five years. It is probably the most frustrating aspect of infertility in my mind. It's horrible, living in limbo. I think it affects your every waking moment—thinking about what you should be doing, what you could be doing, and what you want to do, and yet you

can't. You are putting so much emotional energy into surviving all of this medical shit and emotional stuff. I don't have what it takes to do it all at one time. Maybe some people do, awesome people I guess, but I think it is very hard.

It's just limbo, it's all limbo. I just was elected to this office that I told you about within [a feminist organization] and it's a serious commitment. It's a commitment of time, time, love, and money, but it's not—my other work is real estate renovation and management work, which I'm some days thrilled with and other days bored shitless with, and it's like, "Why make a change? Why do something when tomorrow it may be totally different?" That's why I say intellectually it's so crazy because it's so stupid and you know it's stupid and yet you don't. I don't deal with it well at all. Part of it is hope. If you go ahead with your life, you are somewhere, someway giving up.

Although living in limbo was at odds with Carrie's explanatory system of the order supposedly intrinsic in daily life, the limbo metaphor enabled her to begin reorganizing her experience. Her search for continuity through fertility necessitated, in her view, a decision to stop her life to pursue medical treatment. Going ahead with life meant giving up the hope of becoming a parent and, thus, losing her sense of continuity. At the same time, however, she was beginning to reframe the meaning of hope.

Taken out of context, the text does not directly reveal how Carrie's struggle to deal with her disrupted life was connected to her struggle with and resistance to biomedicine, a struggle that was fraught with contradictions. Not only had Carrie undergone years of medical treatment, but her infertility was iatrogenic: her difficulties in conceiving and carrying a fetus to term were caused by the effects of her mother's having taken DES (diethylstilbestrol) during her pregnancy.[5] Physicians readily acknowledged that DES had caused identifiable bodily defects.

I had some cervical abnormalities, some pap smears that weren't normal. Because of my involvement in the woman's movement, I was aware of DES. I had a suspicion. I was the right age. It turns out I am a DES daughter. But now that I'm in infertility treatment, it's very hard for me to sit around and do nothing. I find it extremely comforting to be doing something [pursuing a specific medical treatment]. It's sick because here I am pumping drugs into my body, which is the same reason I'm in the fix that I'm in right now.

In her efforts to recast her experience to make it more personally acceptable, she addressed the ways in which her identity changed through her
association with the women's movement. She viewed her efforts at resistance to biomedicine as attempts to empower women and better their
health care. Nevertheless, she continued with medical treatment because
she equated it with hope.

Metaphors of hope and persistence are central to Americans' efforts to
create a sense of continuity after a disruption. Both lay and medical literature attest to the importance of maintaining a hopeful attitude as part
of responsibility for the illness. In North America, persistence is valued
in persons seeking medical solutions for a range of conditions.[6] Doing
nothing is equated with the failure to take responsible action, whereas
doing something is viewed as leading to the betterment of a given situation. Conceptive technology may mobilize and reinforce this cultural
faith, held by both couples and physicians, that persistence will ultimately pay off.[7] The hope that persistence will prevent later regret is central to decisions to use medical technology,[8] and Carrie voices this hope
in her narrative.

> Eighty percent of DES daughters eventually carry to term. I find it very
> depressing. At the last symposium, we sat and listened to this woman
> who had gone through five miscarriages and was still at it. I think mis-
> carriages are the worst. Living through the emotional turmoil of miscar-
> riage is something that I wouldn't wish on anybody. But after the second
> miscarriage, I said to my husband, "I think I could handle one more."
> My rationale was, if we stop now, I will always wonder, "What if we had
> tried that?" I can't rationalize not doing it. Maybe nothing will come of it.
> But if we don't try, we'll never know.

Carrie's narrative epitomizes the tension between (1) the effort to find
a personally acceptable route out of disruption and restore order and
(2) the difficulty of accomplishing this in the face of the moral force of
normalizing ideologies. In Carrie's case the tensions that contribute to
her dilemma are especially clear. As a DES daughter, she has the moral
authority of someone whose condition was imposed by the medical dictates of a previous era. Yet she can't give up the effort to conceive. She
acknowledges the conundrum posed by using fertility drugs to fix a con-

dition created by other fertility drugs. Meanwhile, she is actively engaged in resisting normalizing ideologies about women and their bodies through her work with a feminist organization, and, in addition, she is struggling with cultural issues of hope versus "giving up."

For Carrie, as for everyone else in this book, the conflict between meeting their need to restore order and living up to normalizing ideologies was one that went on not simply for months but for years. People whose lives are disrupted are often thrust into a limbo-like state for long periods of time, sometimes even for life. Living with this kind of tension for a long period reshapes the way people think about their lives. They may become increasingly aware of the disparity between the voice of the body and the voice of society. Carrie addressed the agony she experienced in living with this disparity.

> As a woman I get so upset over the societal conditioning that you have to be a wife, you have to be a mother. There are all these have-tos. There are days when I ask, "Why do I want this?" Am I that badly keyed into societal conditioning? I can't answer that question. It is one of the nightmares of my life. On one level you struggle so hard for what is personally intimate, which is the relationship that you have and what you want that relationship to bear. And on another hand, it's being knowledgeable of society and its pressures and maneuverings. Is that because of the kind of work I do? Are we going through this hell because I can't meet society's expectations for women? Give me a break.

Carrie teases apart these two voices in an effort to resolve the tension she experiences. Her growing resistance to the moral force of normalizing ideologies prefaces her eventual decision to stop seeking motherhood and pursue other goals that are personally meaningful and within her reach.

UNCERTAIN ILLNESS TRAJECTORIES

Biographical disruption is triggered not only by the onset of chronic, disabling illness but also by any major change in that condition.[9] The illness, and it's meaning for a person's life, must be continually rethought. Men and women must integrate each disruption into their lives, yet when they experience one disruption after another, the task of integration becomes extremely difficult, if not impossible. That normalizing ideologies must be addressed at each phase of an illness makes the task even more complex.

The trajectory of an illness—the way the illness unfolds, the efforts a person makes to integrate the illness into daily life, and the impact of the illness on those involved—dramatically affects how people attempt to mediate disruption.[10] Illnesses that fluctuate unpredictably and require frequent medical intervention will be interpreted in quite different ways than illnesses that are characterized by gradual, continuous decline or by decline and subsequent restabilization with decreased functional ability. The various kinds of illness trajectories may affect identity differently, but the effects are always profound. Continuously shifting experiences of the body undermine efforts to repair disruption. People who have chronic illnesses experience uncertainties about what symptoms mean and what the future holds. Management of a serious chronic illness that has frequent ups and downs entails a continual reworking of identity. Don, a forty-year-old Anglo man with severe asthma, is engaged in this reworking process.

> I think I'm in the process of really trying to find out who Don is in the relationship to chronic disease and in relation to really accepting it. I really don't think I've accepted it yet.

Don's illness is erratic; he experiences continual ups and downs. His physical difficulties increase with each acute episode. His illness is getting worse, forcing him to rethink many facets of his life, including how the physical changes he is experiencing affect who he is. In a moment of anguish, Don attests to the idea that uncertainties about the trajectory of an illness affect every aspect of life.

> My doctor told me, "Don, this is not the time to take up skydiving." You get those monkey wrenches thrown in that say, "I'm forcing you to accept the fact that you're not going to be able to do these things." You go, "Who am I? How am I going to deal with this? What hobbies am I going

to take up? Should I start playing solitaire? Should I start playing chess? What should I do?" Maybe I should become a hairdresser or something, I don't know.

The recurring question "Who am I?" haunts Don as he attempts to deal with one assault on his body after another. The questions he asks about his identity are posed in the form of questions about social roles, questions about relinquishing those roles, and in posing them in this way, he acknowledges the force of normalizing ideologies. Giving up roles in midlife is not part of the ideology of manhood in the United States.

As Don tries to come to grips with the damage his body has sustained from his illness and the limitations it places on his daily life, he searches for new anchors for his identity. The high-energy athlete may now be gone. How will he fill that place?

I still ask, "Who am I?" I still ask, "What do I believe in?" I think it is constantly under process of revision or editing—who Don is. And the reason why is because the crises that we face and even the victories that we enjoy get absorbed in our lives in different ways or we deal with them in different ways.

By asking "Who am I?" and "What do I believe in?" in the same breath, Don acknowledges that his sense of self is in a process of metaphoric "revision or editing" and notes that the way in which both crises and victories are "absorbed" into life is contingent on changes to personhood.

His uncertain illness trajectory raises additional questions for him apart from questions about the course of the illness over time. What will life be like, and how long will it be that way? How much time is left? Discontinuities in life force individuals to reconstruct their biographies.[11] In trying to place his illness in his life in order to maintain his sense of coherence, Don is engaged in an ongoing process of biography reconstruction. For those who have faced the threat of personal destruction, biography reconstruction can be a therapeutic tool.[12] A health biography includes highly personalized and particularized memories, conceptions and meanings of events, pain, and discomfort, experiences of past illness, and health-care experiences. The body itself evolves within the context of this biography and is transformed in interactions with other people.[13]

The biography, then, is the conduit through which embodied knowledge of self is presented to oneself and to others. Meanings associated with an illness are interpreted within this biographical context, through social relationships as well as through the most mundane aspects of life.

In addressing his biography, Don uses a military metaphor.

> People in midlife are wounded soldiers. And weary soldiers. We've been to the front and back.

He identifies himself with the social condition as he sees it. Part of the fight metaphor so dominant in U.S. life, the soldier metaphor gives his life a sense of coherence and simultaneously aligns him with others. As a soldier, he is able to place himself within dominant ideologies about perseverance. This metaphor is a guiding metaphor that facilitates his efforts to integrate the long-term effects of a chronic, incapacitating illness. He tries to link the past to this metaphor when he says,

> I was much more vociferous when I was young. It was easier for me to take the big risks, and I had the energy to take the risks. I don't have the energy anymore. Maybe I'm just less naive than I was then, smarter now, more gun-shy. Stuff that's happened in the past ten years has just worn me out in some ways.

Don extends the metaphor from his illness to his entire life by talking about his willingness in youth to take risks, a willingness that has been curtailed by his limited energy.

His ongoing illness has affected his view of the world.

> I'm struggling with the disease. Part of me says I accept it and part of me refuses to accept it. I battle it—there's a part of me that probably will never ever really accept it. I don't ever want to let go of my whole book of being able to do things that I've wanted to do. The hope has really been shattered. But part of my personality is I'm a fighter. I refuse to give up fighting. I'll fight the damned disease until they take my last breath. Or until something else gets me. Sometimes I feel like I'm winning and sometimes I feel like I'm losing.

Don describes his "war" with his illness: he vacillates between accepting and rejecting, doing "battle" with, his illness, but he concludes he will "never ever really accept it." He adds another metaphor: all the things he does and wants to do comprise a "book" that he is unwilling to relinquish to his illness. Although hope has been shattered, he insists that he will persevere; in other words, he will fight to the death.

In these statements Don is exploring the role of metaphor in reframing disruption. In using the soldier metaphor, he makes it clear he has identified how to pick his fights and identify which ones are important. He situates his experience temporally, contrasting the young Don who took risks with the more mature, "smarter" Don, who knows where to place his energies in a life or death fight. In doing so, he reconstructs his biography around an aging warrior theme.

Don observes the overwhelming impact of disruption and identifies the various facets of his life that are at stake.

> It interrupts every aspect of your life. My chronic disease has interrupted my marriage, the time that we spend together, our sexual relationship is interrupted, my work, my relationship with my child . . .

Everything meaningful to him is at stake in this life or death fight, from physical functioning to family and social world.

Don reflects on the impact his illness has on his life and his identity.

> About chronic disease—you really go through periods of highs and lows and depressions, and sometimes it can just really become an incredible burden. It compresses your life down to a really short period of time. The feeling that life seems to be going so slow regarding my health, yet it seems to be going so quickly because you can't do the things you want to do and things seem to be passing you by. You can get really depressed, and in that depression you just really wonder if you're losing your identity because of the disease. It changes your life focus; you don't do the things you were able to do. And you wonder if you're ever going to be able to do them again.

In this statement Don underscores the ever present uncertain trajectory and its effect on his body, his emotions, and his identity. In addition, he calls attention to a frequently experienced aspect of chronic illness: the compression of life. This compression and the curtailment of activities one is accustomed to have a paradoxical effect: life goes slowly and quickly at the same time. The ultimate effect is one of being passed by, resulting in depression and a shift in "life focus": he shifts from doing things to questioning whether things will have to be given up.

No matter how ill they may be, people have lives beyond their illness. Although a severe illness may *appear* to shape identity, illness does not define the self, nor does the person become the illness. Yet the person may have to struggle to avoid becoming engulfed by the encroaching illness. The notion that the identity becomes embattled suggests a war, or fight, between the self and the illness.[14] For Don, the illness has become an almost tangible "thing" that he struggles against.

Identity is fluid, not static. As we have seen, different illnesses have different effects on identity. In addition to his asthma, Don struggles with another illness, osteoporosis, and the weakened body it implies. Without careful scrutiny, he appears to others to be an ordinary, "normal" person with a normal body. Acquaintances and coworkers are unaware of the *felt* destruction of the body, which is very private and seldom articulated verbally. Unless Don were to wheeze audibly or call attention to the broken arm that is the result of osteoporosis, no one would know that his body is profoundly affected by his illness.

Don is also addressing his gender identity. He is dealing with the erosion of some of the activities he associates with being a man—his work, his sexuality, his role as a father. Don questions who he is and whether he has become so altered as to become another person. He clings to the still recognizable vestiges of himself and portrays himself as a veteran, a soldier in a war for his life. He faces an ongoing effort to reconcile, through biographical reconstruction, the inroads his illness has made on his gender identity.

In his narrative portrayal of his efforts to regain a sense of continuity, Don is engaged in an endless process of reworking what normal means for him. He questions the cultural discourse on normalcy at the outset by asking what he has to give up and what he should take on. He uses irony in his discussion of the comings and goings of vocations and avocations, such as skydiving and hairdressing, to indicate that what is considered normal is not clear-cut. At the same time, he is voicing his frustration that he must move toward more sedentary activities, such as solitaire and chess. In these and subsequent comments, he challenges the cultural discourse on normalcy, resisting the moral force of normalizing ideologies.

Don uses narrative in his process of biographical reconstruction. Through narrative he weaves together the many different strands of this ongoing disruption: his bodily experience and expression, his identity and sense of self, his emotional response to his illness, the changes in his roles as husband and father, and the broader social worlds of work and society. He uses narrative to promote self-healing and regeneration.

People's understandings of their illnesses must be viewed in the context of their entire lives and their interpretations of their lives. Don's story, as presented here, is a story within a story. The story of disruption was framed by the larger story of his whole life. Personal histories shape how people view the future. An illness is experienced primarily in terms of personal history and the meanings that are constructed out of that history. Personal histories shape people's sense of the future and the enactment of that future.

Although he has never been a soldier, Don uses the soldier metaphor to emplot his story and give it a sense of the future. This metaphor reveals the cultural foundations behind metaphor: Don uses it to recast the story of a long-term illness into a larger metaphor about society's ideology of perseverance and endurance. Although he also tries to resist the moral force of normalizing ideologies, by framing his story in this way Don situates himself within a moralizing discourse. He redeems his status as a person who is ill by positioning himself as a full member of society.

Don's wife, Laurel, has had her sense of the future altered by Don's illness, as well. She, too, addresses what is at stake in the context of her history of their marital relationship.

> Here he is with osteoporosis. He found out today it's not as bad as they thought, but still! He's forty years old with osteoporosis—my jock husband! This guy I married would backpack for weeks, played tennis, played racquetball, skied, was a ski instructor. He was a jock. Finally I can keep up with him, and I never could before. I feel so much of the time that I'm losing my husband. Every time he comes home with one of these little bits of news, I feel like he's being taken away a little bit at a time.

Laurel presents a set of contrasts different from Don's: she compares her husband the one-time "jock" with her husband who is "being taken away a little bit at a time."

Their daily lives are affected by frequent life-threatening medical emergencies. She ruminates about how her husband's illness has affected her.

> I hear myself thinking all these things in the past year or so. Kind of a survivalist mentality, or the sergeant taking the troops into battle, or like I'm on a ship at sea and I'm going to batten down the hatches before the storm. I hear myself thinking, "The storm hasn't come, it's right ahead, and I'm gonna brace myself and get through it." I have no sense of how long that storm is going to be. In the back of my mind there's quite a bit of fear, especially now that we have a child. I fear being a widow young.

The storm metaphor readily lends itself to a marital relationship in which one partner is chronically ill: storms are sporadic, they eventually end, and they leave a period of calm in their wake. Laurel worries about the length of the storm and conveys her sense of urgency and concern about her ability to weather the storm by using multiple fight and survival metaphors for her actions. She situates her concerns in the here-and-now.

Laurel's current situation informs the way she sees her life unfolding. Her concerns are not only with the immediate future but also with the long term. She wonders with trepidation whether she will have to go through the middle of her life, whether she will have to raise her toddler son, without her husband. This scenario for marriage and family life is very different from the one Laurel envisioned when she and her husband met and married. As she faces each day with uncertainty, the loss of her expectations about family life threatens her sense of coherence about her life and magnifies the fears she experiences. Her instrumental role in the storm metaphor enables her to rehearse her role endlessly and thereby mitigate some of the uncertainty of her situation. Laurel, too, is engaged in biographical reconstruction. Although she does not have an illness, the disruption of her life by his illness necessitates that she reflect on her fears and thereby transcend them.

By placing herself in the heroic role of a sergeant in battle or a ship captain fighting a storm, Laurel also uses the soldier metaphor. In doing so, she places her role as the spouse of someone who is ill within the bounds of normalizing ideologies. Although she, too, struggles against the moral force of such ideologies, she must contend with her social roles in the present, including her caregiver role, as well as her anticipated future role as a young widow. She must find a fit between herself and society, as her experiences are not in synchrony with those of other married women her age.

LIMBO IN OLD AGE

Old age is about limbo, as the question of *when* life will end becomes increasing pertinent as people age. Even those who appear to be in good health live with the increasing likelihood that they could become ill or die at any time. In the following story of repeated disruption, the narrator works to reduce her sense of being in limbo by emplotting her story in a certain way. Miss Frieda Mintz, an eighty-year-old Jewish woman in the late-life transitions study, was a refugee from Eastern Europe after World War II.[15] Miss Mintz, who has had little formal education and speaks heavily accented, imperfect English, has led a quiet life working as a clerk while carrying on a rich, inner life.

Miss Mintz described a complex series of events that resulted in her eventual move to an institution.

> Before I was here I was at a board and care home.[16] They put me there from the hospital. It wasn't my choice. I fell down and broke my hip bone, and that's how it all happened. Before I fell I was okay. I took care of myself. I was independent most of my life. I worked for a living. Just when you get old, this happens. When I fell down, I was seventy-nine years old. I don't know what happened after that. They picked me up in the street and took me to the hospital. While I was in the hospital, they took my breast off. I have a cancer. I was in the hospital when they found that.

This fall dramatically altered the quiet, self-sufficient life Miss Mintz had led during the fifty years since she came to the United States. Before she fell she was "okay," that is, there was nothing wrong with her. Because she had lived on a tiny social security benefit from the time she retired, she had no financial resources. She told me that it was important to her to not have to worry about paying for her burial when she died, and that the institution would pay for this cost. The institution offered security, but the emotional and social price was high. In moving from the board and care home, she had had to leave behind friendships formed there.

Sometimes people are able to overlook or manage their gradual impairment without giving it much attention until a specific event, such as a fall, catapults them into an acute care hospital or a set of changed life circumstances, Miss Mintz, looking back on the time before she fell and broke her hip, amended her picture of herself as healthy to include an initial sign of increasing impairment when she added,

I was perfectly healthy then. I was using a cane, just for a little stability.

When Miss Mintz was moved from the board and care home to the large nursing home, things changed dramatically.

Maybe every three or four weeks they think of something so we have always a surprise coming. [Yesterday] it was a big treat to go to Half Moon Bay to see the ocean. I was the only one who saw the ocean because I walked out a little bit on the sand. One of the women [caretakers] stood by me. The other ones stayed on the bus. But they had to turn the bus around for them to see the ocean on the way back. It was nice. I saw the country. It was a nice sunny day. That's my only peak since I got here. I sit in this chair. I turn it into the sun to read. The whole mood changes when there is sunshine around. It does something to you.

This story clearly delineates how Miss Mintz contrasts herself with the others living in the institution. She continues to view herself as autonomous, independent, able to take a walk in the sand at the beach, which gave her a sense of freedom. This image of her walking on the beach is juxtaposed against that of the others unable to leave the bus, that of the bus being turned so they could see the ocean.

She talked further about how she saw herself in relation to the others at the institution.

I had a hard time to get acclimatized to here. It was a shock to me. Seeing everybody in a wheelchair. *Everybody.* And all of them sleeping all the time. It was quite a shock to me. . . .

. . . I always have to have a few books. Just give me something to do. I didn't think I could stand it. Most people sleep around in their chairs. I want to keep my eyes open. . . .

. . . I got used to it [being in the institution]. I don't brood over it. I found out the less I think about it, I'm better off. This way I keep my mind. I have an active mind, anyway. I like to move, too. I enjoy finding out things. I was today a few hours at the art department. They've got an art department where I paint a little. I've got a painting to my credit. In my reading, you know, through reading you find out everything. You find out about art, about everything. And there was a whole . . . oh, maybe two or three years I was absolutely loving art. And in this time, I read many books on art. And one picture I got acquainted with. It's in my bedroom. I copied it. [Enthusiastically] I've got to show it to you.

Miss Mintz is determined to keep herself intact, both in mind and body. She has observed that to maintain her autonomy she must stay active both mentally and physically. She paints, she reads, she continues to satisfy her insatiable curiosity.

Starting towards her room, pushing her wheeled walker, she said,

After dinner I go home and listen to the radio. I have my radio. I like it very much.

Miss Mintz, in calling "home" the room she shares with another woman who is bedridden and cannot talk, has begun to transform the undesirable situation of being in the institution: she goes home at night and listens to her radio, thus escaping from the aspects of the institution that she finds oppressive. When we arrived at her room, she said,

The picture I painted. It's my pride and joy. I was absolutely . . . I was in love with art. I read books on everything about art history and everything. That was my life for a long time. I think that was the happiest time in my life . . . when I was painting and reading books on art. There's nothing as nice as art. It all came to me through my reading, my interest in art. I think modern art is best.

Later, after she showed me her painting, I remarked, "You have a lot of things going on." She agreed and concluded, "I've got to keep my mind going." The key to Miss Mintz's philosophy is an active mind. She is resourceful and self-sufficient in keeping herself busy and rejects the cultural image of the aged as being moribund. Miss Mintz remains undeterred by the issues about the end of life as she goes on with her life. She is surrounded by the other, the people "sleeping around in their chairs." Miss Mintz shifts her vision away from this specter of moribund old age, back to books and art. In spite of her strong desire to keep a sense of personhood intact and her desire to continue to live a full life, Miss Mintz wanted to come to the institution because it gave her the security of being taken care of in death, something that many people worry about in old age. Although life and death remain very close to each other, Miss Mintz intends to carry on. She lives in the present.

As people age or become seriously ill, the symbols they use to keep a sense of continuity alive may stay the same, but the expression of these symbols may change. Although Miss Mintz refers to her involvement with art in the past tense, "that was my life for a long time," art is obviously still important to her in the institution; she attends art classes and continues to read about the lives of artists. Her passion for art infuses her days with meaning.

Although it may not be readily apparent without a fuller contextualization of her story, Miss Mintz is resistant to the moral force of normalizing ideologies. She does not subscribe to the cultural ideology of advanced old age that views people as being decrepit and unable to think for themselves. She resisted being given a wheelchair when she entered the institution and compromised by accepting a wheeled walker so that she would have the freedom to walk around. Miss Mintz eagerly volunteered to show me how well she walked without it; she was proud of this marker of her independence. Moreover, she turns her back on her peers at every opportunity, in an effort to maintain her distance from them.

Miss Mintz is weathering one of the most difficult transitions people experience in U.S. society: the loss of independence. Despite the dramatic change in how she lives her life, she is attempting to restore a sense of continuity. Her story demonstrates perseverance, acceptance of her situ-

ation, and efforts to reestablish control over her situation. When she was first faced with no longer living independently, she chose—in perhaps the final major choice of her life—to go to the institution because she wanted the security of not having to worry about not having enough money for her burial. Controlling what will happen after death is a way of maintaining control over one's life. Her choosing to go to the institution contrasted with the kaleidoscope of events that had been triggered by her fall, in which she did not have a choice. In looking at her situation in this way, she transformed it; she brought it under her control.

As she acclimates herself to the institution, she is taking advantage of its benefits and trying to ignore everything else: she reimmerses herself in art and in reading, which she finds immensely satisfying and fulfilling. Indeed, they are key to the further transformation of this experience. She spends as much of her day as possible in the art department. When she is not there, she is sitting in a window, immersed in a book. She always turns her chair so that she faces outside, away from the other inhabitants. She thus avoids *seeing* them. She walks around the grounds and buildings daily in order to get as much exercise as possible and keep her body fit. At night she goes "home" and listens to the radio, engaging other worlds outside the institution. In orchestrating a new life for herself that carries into it meaning from the old life, Miss Mintz begins to leave an extended period of limbo behind. She has maintained her interests and her zest for life; she likes to move about, to feel the sand under her feet, to wield a paintbrush on a canvas. Her embodied knowledge, shaken by the physical trauma she experienced after the fall, has been restored, and with it her ability to create continuity.

8 Creating Order out of Chaos

Efforts to reorder the world after a disruption begin with the body. After a period of chaos in which a sense of being disembodied reigns, efforts to integrate past and present are initiated. When embodied knowledge is reestablished, notions of order in daily life begin to resurface and take shape.

Jackie, a thirty-year-old African-American woman, had been married for five years. During that time she had worked at a variety of jobs while she completed her high school education. She and her husband had been trying, without success, to conceive since their marriage. Because they had no health insurance and could not pay for treatment out-of-pocket, Jackie had focused on changing her self-image in order to prepare her body for a baby.

> Being a woman is being in my body for the first time in my life. I lived from the neck up because of all the abuse that I went through. I hated my

body, and I did a lot of destructive things to my body as a result of not liking it. So being a woman for me is being in my body and being in touch with being feminine. I just was not in touch with my woman, the woman inside of me. So for me, it's working through that stuff and just feeling good about being a woman. And liking my femininity, I do—it is nice being a female. It feels good, and I feel like I am fulfilling that because I feel as a whole person—mind, body, and spirit. I am really connected to that.

Talking to her body, she added,

Let's get pregnant. Come on, body. Start working.

The metaphoric transformation of the body is introduced: in the past, Jackie lived only in her head, disconnected from her body, but now she has a new feeling of being in her body. Referring to her inner self as "my woman," she takes metaphoric ownership of her body, and she talks directly to her body. Embodied knowledge has been restored.

SHIFTING BODILY KNOWLEDGE

Embodiment encompasses people's historical experiences of their bodies. As I noted in chapter 3, creating order after a disruption begins with this historically situated and contextually informed body.

As I indicated in chapter 7, people in the late-life transitions study were often not truly new to impairment, but until a specific event forced them into a set of changed life circumstances, they had been able to manage their impairment without giving it much attention. Mrs. Sarah Fine, a ninety-year-old Jewish woman, reported this sudden awareness of incapacity while she was discussing how her life had been disrupted when her daughter-in-law moved her three thousand miles to a long-term care institution on twenty-four hours' notice.

I had a big change because my sister was living with me after my husband died. Then I fell down and hurt my back. Then she [the sister] got sick and was taken to the hospital. So my son says, "Mother, you've got to come here so I can keep an eye on you, and you'll get very good care."

He's very interested in my health. He's my only child. He says, "You cannot be alone." So my daughter-in-law flew to my hometown and moved
me here the very next day. A lot of my possessions were left there—all
my furniture and most of my clothes and most everything. So I came,
like, overnight.

When asked how she was dealing with this abrupt move, she responded,

I'm very lonely. I'm trying to adjust.

Sudden changes such as this often brought an entire array of infirmities to people's attention. Mrs. Fine remarked,

I can't play cards anymore because my hands are very unsteady. And I
can't write, and I've had my eyes tested I don't know how many times.
But it's not the glasses, it's that my eyes are going! Like everything else. I
need a transplant from head to foot! My friends, in my age group, are
nearly all gone. I'll be ninety next month. I don't know if I was lucky to
live that long or not.

The abrupt transition that was forced on her by her daughter-in-law's
moving her to California led her to look at herself anew and brought
previously ignored bodily changes to her attention. Mrs. Fine acknowledges that her body is wearing out. Nothing functions as well as it once
did, and consequently her daily activities are severely constrained. In
assessing her bodily changes, she acknowledges her longevity, and she
questions whether living so long is a positive thing.

The disjunction in her life is further exacerbated because she has few
of her own clothes. Her daughter-in-law has replaced Mrs. Fine's ward-
robe with her own unwanted clothes, thus furthering the disruption of
the known and familiar. Clothes do more than simply cover and fit the
body. They are an extension of the body, an extension that proclaims personhood, because people choose clothes that represent who they are.
Without such reminders of identity, a major linkage with the known
body is dissolved, and a guidepost of continuity is destroyed. This is why
some old people become disoriented when they must live in a hospital
room and wear a hospital gown.

Despite her advanced age, Mrs. Fine is trying to find a new life for herself in the nursing home. Her renewed bodily awareness reminds her of the limits of this endeavor: she can no longer write or play cards, two activities that have endured throughout her life. Her bodily constraints shape the activities in which she can engage. Increasingly, television fills her days.

Mrs. Fine anticipates that, because of her age, her bodily impairments cannot be altered for the better, but many people in the stroke study did not accept abrupt disruption to the body as permanent. For these people, trying to get the body to return to normal after a disruption was central to the creation of a sense of continuity. Gerald Leong, a sixty-six-year-old married Chinese-American man, had a stroke shortly after he retired. The list of changes Mr. Leong has experienced is so long that he views himself as a different person.

> Naturally, I'm not the same person I was before the stroke . . . but, like they say, one day at a time. I don't talk as good as I used to and I don't walk as good as I used to. I've got to get my judgment back. I know I don't drive as good as I used to. I drive just as *much* as I used to. It's just that I don't drive as *good* as I used to. I know it. And I can't dance anymore.

Mr. Leong, like Mrs. Fine, assesses his loss of bodily functions, but he couches those losses in different terms. Mrs. Fine associates her bodily losses with advanced age and appears to view them as normal, whereas Mr. Leong identifies his bodily changes as abnormal. Six months after the stroke, he mulled over the meaning of normal as he tried to return to his former life despite his residual disabilities.

> I don't know what is normal or not normal for people who have had strokes. My right hand—I don't have the dexterity that I used to have. I refuse to use chopsticks. I used to use chopsticks when I had Chinese food but I use a fork now.

He is trying to ascertain what *degree* of normality to aspire to—what is normal for people in general or what is normal for people who have had a stroke. He deals with some bodily changes by changing habitual behaviors, by, for example, using a fork instead of chopsticks. But he is determined to recover from other bodily and cognitive changes: for example, he wants to get his judgment back. His impaired judgment affects his ability to drive, an ability which, for him, represents normalcy.

One year after the stroke, Mr. Leong gauges how these losses have affected his daily functioning.

> I don't consider myself helpless. I do things but I don't do them as rapidly. Before the stroke I didn't have to hang on when I go down the stairs. Before I just zoom down. I walk as fast as I can. Going up hill and downhill I find it more difficult now than before. I lose wind faster. In other words, I'm breathless.

As Mr. Leong talks, past and present become entwined. He asserts that he is not helpless; he does many of the same things but more slowly. His bodily changes have occurred, for the most part, in degrees. He has experienced an across-the-board slowing down: he now lacks the coordination to dance, and in general is forced to move more slowly and methodically. These reminders of his changed body are always with him.

In cataloguing the many changes he has gone through, Mr. Leong identified activities that he liked, activities that made him feel normal.

> I like to drive. When I'm behind the wheel, I can pretend I'm normal. If I have to go anywhere, I drive. I'd rather drive than take public transportation. Because I don't have to fight for a seat. I know I have a seat. Then I go fishing once in a while. When I sit in the boat or when I drive, if I don't think about it, I forget about the fact that I had a stroke. Because I'm like before.

Mr. Leong is not content with adjusting to what is normal for a person who has had a stroke. He wants to fulfill his idea of what is completely normal, and he chooses his favorite activities—driving and fishing—to reinforce that sense of normalcy and diminish the importance of his impairments. Nevertheless, one year after the stroke he has reworked his notion of what is normal for his age.

> My friends tell me I should practice talking and using my right hand. But my philosophy is different than theirs because I tell them in my situation I don't consider at my age I have to learn unless I really need it. But

they believe in being perfectionists—they like to talk and speak good and be able to use their hands.

Mr. Leong tries to rationalize his impairments.

> Maybe this is the best thing that ever happened. It forced me to rest, and I don't have to think like I used to. It's hard to separate whether this is a result of the stroke or old age.

Because daily life revolves around what the body can do, a body rendered unpredictable by disruption may become a source of frustration. Renewing a sense of predictability of the body after a disruption gives people opportunities to retrench and make necessary alterations in daily life over time. In old age, the predictability of the body is gauged not only in terms of the problems and prognoses associated with illness but also in terms of a cultural discourse on old age, in which physical impairment is considered a normal part of advanced age.

Mr. Leong's and Mrs. Fine's stories illustrate how people have different ideas about what is normal at different times of life and show that these ideas reflect cultural notions about what bodily losses are expected for a particular age group. As we have seen, people's notions of normalcy differ depending on their gender and ethnicity, but here we see how ideas of normalcy depend on their age also. What Mrs. Fine tries to accept as normal for ninety is very different from what Mr. Leong initially views as normal at sixty-six. One year after his stroke, however, Mr. Leong begins to view his impairments as acceptable, and even normal, for his age. Doing so enables him to come to terms with the changes in his body, which he would otherwise view as abnormal. Mr. Leong's friends, in contrast, reflect a different view of what is normal in one's late sixties, a view to which Mr. Leong previously subscribed.

While Mr. Leong strives to appear normal through driving and fishing and thus to maintain a semblance of continuity with the past, Mrs. Fine has had to abandon her lifelong activities, but she attributes this necessity to her age. Continuity—experienced through habitual behaviors and familiar possessions, including the very clothes she wears—has been significantly reduced for Mrs. Fine, and thus she must turn to other sources of continuity. She consequently stays in her room, surrounded by her familiar pictures and plants.

The stories of Mrs. Fine and Mr. Leong illustrate both the ambiguity that surrounds age norms and the moral force of normalizing ideologies. Society's opinion of Mrs. Fine's physical status was ambiguous until her son declared her unfit, by society's standards, to live alone any longer. Although she acquiesced in his plan, she continues to resist in small ways, primarily by complaining about her daughter-in-law's assumptions that Mrs. Fine would enjoy wearing her hand-me-downs. Mr. Leong, resistant to being told what parts of his body he should try to fix, clings to his own notions of normalcy—being able to fish and drive a car. These activities reflect cultural notions about what men, old and young, do throughout their lives. Thus, his ability to continue with these activities enables him to view himself as being in line with cultural ideologies of manhood.

RESTORING NORMALCY

For the creation of a sense of continuity, the life story must be reconstructed to fit a set of life circumstances different from those originally anticipated. It is not possible to move on with life until the future has been reorganized and given new meaning. The restoration of normalcy entails the preparation of a place in the life story for an altered set of hopes and dreams. In this reorganization process space is created for new and different ideas about one's life. If the new possibilities are ultimately found to be acceptable, they are incorporated into identity. The integration of bodily changes is an integral part of this process.

Mr. John Goodson, a fifty-year-old African-American man in the ethnic minorities study, has serious health problems because of complications from diabetes. Because of renal failure, he must dialyze himself every four hours. He has had a leg and part of his remaining foot amputated, and he has a prosthesis. He is very knowledgeable about his health condition. He contrasts the health care he receives currently with the treatment he received in Mississippi, where he had lived until two years before the interview. Indeed, his search for better medical treatment was what finally made him decide to uproot himself and move to the West Coast. At the time of his first interview, he was living temporarily with his ex-wife while he waited for a wheelchair-accessible apartment to become available in public housing.

After Mr. Goodson talked at length about the poor care he had received, the interviewer asked, "Don't the doctors there care about you as a person, or is it racial?" He responded,

It's both of them if you really want to hear the truth. Mostly it's race. It's a racial thing. I'll tell you what happened. I was in the hospital. I had a catheter in my chest, and it wouldn't work. He operated on me, took it out. Told me he didn't see anything wrong with it, and he put it right back in the same place. That night I started bleeding, and I bled just about all night. I like, bled to death. I was scared. I bled about three hours, and all they was doing was changing patches and changing the bed. Blood was all over the bed.

He [the physician] didn't come. He didn't show. He's telling the nurse what to do because she told me. That's why I know that she contacted him. He told her, "All you do is keep your hand over the hole. He'll finally quit," and really it did. She had held it so long that I told her, "I'll hold it," and I held it and finally it stopped. I didn't see him the next day. He's the type of doctor that would cuss you out. He'd be cussing and raising hell. Saying everything. Like I lost my leg, you know. My toe was infected, and he looked at it and he told me, "All we got to do is cut it off." That was his diagnosis right there. I said, "Well, wait a minute now. I just got a little blue spot on the end. Can we do something about that?" "Cut it off is all I know to do." And you see I have one leg.

Here, I got pretty good doctors. They call and check on me to see how I'm doing. People come and get me and take me to the doctors. Anywhere I got to go, I got a way to get there. Totally different. I got cab vouchers. In Mississippi you don't even have a cab! Now they got an ambulance there, but they're going to take their own time about getting there. Controlled by the whites. No blacks. Yeah. I'd rather be here.

Mr. Goodson tells a story of neglect. He indicts the health-care system, as he experienced it in Mississippi, of racism. These traumatic experiences finally resulted in his decision to move to California.

After asking Mr. Goodson about his health, the interviewer shifted to issues of identity and asked him, "So how would you describe yourself as a person?" Mr. Goodson responded,

> Well, I think, to me I think, I'm a nice person, you know. I try to be in no moody moods. I try to wake up everyday and be the same. I'm a church person.

He makes it clear from the start that religion is part of his life and identity.

He later combines a statement of acceptance through religious faith with a statement that reflects the value placed on perseverance in the United States.

> Well, I'm at a point that I don't let it [my health] bother me because I put it in my mind that this is something that the Lord . . . something just happened, you know what I mean, and it's one of them things there ain't nothing you can do about it, so I just live with it everyday as an everyday thing. I don't be looking at me and saying, "Oh look, I lost a leg." I don't do that. I just look down and get up and go. I don't like my leg to take control over me. I try to control it. Instead of looking pitiful. Depressed. All that kind of stuff 'cause I know I can't get my leg back. I know I ain't getting a foot back, so I thank the Lord for what it is. The old saying is to use what you got.

Mr. Goodson is trying to be practical about the loss of his leg and his other foot. He is taking personal responsibility for living with this loss by saying that he doesn't like his leg to control him. Although he acknowledges that the amputations are permanent, the amputated leg is embodied, still part of him, and therefore subject to his control.

> I ain't got nothing else so I use that. At least I'm left with a leg to stand up on and could walk. Some people can't even walk. Many people can't even walk over to their own to get a drink of water or get up in the morning and put their clothes on. See, I can do all that. Brush my teeth. Go to the barber shop. I do all that. Tomorrow I'm going to start school. I'm going to take up reading. I'm not a good reader. That'll give me something to do.

Mr. Goodson compares himself favorably with others. He points out that he is independent—he can take care of himself. Moreover, he is taking the extra initiative to try to learn to read.

I'm not living in the past, I'm living for the future and, like I said, the environment I don't like. The status, the way I'm living, I never lived like this [in someone else's house]. I worked for myself. I've been independent, and I owned my own business when I was in Mississippi. I put out music machines, juke boxes and pool tables and video games and stuff like that. I was in the restaurant business. I owned four or five restaurants. I had people running them. I always had a nice car to ride in. A truck. A telephone. All that stuff. I'm used to all that, but now I've fell off the end of the cliff and I can't get back up on the hill. I don't know.

Mr. Goodson contrasts what he is used to and what he is living with: he contrasts being completely independent, owning his own business, with keeping going, but at a slower pace. When he says he is living for the future, he calls attention to differences between his past and his future. He uses a metaphor of falling to capture the experience of his illness. He concludes,

I'm just only fifty years old, and it's not like I'm dead, I just lost a few limbs.

Mr. Goodson is trying to restore a sense of normalcy to his life. He summarizes his life situation, thus putting his situation into perspective, as a temporary hiatus in a stream of continuity.

Several months after this interview, Mr. Goodson came to speak to a class I was teaching on minority health and aging. Since his first interview, he had moved into his own apartment. After describing his health problems to the class, he volunteered,

I don't feel like I'm sick. I'm living by myself. I'm independent—I don't depend on anybody. I feel just like I did before I lost my leg. I drive a car. I go places. It's a blessing to be here. I could be dead.

Mr. Goodson's story of disruption and recovery illustrates how the experience of disruption is shaped within the framework of the cultural discourse on continuity. A series of disruptions were followed by a period of limbo, which was characterized by uncertainty about the future. The crisis of bleeding after surgery was followed by the loss of his leg and part of his other foot. He undertook other changes himself, such as the move to California, a bold effort to take command of a situation he viewed as jeopardizing his well-being. This move, however, resulted in a long period of limbo during which he slept on his ex-wife's living room couch. Moving into an apartment of his own is a major step in ending this period of limbo and restoring a sense of continuity to life. The apartment represents independence and autonomy. His plan to improve his literacy through a course at the library symbolizes a fresh start, another effort to take charge of his life. Mr. Goodson shapes his life, and in doing so, he fulfills U.S. values about taking the initiative and persevering through self-improvement. Through his actions, he upholds U.S. values of autonomy and independence and lives out cultural notions of continuity. Moreover, Mr. Goodson's religious beliefs enable him to make sense out of the disruption he has experienced. His religious faith has enabled him to integrate the many discontinuities in his life.

In living out cultural expectations about continuity, Mr. Goodson deemphasizes his impairments. He works to control the leg he no longer has; that is, he tries to shape the situation created by the loss of his leg. He also diminishes the significance of self-dialysis. Although dialysis not only occurs several times a day, thereby considerably curtailing his activities, but also signifies a significant level of kidney damage and portends a shortened life, dialysis has become a bothersome detail rather than a major interruption to continuity.

By downplaying his health problems, Mr. Goodson is also able to maintain his sense of personhood. Despite his disabilities, he reassures himself and others that he is the same capable man who has always been in charge of his life. Although he has had serious physical changes, his sense of who he is has not changed. He reaffirms who he is: "a nice person." His sense of internal coherence is thus preserved.[1]

As Mr. Goodson mediates this disruption to his life, he addresses the moral force of normalizing ideologies. He resists any notion that he is not whole. He defines himself in the context of cultural expectations about manhood for men in midlife. He subscribes to U.S. ideologies about perseverance and endurance. He attributes his lack of literacy and his illness to racism. The moral authority of his narrative is thus characterized, most of all, by his experience as an African American who has spent most of his life in the southern United States. In this instance, he resists

dominant normalizing ideologies about personal responsibility for preventing illness—he is saying the impairments resulting from his medical
treatment are not his fault—while subscribing to normalizing ideologies
about responsibility for taking care of oneself in the circumstances of
having an illness.

REORDERING LIFE

Restoring a sense of normalcy is essential to the creation of continuity,
but it is possible only for those who have a health condition that is relatively stable and does not interfere significantly with the daily routine.
The process of restoring normalcy has ups and downs and is replete with
uncertainty. Searching for and developing markers of continuity with
one's former life may be wrenching tasks that sometimes result in feelings of hopelessness and defeat. Although people in the stroke study began to consider the meaning of the stroke while they were in the hospital,
its implications for their lives did not emerge fully until they returned to
the outside world and attempted to live at home.[2] Returning home forced
people to confront their limitations. Furniture had to be rearranged and
special equipment brought in, such as bedside commodes, wheelchairs,
and canes. They had to learn how to cook in their own kitchens again, to
walk down the hall, and to move around in the bathroom without falling.

The profound changes to both body and mind led people who had
had a stroke to question whether they were still the same person. After a
period of time spent confronting the loss of the known and familiar, most
people began to search for ways to link their past lives with the present.
Their efforts to go on with their lives focused on mundane, everyday
tasks and reflected an attempt to reinfuse their lives with meaning.[3]

Mrs. Mary Jordan, who told of her distress after a stroke in a previous
chapter, demonstrated sustained efforts to create continuity after a stroke
in four interviews spread over two years. I first interviewed her shortly
after she went home from the month-long hospital stay that followed her
stroke. At that time she remarked, "I'm anxious to have a full recovery."
On my second visit, six months later, she talked about her goals for her-

self. She saw restoration of her bodily abilities as the linchpin of her recovery.

> I'm just anxious to really get back to normal when I can because I would like to be able to get out of the house on my own, to get out the front door and go down the stairs and get in the car or bus or something and go on my own, like I used to. I think that is going to be another two or three months because I can sort of tell by my body.

Mrs. Jordan is listening to her body. She links her bodily knowledge to ordinary, everyday activities, activities that signify the end of chaos and the resumption of normal life.

At the third interview, a little over a year after the stroke, she had just begun going out of the house on her own, and she felt that doing so was wonderful. Meanwhile, however, she had experienced new disruptions: her sister, who was also her best friend, had been diagnosed with terminal cancer. About the same time there had been an earthquake in which she lost some possessions, such as china and glassware. It was not these losses but the severity of the earthquake—the television toppled off a table and she was unable to walk across the room because of the severe shaking—that unnerved her.

> The whole thing is, I was doing so good, that's what kills me. Well, I shouldn't complain 'cause I'm still gaining ground. I really am. I can see it in myself. But I work—I still exercise every morning and I go to class at the Y twice a week for exercise. They're not the greatest, but they give me a little exercise and the class is lovely. They are all stroke victims. This lady [Mrs. Jordan] happens to be the best one in the class.
>   Everything else seems to be—thank God—coming back, you know, and I'm walking and walking. Well, I haven't been because I just . . . that stuff [her sister's illness and the earthquake] takes the strength out of you, too. All that trauma. But now I'm back to walking and feeling better. And so I just may be out of the woods now. I certainly hope so, but it's a terrible feeling. It's not a deep, it's not a depression . . . I didn't get too deeply depressed, you know. Sometimes some of us do, anyway. But I wasn't depressed, it was just . . . Well, as somebody said, "overanxious." It was right after the earthquake. I really thought I was going out of my mind, and there's nobody here. And everything is worse at night. I just, you know, the terrible, terrible thoughts that one gets and I'm sure I'm not too much different from some people.

I'm very careful and cautious. Maybe that's why I get so anxious, it could be, you know. I'm kind of a worrier. But I've made up my mind I'm going to be very careful. I don't want to fall. I don't want to tip over or anything. I think there's hope for me. I'm still making progress.

Mrs. Jordan, throughout the period of her recovery after her stroke, wrestled with the hope metaphor. Having hope meant having a future. It meant a return to normalcy. The earthquake and her sister's illness were further disruptions to her goal for a normal life. They dispelled, for a time, her sense of hope and, thus, future. In the first year after the stroke, her sister had been her primary caregiver, running errands and doing grocery shopping for her. She had also been a major source of support, always dropping by to talk and cheer Mrs. Jordan up. While the most upsetting event, by far, was her sister's illness, the earthquake frightened and jolted her out of a gradually returning sense of normalcy. During Mrs. Jordan's convalescence her sister's boundless energy and enthusiasm for life had been contagious. Mrs. Jordan, reassured, had responded by giving all her attention to recovery. With the onset of her sister's illness, however, Mrs. Jordan's tenuous sense of continuity was again disrupted. Her comments reflect her efforts to focus on her progress and reassure herself about how she is "still gaining ground." "Hope" equals "progress" toward her goal of full recovery.

One year later I went back to visit Mrs. Jordan. She had recently had another setback.

I had a bad fall in September. I think I told you on the phone. September was very bad because I had reached the point that I was in fairly good shape. And I had been struttin' around in the morning, without my cane here, and I got in my car—I think I told you I took lessons to drive my car again. I've gotten so I drive around the neighborhood. The car is right there. So I didn't bother with the cane. I got downstairs, and I thought, "I forgot my cane." I never usually go without it. So I thought, "Well, I can do it. I'm all right."

So I get the car out, and then I spray the rose bushes and pick up the hose and roll it up and nothing happened. So then I think I'll go in the backyard and pick a rose for the living room. So out I go without thinking I don't have my cane. I got out to the entrance of the garden, and whether something happened to my head, or I tripped, or what . . . I think I lost my balance. And I could not stop myself from falling. And I fell so hard on the cement, the whole weight of my body, and I'm no lightweight. I laid there and couldn't get up. And I had forgotten to put my Lifeline on.[4] I called over to the yard next to me, but they couldn't hear me. So eventually I got myself up and went upstairs. Fortunately, I didn't break anything. And the doctor said, "Anybody else your age or younger would have broken her hip." My femur bone was sore for months. Black and blue. I cut my hands on the rose bushes. They were bleeding all over. I don't know what happened to me. And I went into shock, I think, without realizing it. And finally my son got there, and he said, "Okay, Mom, we're going to the hospital." But I had no fracture.

It set me way back. I couldn't walk so good, anymore. My head was not good anymore. A stroke affects your head. You get dizzy and light-headed, and you don't think so good. And I had just about gotten all over that. So it [the dizziness] started again from that fall. It was such a hard one, that it must have shaken up my whole body. I must have hit my head, or maybe I might have had a very slight stroke again. But I don't think so. I don't go [walking through the house] without my cane. I think I have lost part of my sense of balance or something. And I hope that mine [her balance] can recover.

Mrs. Jordan's efforts to live her life as fully as possible emerge in this story. Her only concessions to having had a stroke are a cane and an emergency alert system. But she leaves these aids behind as her habituated body returns to her. Through it she experiences the resurgence of being-in-the-world. When she falls and her carefully restored world starts to fall apart again, her physical being has new immediacy: cuts, aching bones, black-and-blue marks, light-headedness, and a narrowly averted hip fracture now preoccupy her. She looks to her body for an explanation of what happened: perhaps the hardness of the fall "shook up" her whole body, or perhaps she had another stroke. In spite of this troubling fall, she perseveres.

I figure I have to do my own therapy. I have to get out and walk every-day. Because it's going to help my walking and strengthen my legs. And after that, I was wobbly again, and now I know I have to walk every morning. I can only go two blocks, two short blocks and back now.

Looking back on the stroke she had had two years earlier, Mrs. Jordan tries to put her illness into perspective.

I saw the patients in the hospital when they'd wheel them down in the chair in the morning to wait for their turn [for rehabilitation therapy], and they'd wheel me down, too. I couldn't walk then, either. And they're all sitting like this [she imitates a blank stare]. And I am sitting up and smiling. But of course, they were worse than I was, maybe. It's a pretty bad thing when you come to and realize what's happened to you. And I even cried for me. Especially when I couldn't do anything.

Remembering how bad things were reminds Mrs. Jordan of how far she has come in her recovery: she is not, as she was in the beginning, sitting in a wheelchair. Nor is she like the other people she was with, whom she portrays as not really there at all. Concluding, she said,

So, it's two years and two months [since the stroke]. I'm hoping I can still make progress.

Mrs. Jordan maintained her determination to return her life to normal throughout two years of interviews. She never gave in to a sense of hopelessness about her situation. Like everyone else in this chapter, she demonstrates unrelenting perseverance in the face of adversity. Indeed, she prides herself on her perseverance, and it was a source of continuity as she worked to regain her strength and previous level of daily functioning. Perseverance is a key part of the cultural discourse on continuity in the United States.

Markers of continuity emerge from life experience and the layers of meaning people attach to their lives over time. Indications, no matter how limited, of the ability to return to activities engaged in before the onset of disability are cause for hope. An increase, however modest, in positive social interactions, and successful substitution of one activity for another so that some form of familiar daily life can resume, are necessary for people to forge a sense of continuity. Markers of continuity may be simple—the ability to walk across the floor or sit in familiar surroundings in the midst of one's possessions—or complex and dependent upon meaningful definitions of self—engaging in lifelong activities such as playing cards, going fishing, or driving a car. If markers of continuity cannot be identified and expressed, life loses its meaning.

The routines of daily life are crucial in establishing continuity. The repetition of events of everyday life gives structure and logic to people's lives. Robert Rubinstein's work on the symbolic meanings of home informs our understanding of this phenomenon by calling attention to how identity in old age is anchored in the most everyday aspects of life.[5] When people cannot perform routine activities they once took for granted, they experience disorientation. Meaning is restored by the reestablishment of these activities or the substitution of new ones.

A sense of continuity requires much more than the ability to carry out routines and activities, however. For some people, a sense of continuity depends on involvement with loved ones. For others, continuity depends on the fulfillment of a specific role that is key to their self-definition; the loss of that role may prevent the reestablishment of a sense of continuity. For still others, continuity is maintained through other symbols that preserve a consistent sense of self in the face of change, such as character traits that remain unchanged.

Some people are simply not able to restore a sense of continuity, especially late in life when physical and cognitive losses may overwhelm personal resources to deal with those losses.[6] In the stroke study, I frequently observed people who were so physically and cognitively impaired and whose personal situations were so constrained that they could not regain a sense of continuity. Their lives appeared to become devoid of meaning. They appeared to be, and sometimes stated that they were, simply waiting to die.

Restoring a sense of continuity depends, in part, on addressing normalizing ideologies and their effect on one's life. Mrs. Jordan, like the others in this chapter, is concerned with redefining normalcy for herself. Like the others, she is also concerned about how she measures up to cultural norms. Nevertheless, she insulates herself whenever she can from experiences that might suggest she does not measure up to these notions. In order to sustain her embodied knowledge of herself as whole, she engages in a continual process of comparison with others. Reassuring herself that her setbacks are part of the normal process of recovery, she carries on.

9 Healing the Body through the Mind

Narratives of healing—both the story told to oneself and the story told to others—are part of a process of healing disruption. Healing is performative.[1] The performance of healing by the healer, the sufferer, and any other participants may initiate change, signaling the restoration of order.[2] The healing process is not only potentially transformative but also empowering, especially when people attempt to heal themselves. The narratives in this chapter explore these phenomena and, in particular, examine two specific assumptions about healing in the United States: (1) the assumption that the route to the body is through the mind and (2) the assumption that taking responsibility for one's health is important. Each of these narratives illustrates a different healing philosophy or technique, yet these underlying assumptions remain the same. They have implications for the ways in which people attempt to assuage disruption as well as for the process of regaining bodily knowledge after a disruption.

MAKING SENSE OF EFFORTS TO HEAL

I start with my own experience of efforts to heal disruption. My personal experience of healing is intimately connected to my professional study of the healing process. Moreover, certain elements of my personal experience have shaped what I focus on in studying illness experience.

I was raised by a healer, my grandmother, who was a Christian Science practitioner. The process of healing shapes the contours of daily life for all those who are concerned with it—the person who is the focus of healing, the family, the healer, and, when healing takes place in the healer's home as it did in my family, the healer's family. My grandmother and her healing practices were the focus of our family life. A healer's life is not her own. It belongs also to those who seek her out for help. The healer's family must share the healer with an array of supplicants, whose needs sometimes appear to come first. Indeed, that they often do come first can lead to problems in the healer's family; these problems have been well documented, especially among physicians.[3] Underlying this way of life is a basic assumption: that the healer has unique and special power—power that gives the healer not only special status but also a special responsibility to others.

I never heard the word *shaman* until I took my first anthropology class and read Bronislaw Malinowski's work on magic, healing, and religion. I realized then that I already knew a great deal about shamans. From my child's-eye view, my grandmother seemed to be a shaman: as she prayed and comforted, people felt better. They came back bearing gifts. They sent friends and family members to be healed. My grandmother seemed to be larger than life, as healers often do. She stood in front of large congregations of people every Sunday, speaking in her ministerial voice; she consoled and advised others in her office and on the telephone in her confidential voice. She had seemingly psychic powers that were both frightening and reassuring. Scariest of all, she was responsible for life and death, sickness and health. Often her patients recovered, but sometimes they remained sick or even died.

Across cultures, healing power, or at least the potential to capture and focus that power, is often passed down in families from one generation to the next. Just being kin to a healer may confer this spiritual power on the relative. When I was still a child, I understood that I was my grandmother's apprentice. Every question I asked became a lesson; every action became a testament to the power of healing. I was ambivalent. I knew that she wanted me to follow in her footsteps and was exerting her considerable will to shape me in her image while, at the same time, trying not to rigidly mold me. Even as I was fascinated and drawn to the healing process in all its complexity, I struggled against being consumed by it as I saw that she was.[4] I didn't want responsibility for other people's lives. I was tired of being different from others. I wanted to be like everyone else. Being like her would mean being abnormal. My refusal to follow the path that she had chosen for me, one for which she gave me so much preparation, was another discontinuity with which I had to contend as I moved through life.

Christian Science clung to me like an extra skin as I entered adulthood. For many years I did not appreciate how profoundly I was affected by being raised in the midst of a form of what anthropologists call folk healing. I was too embarrassed by my marginality as a member of an aberrant and atypical Protestant sect to be able to see beyond my own predicament.

Growing up in a culture of healing—for that is what Christian Science is—gave me an intuitive understanding of folk healing, an understanding that I did not appreciate at the time, but it also gave me blinders, which I continue to struggle with as an anthropologist. I was too close to the phenomenon of folk healing to look at it dispassionately; it was fraught with myriad conflicting emotions. As I sorted through my own ambivalence, it was easier to study biomedical systems of healing, to which I was a comparative newcomer, than to study the type of healing I already knew. Because I was not socialized into biomedical forms of healing until I reached adulthood, they were not emotionally charged in the same way that Christian Science was. Indeed, studying biomedicine was, for me, like studying another culture, like traveling to a distant land to do fieldwork.

As a child who had asthma, I was my grandmother's patient. She never stopped trying to heal me, and she considered her inability to do so to be one of the failures of her life. At the same time, however, my grandmother frequently voiced an underlying expectation, consistent with Christian Science beliefs, that I would do my part to heal myself. The necessity for doing one's part is one of the dictums of Christian Science. Praying, thinking "right" thoughts, living the Christian Science way were the only ways to keep "mortal mind," or evil, which would otherwise cause illness, out of me. The power of mind, or thought, dominates Christian Science beliefs about health and illness. Christian Scientists believe that people are inherently good and pure but that society is impure, "evil." The essential task of each person is therefore to keep evil forces outside the body by means of prayer and thinking the right thoughts.[5] As a child, I was constantly told to "stand porter at the door of thought [and let no evil in]." This metaphor captured my imagination. Throughout childhood, I imagined myself in a doorway, standing guard against evil.

Christian Science, which has its roots in Christianity and American transcendentalism, embodies many core U.S. values. Chief among these is personal responsibility for health. My inability to rid myself of my chronic illness meant that I was somehow letting evil in despite all my efforts. My sense of responsibility for my illness grew, and for a long time I worked hard at overcoming and managing my illness through Christian Science.

As my symptoms grew worse, I stopped trying so hard to be a perfect Christian Scientist. I felt as though I was suffering more than a "good" Christian Scientist should. Christian Science was not only not helping me get better but also not helping me make sense of my suffering. Its explanations didn't comfort me. I was doing everything I was supposed to do, but it wasn't doing any good. My disillusionment with Christian Science was furthered by my uncertainty about the nature of my illness—I had so many symptoms—and by the fact that my grandmother never named my illness. She lived in a Christian Science world, where giving a name to something it made it worse rather than healing it; giving it a name was giving a foothold to evil.[6]

I began comparing myself with others around me who were ill. Observing my grandmother with her patients gave me ample opportunity to do this: people sometimes came to our house, and she took me with her to visit the homebound. In retrospect, I realized this was part of my apprenticeship. I saw that people were comforted, that these beliefs worked for them. My grandmother's patients were mostly older people who had chronic health problems such as heart conditions, arthritis, anxiety, or depression or problems in their relationships with others. Biomedicine had little to offer these people at that time. Christian Science, however, offered hope and a healing process that shares many characteristics with psychotherapy.[7] My grandmother's patients were part of the subculture of Christian Science, a social world that can be completely absorbing. Some of them were socially isolated, however, and my grandmother was their link to the world.

By the time I was a teenager, I saw big differences between her patients and me. The age difference was the most obvious. Christian Science was a religion of the middle-aged and old, not the young.[8] Although I still believed in the power of these practices and saw their efficacy for others, I began to look around for another way to ameliorate my own suffering.

When I turned eighteen and became legally independent, I sought out a physician in search of some answers for—and relief from—my illness. My doing so represented a major break from family traditions. It was my very first anthropological excursion. Before long I intuitively grasped a thread of continuity in these two forms of healing—the theme of personal responsibility for health. The methods of healing were different, but my role was essentially unchanged: it was up to me to manage my illness, to stay in charge of it, and to follow prescribed regimens. The difference was that once I started using the biomedical system, I started to get better. Although asthma medication was then in an early stage, it did improve my daily functioning, especially when combined with home remedies.

Because biomedicine was so essentially foreign to my lifelong way of thinking about health and illness, it held a fascination for me. This fascination lasted until I began to see the similarities between my grandmother's techniques and those of physicians. They learned the patient's history; so did she. They asked the patient to identify the problem; so did

she. Her treatment consisted of constant prayers combined with a pre-
scription for specific readings from the Bible and other Christian Science
religious works—essentially a religious course of study. Such a system
can be effective only in cultures where personal responsibility is a prime
cultural tenet, because the work of getting better rests on the shoulders
of the person seeking help.

Biomedicine had other facets of healing that I was familiar with
through my grandmother's practices. Physicians—at least the ones I
thought of as "real" healers—provided support and care as my grandmother did. They had mystique, as she did, which gave people hope at
the same time that it kept them enmeshed in the healing process. The
"good" ones—the ones who allowed themselves to be seen as people,
not just as physicians—I thought of as "wounded healers," people who
have become healers as a result of their own troubles and the resulting
transformations.[9] Shamans around the world often attribute their special
power to their own initial life struggles, which they view as connecting
them to higher powers than for most mortals. Certain physicians I encountered had, in my view, looked inside themselves for answers, as my
grandmother had done in preparing to become a healer. They were willing to acknowledge their human frailty to patients; this willingness had
always been the secret of my grandmother's success. I began to see what
the business of healing was all about.

As I have pointed out already, it was repeatedly brought home to me
that personal responsibility pervaded the biomedical system in which
I was a newcomer. As I became increasingly intrigued with the role
this tenet played in biomedicine, I found myself examining how people
interpreted personal responsibility for health in the various studies I
undertook.

TAKING PERSONAL RESPONSIBILITY FOR HEALTH

Because personal responsibility is so highly valued in the United States,
it follows that taking personal responsibility for health is part of the
process of making sense of suffering after a disruption to health. Making
sense of suffering is part of self-healing, for it provides the sufferer with

peace of mind. It is specifically within the context of personal responsibility for health that I turn to narratives of healing, especially self-healing. In previous chapters, we have seen how personal responsibility for health is played out in people's efforts to create continuity in the face of disruption. Here I examine the complex ways in which different approaches to healing are combined in the United States, and the role of personal responsibility in efforts to bring healing about. Although people in the United States, both in the past and in the present, have engaged in self-healing processes just as often as people in other societies have, non-biomedical forms of healing remain unsung in daily life. People draw on various types of healing as they attempt to integrate loss and change into their lives.

In the ethnic minorities study, we have made a special effort to elicit narratives that include people's religious beliefs and their ideas about healing modes other than biomedicine.[10] In interviews with African Americans, personal responsibility for health is a central motif. Treatment through a combination of biomedicine and religious faith is repeatedly described. Although there is a tendency to separate the sacred from the secular in U.S. society, religious and biomedical beliefs are often intertwined at the level of illness experience.[11] People who have life-threatening or long-term illnesses or disruptions in their lives usually understand healing to be a complex process that encompasses more than one healing system.

After a serious illness, people often assume greater vigilance over their health. They may monitor their bodies continuously. Mrs. Leona Turner, a sixty-nine-year-old African-American woman in the ethnic minorities study, has both diabetes and high blood pressure. She had a mild stroke three months before she was interviewed. She combines a knowledge of biomedicine and her own religious beliefs to care for herself. Having worked for many years as an office assistant for internists, she is well informed about biomedicine. Physicians for whom she worked now provide her medical treatment.

Mrs. Turner's story exemplifies how personal responsibility for health affects the way people monitor their bodies after a serious illness. She demonstrates her sense that she is responsible for doing everything she can for herself before turning to others.

I had one retina repaired on the left eye. Everything looked like a cloud. It gets dark. So I gave my car to my son, and he takes me to some of my doctors appointments, grocery shopping, and friends. And the more that I have to do or think about is better for me because I won't sit here and go lulu. I always—when I pray, I say, "Please, dear God, don't let me go blind, and don't let me have to lose my mind because they [cognitively impaired people] can't do anything." I've seen this and that's why it's frightening, so I say, "Let me keep my right mind and my eyesight." Sometimes they [her eyes] get very blank like a haze, and then all of a sudden it clears up. That's one of the diabetes symptoms. Cataracts, strokes, heart attacks. When I get into bed at night I say my prayers and I put my hand across it [her heart] and I put my hand up here and say, "Please don't let me have a heart attack." With the stroke I wasn't para-lyzed any place, but it was all in the left side, so that means the stroke was on the right side, and I exercise. I've lived this long. I'm sixty-nine. Next year, if God lets me live, I'll be seventy, so I thank Him for that, 'cause He did what He didn't have to do.

When the interviewer asked, "Is there anything, being black, that you work on or that helps us to take care of ourselves, do you think?" Mrs. Turner responded,

I think you should watch your diet. I think everyone should watch their diet. I guess if I had watched mine I wouldn't be like this, but with diabe-tes you just don't catch that. It comes from a family member. My mother had it.

Asked if she has had any problems with the health-care system, Mrs. Turner responded,

No. My doctors, I can call them any time of the day or night, but I try to do the best I can for myself, and then when I'm feeling bad I call and they say, "Well, why did you wait so late?" "Oh well, I was trying to help myself."

The interviewer queried her further: "So what would you try to do? In-stead of calling them, how would you try and help yourself?"

There are certain things that, you know, you read in your medical book—how to lie down, sit down, walk, exercise, and if that doesn't work, then you get in touch with your doctor. And by me working in the medical field, it's quite a few things that you learn on your own. So I try to do that. I take my medication and do what I'm told, if I think it's right. But if it doesn't work for me, that doesn't mean it won't work for someone else. Then I try something else. So I haven't really had no big problem.

I try. I have the walker. I have a cane, and I walk down the stairs and walk up. By the time I get back in, I am too tired. I have to do it sometimes. Sometimes I don't want to do it, and I said, this is for me and I do it but not right after [being ill] in August, when I fell three times. Monday, Tuesday, and Wednesday right out there, getting in the cab. Right out in the front. And the man said, he looked around and suddenly when I stepped off the curb, when he looked again I wasn't there. I said, "No, I'm lying on the sidewalk with my legs under your cab." He said, "Do you need any assistance?" I said, "No, let me do it. Nobody helped me fall here."

Mrs. Turner tries to diminish the effects of the stroke and her other illnesses. She is so independent that even when she falls repeatedly, she will accept no help from others. She concludes,

I feel pretty good. I can't let a pain stop me.

Mrs. Turner's independence and her religion inform her sense of personal responsibility, and together they have led her to develop her own complex system of self-care, which combines both religious and biomedical approaches. Some aspects of this system are preventive, such as praying to God, doing exercise, and watching her diet. Some involve illness management, such as taking her medication and doing what she is told (if she agrees with the medical regimen), as well as paying attention to body mechanics and asking God for guidance. Mrs. Turner's narrative illustrates how the moral force of normalizing ideologies informs people's actions with respect to their health.

TRANSFORMATION THROUGH SELF-HELP

People have multiple, often conflicting, understandings of their illnesses and may utilize more than one type of healing. In the United States, people often turn to other modes of healing while they are engaged in biomedical treatment. But doing so often goes unacknowledged in biomedicine. How people select and use specific modes of healing changes continuously depending on their condition and their absorption of information about healing: information about specific religions, types of psychotherapy, self-help remedies, and the latest biomedical advances. The sources of such information are many: television and radio, the various print media, friends.

What types of healing people turn to when a disruption occurs depends on a variety of factors, such as ethnicity, class, age, and gender, as well as the social and cultural context, the specific illness or illnesses, family beliefs, and life experiences. By the time a disruption occurs, most people have already become accustomed to particular types of healing, but because disruption usually causes people to question many aspects of their lives, this is the most likely time of life for people to experiment with new beliefs and practices. People often increase their participation in healing forms they already know. After a disruption, it is common for people to reimmerse themselves in their religion and in healing modalities they have utilized in the past.

Experimentation with new modalities is apparently most likely to occur among younger people, especially women. In all my research over the years, I have consistently observed that women turn to other forms of healing more often than men do. This should not be surprising. Women have traditionally been more focused on health than men. They have been responsible for family health in the United States.[12] In the nineteenth century, women were in the forefront of the popular health movement.[13] If my data are any indication, women more readily embrace alternatives to biomedical healing than do men, and they give the healing process more attention. Women's engagement with healing is a creative opportunity to take control over their lives.

Age is also a key factor in the type of healing that people turn to. In the infertility study and the midlife study (mostly people under the age of sixty), I frequently encountered people who used alternative healing techniques, but I seldom encountered these healing techniques in the stroke study, the ethnic minorities study, and the late-life transitions study (mostly people over the age of sixty). An eclectic mix of healing practices has emerged among younger people of various ethnic backgrounds in the studies I have done. This may be due, to a considerable extent, to the fact that all these studies were done in California, where there is widespread access to various forms of healing. Some of these healing forms, for example, twelve-step programs, are widespread throughout the United States, however.

The story of Jackie, a thirty-year-old African-American woman in the infertility study, illustrates that many forms of contemporary self-healing are grounded in core values of U.S. society. Jackie, a high school dropout, had been recovering from several addictions for a number of years. She discovered psychotherapy and therapy/self-help groups for the first time when she participated in an addiction program. She had combined the work of recovery with her effort to get a high school diploma and job retraining. At the time she was interviewed, she was completing a program in business and office management. She had been married for five years and was trying to conceive.

> I am recovering from substance abuse. In fact, I am going on twelve years off alcohol and drugs. That is a miracle. I don't even use sugar anymore. When I do get pregnant, I don't want to put sugar in my body. That was the first thing that I was addicted to. Going to make sugar sandwiches. I am just trying to get this body healthy so when I get pregnant, I want to be healthy. So I am working towards that.
>
> I come from a dysfunctional family. I have come a way from substance abuse to cigarettes, from being a street person, really. I didn't like myself, I hated myself. I wanted a child at thirteen because that would have given me something to love, and now I'm glad that didn't happen for me because I would have passed on to that child what I knew, which was anger and hate because that was all I had inside of me. So I have come a very long way. And moving to a new city would really be wonderful because it would be saying good-bye to the old and starting a whole new life. Not saying good-bye, but it would be symbolic . . . New people I don't know.

Jackie begins the story of her addictions by calling attention to her history and who she has become despite that history: a person free of addictions. She contrasts her childhood addiction to sugar sandwiches, food that is associated with poverty and deprivation in the United States, with her efforts to develop a healthy body and live a full life.

Jackie calls attention to her ongoing need for help with the process she is engaged in, and twelve-step programs have been the primary source of assistance. Jackie articulates a core tenet of U.S. values that is embedded in these self-help philosophies: that changing how she *thinks* will lead to personal change and, ultimately, to healing.

> I had to go to Alcoholics Anonymous and a lot of different twelve-step programs for my sugar addiction. I will call it an addiction because I couldn't stop on my own. I had to do some work. I had to go to Over-eaters Anonymous. So I work on myself through those programs. My problem is centered in my thinking. I need a lot of help with that, so I go out and get help.
>
> I am not that person any more that I used to be. I had to do the work [therapeutic work]; something was put inside of me to want to do something different. I was on this destructive road, and I don't think I could have gotten off it if it wasn't for a power working for me that wanted to get me to change my life so that I could have something better, because I couldn't have done it. I really thought I was going to be dead at age twenty-one, I really did. There were many times that I wanted to die and took pills, sleeping pills; I remember taking a bottle of sleeping pills and ended up in the hospital getting my stomach pumped because I just didn't want to live. So I am a miracle.

Metaphor mediates not only illness but also cure.[14] Jackie uses multiple metaphors in discussing how she has changed as a person. She contrasts her former, self-destructive life with her present life in which she feels the power within her. She extends the metaphor of body as healing force with a metaphor of self as a shrine. As she tells her story, a narrative of healing emerges, in which the healing force is embodied within her. Her body is thus a metaphor for the healing force.

In the process of healing, Jackie has undergone a multifaceted process of transformation. The process of transformation involves growth and giving to others and has a natural conclusion for Jackie: a child. She reflects on the concrete changes she has gone through.

> I think the biggest thing is just not taking anything. Not putting that alcohol in my body and the cocaine and all that. Just not doing it. And just

one day at a time. I have done a lot of work, I am not saying that. But I think that over the years, I mean even after five years of sobriety, I wanted to commit suicide. It has been real painful, just like having a baby and giving birth. That is real painful too, and it is like I am giving birth to a new person.

She has resisted her addictions and engaged in therapeutic work, which she has approached with the slogan adapted by Alcoholics Anonymous, "one day at a time." In describing the changes, she has undergone she addresses the rebirth of the body.

I look at it that way. It is painful for a reason, but once I get through it, I am like, "Look at me now." I look in the mirror, and I am the person that I used to point at. I used to point at that lady and say, "I want to be like her. I want to be like that lady." I am becoming her, and I continue to grow and I just have so much to give, so when I am ready, a child will come.

I remember this woman telling me, when I had the ectopic pregnancy, I went to her because she is kind of a psychic—she works spiritually with people. She said, "When you begin to love yourself like you think that you will love that child, when you begin to love you, those parts of yourself that you reject, then you will have a baby." I held onto that because that is telling me that I will conceive.

Having successfully used other healing modalities, Jackie turned to a psychic who gave her the next task in the healing process: learning to love herself. In other words, self-acceptance will complete the healing process, and she will conceive and, through conception, will regenerate herself.

Jackie directly addresses the transformation process as she describes the fate she escaped and the contrast she embodies.

I am the kind of person that ends up prostituting on the street with a needle, dying with a needle in her arm, because the people who have gone through the kinds of things I have, that have been affected by the things that I have been affected by, that is where they end up, a lot of them. It is too much, too much pain. But I know I can do it, and I have. I work on being a better person. I know that I need to enlarge my spiritual life. We are looking at holistic ways of having children.

I am growing so much. I am such a gift to me. I think that is my life. The kind of therapy that I am doing right now, Feldenkrais body work [a system of postural body movements] and rebirthing is really changing me at levels that I can't see, but I see in my daily activities that I am not the same person that I was. I am wanting to take risks, and in fact, I am not so fearful to step out there. So I see my life unfolding. I am trying to stay out of the way so I don't screw it up.

Jackie describes the process of personal change she has undergone with the help of various healing techniques. She vividly contrasts the fate she narrowly avoided with who she is becoming, describing herself as a "gift." She acknowledges some fear but at the same time is becoming less fearful and more hopeful. In her description, she repeats the theme of death and rebirth of the self that is central to psychotherapeutic perspectives in the United States and is reflective of Western views of transcendence. The old self dies out and the new self takes over, in a process that is difficult but nevertheless necessary in Western ideas of rebirth and regeneration.

The forms of healing that Jackie deals with are complementary. They embrace a unified philosophy about the process of transformation that is grounded in one pervasive, guiding principle: transformation occurs through the process of taking personal responsibility for oneself and being open to change. Working on oneself through various interactive healing programs and therapies is seen by people who follow such a pathway as the route to transformation.

Jackie's story epitomizes the cultural approach to making sense of suffering and engaging in self-healing that is unique to the United States. The theme of personal responsibility for health runs consistently throughout Jackie's story. Although explaining why she has survived necessitates that she invoke her efforts to take personal responsibility for health, she does not find fault with those who still live in dysfunctional families or on the streets. She clearly has sympathy for them. In the United States, personal responsibility and success go hand in hand. Jackie is thus able to fit her story into cultural expectations about turning a life into a success story. Her frequent use of metaphors of death, rebirth, and transformation reveals the cultural foundations behind metaphor.

Narrative helps to make sense of suffering. I have suggested that narrative ameliorates disruption: it enables the narrator to mend the disruption by weaving it into the fabric of life, to put experience into perspective. People are able not only to integrate specific experiences with subsequent life experiences but also to understand their own actions and experiences and the behavior of others. We see this process occurring as Jackie narrates the dramatic changes she has gone through. When people are attempting to integrate past and present, they do not take culture for granted: they pick it apart and look at it more carefully, to absorb new understandings from old parts of their stories.

In *Body and Emotion*, Robert Desjarlais tells the story of how he apprenticed himself to a Yolmo healer.[15] Although this was an intentional, self-conscious act that he undertook as an anthropologist, it shares much with the way that people learn about various healing forms in the United States. Narratives of self-healing often reflect a form of apprenticeship. Many apprenticeships do not begin the way that Desjarlais's did, however. Many people in the United States embark on journeys of apprenticeship unwittingly, or even unwillingly, as I did as a young child when I accompanied my grandmother on her visits because she had nowhere else to leave me. Only later do they actually become apprentices, as forms of healing take on meaning and facilitate their efforts to make sense of disruption. The primary goal of these apprenticeships, however, is usually self-healing, not the healing of others. For example, self-help groups and books, as well as new-age healing techniques, have become an industry that offers apprenticeship in self-healing, as Jackie's story exemplifies.

People usually join self-help groups to deal with their sense of difference from a social norm. On the personal level, the groups facilitate the development of a coherent narrative. The story is refined in the group context,[16] and that story gives a sense of coherence to people's lives. Jackie, for example, uses the philosophy of twelve-step programs, "one day at a time," to frame her story of moving gradually from chaos to order and fulfillment.

Self-help groups lend moral authority to the narrator. These groups thus provide tools for mediating the disruptions arising from cultural discourses on the self and normalcy at the same time that they reinforce other dominant cultural ideologies. By joining such a group, people are thus able to configure their story so that it conveys their difference and yet still carries the moral force of normalizing ideologies.[17]

Jackie's story illustrates the U.S. cultural approach to making sense of suffering in yet another way: the philosophy that the route to the body and to the reestablishment of embodied knowledge following physical or bodily disruption is through the mind. This philosophy, an outgrowth of interpretations of Cartesian dualism, does not espouse the *separation* of mind and body so much as it specifies a particular route through the body.[18] This philosophy is common to self-help philosophies and Christian Science, yet it is not a philosophy only of fringe groups. It appears to be a dominant way of thinking about the body in the United States and other Western societies, as it is a basic principle on which modern psychotherapy operates.

This philosophy enables people to visualize their embodiment; it legitimizes bodiliness because preeminence is still given to mind over body. Yet since the 1960s, the trend toward giving credence to *being* a body rather than simply to *having* a body has been growing. Thus, there is currently greater emphasis than there has been in the past on "body work," such as that undertaken by Jackie, in conjunction with other therapies that can be viewed as more mental.

The cultural discourse on the body incorporates various elements of normalizing ideologies, such as personal responsibility, control over the environment (in this case the environment is the body), and the focus on will—the idea that bodily change can be willed. In efforts to promote self-healing, people engage in certain kinds of practices, such as those described above, in which the emphasis is on changing thinking as a means of controlling behavior that affects the body. The philosophies of self-help and self-care now so prevalent in the United States are so successful because they emerge from and fit very well with dominant ideologies in U.S. life.

HEALING RESOURCES AND
THE MIND-BODY CONNECTION

Unlike Christian Science, which excludes other forms of healing, "alternative medicine" and "new age therapies," such as acupuncture and herbal medicine, are complementary, or interactive. Holism is the principle underlying these modalities: they focus on healing the whole person, on the oneness of mind and body. Holism predicates the use of mixed modes of healing: one healing modality may lead to another, and another, so that multiple sources of healing may be utilized simultaneously.

Martina's story of depression over infertility, which was introduced in chapter 5, demonstrates the same cultural phenomenon of personal responsibility as the previous stories have illustrated, but with different types of healing. She, too, chooses an amalgam of healing modalities as she seeks relief from chronic pain related to endometriosis, the cause of her infertility. Six months after the interview in which she described falling off a subway platform, she described her shift from biomedicine to other healing forms, such as acupuncture and herbal therapies, which are readily available in the West Coast city where she lives. These forms of healing are used as both adjuncts and alternatives to biomedical treatment.

> I had in mind that I would go to an herbalist because a friend of mine who had endometriosis quite severely had good results with that. So I thought I would get the surgery and then I would go to an herbalist. It was only because my doctor was quite strong about this [biomedical] drug that I tried it. I didn't plan to take it, nor did I know about the side effects. So I had the surgery. The results were that I had endometriosis and a cyst on one of the ovaries which he removed and little pieces of endometriosis which he vacuumed and that was that.

Despite the finality of her wording, Martina's symptoms did not go away. Several months after the surgery she abandoned medical treatment for infertility and began going to an herbalist for her chronic pain.

> As it has turned out, I still have pain, not quite as bad, but somewhat bad. Sometimes as bad. So my herbalist and acupuncturist think I have some endometrial cysts. Hopefully, through the herbal stuff it [her endometriosis] will be controlled.

When I asked if she was receiving acupuncture too, she responded,

> Oh, yeah, once a month. It's very interesting. It's kind of fun. I mean, it is bizarre. I mean, I have had some strange reactions. The first time I had a

vision of my mama. It depends, I have reactions usually. I mean, tears were streaming down my face, and I felt my mother there being very motherly, you know, healing, and all this stuff. You know, like just before you go to sleep or something, you have these images coming. It's not necessarily good, it's a weird thing. It's dreamlike, almost.

Acupuncture brings Martina's emotions to the fore, which makes her uneasy.

Another time I had a bad reaction. I went and had the acupuncture, and then I was meeting a friend. I met a friend, and I hadn't had a very strong reaction, you know, I hadn't had any while I was there. When I went to my friend's studio, we were looking at a painting. She showed me this one which had an infant crucified. It was a very, you know, sort of gross, ugly thing she was painting. Then the next painting she showed me it was all right. I was holding it [her emotions], right? Then she showed me this other painting with this woman, she had her head shaved and she was in a mirror, and at the point where her uterus would be, there was a skull, and I turned away and I lost it. I did projectile crying. I couldn't believe it. I just said, "I just have to let this out." I pulled out my hanky and just wept.

I just couldn't take that. You know, because of the acupuncture I did not have time to put up the defense and so that it was like . . . I don't know, I just could not handle it. She was apologizing all over the place. I think I just had to let it out. I just looked at myself in the mirror and went to sort of wipe up and stuff, and my eyes were not even swollen. That's what I mean by projectile crying. I mean, the tears just flew from my face. I just had a gut-wrenching cry. She said she had done it [the painting] last week when she was in a very painful situation in her relationship. She painted my fears, you know, the skull at the uterus and carrying it around with you. Instead of emanating creative life, nothing is coming out. Instead, she put death there. So that was one experience of acupuncture that was just too much.

Frightened by the relationship she sees between acupuncture and feeling emotionally out of control, Martina tries to exert some control over the effects of acupuncture by visiting her counselor immediately after she receives acupuncture.

I tried aspirin but it didn't do any good. It didn't work. I just tried to deal with it. A lot of people cope with pain, and that's what I did. So you know, with the acupuncture we're trying to also, you know, to try to put something into my mind, since it seems to be so mind related. It was like after I had acupuncture, sometimes I felt like I was vulnerable. I was afraid to go back in a way because I felt like my skin was gone. You know, I had opened myself up for this. This is what this is about—to supposedly make things flow more easily so that you can get rid of the bad stuff and get your system flowing right. So I'm still seeing a counselor about once a month, and my counselor just moved out near my acupuncturist, so the last two times I had acupuncture and went to therapy for a session afterwards.

She concluded that therapy gave her "a checking point."

I was curious to know how she put all of these events and healing endeavors together, so I brought up her experience of accidents (discussed in chapter 5).

Yeah, that's when I went to the shrink. I realized that I was totally destroying myself. It really seemed that I was not happy, and I wasn't dealing with the question of infertility. That was a big step to realize that something was going on.

In Martina's story we see how she attempts to integrate healing remedies for the whole body. She turns first to biomedicine to cure her infertility, then to psychotherapy. When biomedicine fails to cure her of infertility *or* to relieve her pain, she turns to herbal medicine, then to acupuncture, while continuing the psychotherapy. She then fine-tunes this combination of healing modes by going to see her therapist immediately following acupuncture. By seeking out these various healing modes, she is taking personal responsibility for her health and well-being. Doing something about her physical pain and her well-being is up to her.

As she talks about the forms of healing she uses and her concerns about them, Martina reveals cultural views of women that tap her deepest fears. Although Martina explains the intensity of her response to her friend's paintings as being related to acupuncture, her response to the paintings occurred primarily because "she painted my fears." The replacement of life in the womb with death is a representation of Woman that she fears association with and is struggling against. Images like this one fed into her depression when she was preparing to die several years earlier. She indicates her concern about not being able to get rid of death, the antithesis of creativity. Death, lodged in the uterus, is a negation of the potential for transformation, which is so essential a part of Western views of overcoming adversity and creating continuity after a disruption. The skull in the uterus, a powerful image that elicits an intense emotional response, is the opposite of the representation of women as creative, life giving, and nurturing that is central to the U.S. cultural discourse on womanhood. Martina still fears that she embodies this association of woman with death; hence its powerful effect on her. At moments like these, she experiences such intense grief that it shapes her efforts at reembodiment as a creative, life-affirming woman. Martina's difficulty in resisting these representations of womanhood attests to the intensity of their moral force.

The antidote to the fear represented by the skull in the uterus is healing through therapies that will help to reestablish embodied knowledge. Martina accepts the premise that her pain is mind related, and this premise is reinforced when the painting of the skull in the uterus triggers an intense emotional response and a subsequent return of uterine cramping. Through Martina's effort to reach the pain in her body through her mind, we see again the cultural idea that the route to the body is through the mind. Normalizing ideologies reinforce this cultural idea.

10 Metaphors of Transformation

Anita, a thirty-five-year-old Anglo woman in the infertility study, articulated the kind of paradigm shift she thought was necessary for the transformation of a disruption.

> The whole thing about the infertility experience is the notion of hope. Because as long as you have hope you can keep going, but I think what has to change—what needs to be transformed—is what you hope for.

Notions of transcendence and transformation are embodied in the Judeo-Christian tradition and in philosophical ideologies of the West. The idea of continuity can be traced by examining how concepts such as development, adaptation, and transformation appear in Western cultural traditions and how people use them in their efforts to create continuity.[1] These concepts have been popularized through a variety of cultural routes, from fairy tales and movies to psychological self-help literature.

For example, the concept of development underlies popular notions of how people change. These concepts inform the perception that there is continuity in people's lives; for example, there is a general view that people cope, or adapt, in the face of problems, thereby preserving continuity in life. The transcendent experience epitomizes Western individualism and symbolizes coming full circle from one's beginnings. Transcendence is sometimes seen as the final stage of adjustment.[2]

In the West, people believe that personal transformation begins with alterations to ways of seeing. The Judeo-Christian ethic is replete with examples of the idea that such shifts in vision, for example, shifts caused by miracles and healings, are an impetus to personal change. This motif is applied in contemporary psychology, wherein events in life are seen as a catalyst for personal change. The notion of transformation is a Western interpretation of the effort to maintain order in life: by looking at things differently, people can reorder experience.[3]

Transformation is part of the process of integrating disruption and restoring a sense of continuity to life. The type of disruption people experience delineates not only the meanings they associate with a disruption but also the kind of metaphors they bring to bear in dealing with it. In those studies where the loss was primarily existential rather than physical (the infertility and midlife studies), people eventually dealt with the disruption by transforming it into part of the stream of continuity in which they viewed their life. They used metaphors of transformation in a self-conscious way. That is, they were actively trying to transform or transcend their experience—to rise above it. This was especially true in the infertility study, where people were continuously exposed to the notion of resolution through Resolve, the self-help group that was very active in the geographic locale where the research was conducted.[4] For the majority of people who experienced infertility, resolution was a metaphor for transforming the experience and bringing to a close a phase of life characterized by anguish over infertility.

In the studies where the disruption was a physical impairment (the stroke study, the late-life transitions study, and the ethnic minorities study), metaphors that directly address transformation were not salient. The people in these studies were trying to recover from the onslaught of illness or disability and to live with the resulting fear and frustration. As we have seen in previous chapters, they did not talk about resolution and transformation per se: instead, they talked about recovery and learning to live with new impairments. The metaphors used by chronically ill people can be seen as transformative in a different sense from those used by people facing an existential crisis. Metaphors for hope, perseverance, independence, and autonomy, core values in the United States, are apparently more effective in making sense of illnesses that provoke ongoing uncertainty. So, too, are metaphors that address death and disruption. The use of these metaphors points to the cultural foundations of metaphor and indicates that these metaphors are closely linked to the moral force of normalizing ideologies.

The way people talk about transformation may also be linked to age and educational level. People in the infertility and midlife studies were younger than the people in the other studies, and the former usually were college-educated. Although transformation is a metaphor with a long history in religion, it remained culturally submerged until recently.

THE EXPERIENCE OF TRANSFORMATION

The use of metaphors of transformation to address a loss that is existential can be understood through an examination of the experience of psychotherapy. As a form of healing, psychotherapy provides people with a way of organizing, reframing, and making sense of experience. It provides coherent systems of belief about how to work with and through life problems. Psychotherapy systems are systems of meaning, and, as such, they can transform suffering. Recently, psychotherapy has been viewed as a hermeneutic enterprise which contributes to the construction of healing fictions, which may attain a form of "narrative truth."[5]

Anita, a mental health professional, described how she viewed the experience of transformation in light of her own participation in a therapy group.

> I think what happened was we started to go to the Resolve group, and the group really helped us. It was wonderful to see in the group, couple by couple, people coming to a resolution and what a difference it made. Even if the resolution was not what you had hoped for, it mattered. You

could see people become transformed just by deciding to not pursue something anymore. That really was something to watch.

After she began group therapy, she also sought individual psycho-therapy. She described the process that she thought occurred.

> The therapy group . . . the Resolve group. It's like anything else. People have to hit rock bottom. There has to be a crisis. For me, the kind of therapy that I currently think is helpful and was helpful to me in think-ing about infertility, is my therapist is a Jungian. My husband's therapist was a Jungian and it was his recommendation and then I was referred to mine. What is the most helpful to me about it is that it's more than just you. I mean, it is hard to articulate what you need in therapy. Therapy has taught me about faith and a certain kind of spirituality and how to look at the glass as half full instead of half empty. I guess that is transformation.

Anita articulates the ingredients she sees as necessary to transform experience: a crisis or catalyst and a medium that facilitates faith and hope and eventually enables the disruptive experience to be viewed dif-ferently. In this process, the initial crisis of meaning is gradually re-worked so that a new way of seeing things emerges, that is, new meaning replaces old. Her metaphoric comment at the end of this statement dem-onstrates not only how metaphor works to replace an old structure with a new one but also how a metaphor may mirror the process of transfor-mation as people see it in Western societies, thus magnifying its power.

Western systems of psychotherapy are culture-specific and impart the dominant values of a society, along with specific treatments, correctives, and prescriptions for the patient to follow in carrying out the "work" of therapy. Patient and therapist together construct the meanings in the per-son's story in a reflexive process that reframes the problem to reflect the perspective of a given psychotherapy modality. Similarity in the cultural backgrounds of patient and therapist is often thought to be beneficial because, at the risk of stating the obvious, they draw on shared cultural meanings in the construction of the healing narrative. The new narrative constructed by the patient and the therapist emerges out of a prior nar-rative that no longer fits the patient's view of his or her life circumstances. Anita gives some indications of how this process of reframing proceeds.

In fact, the experience of infertility, it transformed our marriage into a better one. The reason that I went into therapy to begin with was that our marriage was on the rocks, not because of infertility, but because of my psychological . . . I think basically because of my problems of separating from my family. So it gave me a larger, more positive framework to put my experience in and a way to think about it and a way to kind of accept it.

Anita's story epitomizes the idea of reordering experience by looking at things differently. She attributes the problems she had experienced in her marriage not to infertility but to her relationship with her family. She makes it clear that this new way of thinking about her experience comes through psychotherapy when she spells out steps in transformation, as they are seen in the United States: the creation of a new framework, the creation of a new way of thinking, and acceptance.

Acceptance is part of the Judeo-Christian tradition and is a central theme of transformation metaphors. Accepting a situation opens up the possibility of working around it and thus transforming it. The idea of accepting what cannot be changed enables people to focus their energies elsewhere; by looking at a situation differently, they may identify where change is possible, as Anita did. We have seen the phenomenon of transformation through acceptance in various stories in previous chapters; for example, Mr. Goodson loses a leg and a foot and thanks God for what is left, and in doing so, he shifts his focus from the loss of his leg to moving ahead with his life. Acceptance of what cannot be changed is part of the U.S. value of perseverance.

Hope is essential to efforts to create continuity: without hope there is no future. When hope is lost, or absent, people introduce images of death, nothingness, or emptiness into their narratives.[6] People must have hope to live out the cultural notion of transformation.

Metaphors are used to integrate new knowledge about a particular topic through narrative.[7] The integration of new knowledge is a lifelong process that is culture-specific. In the case of psychotherapy, the knowledge that is being integrated is self-knowledge, seen through the lens of psychotherapy, in which cultural values are embedded. As we have seen in previous chapters, hope is one of these cultural values. Much has been written about how psychotherapy systems are culture bound, but little has been said, anthropologically, about why such systems are so effective with certain populations—namely, middle-class, predominantly white members of U.S. and European societies. The efficacy of psychotherapy lies, in part, in its primary tool: narrative. The primary goal of all psychotherapy is to get the patient to take responsibility for getting better and to work toward personal change that will be healing, or transformative.

Reconstructing one's life story by means of psychotherapy facilitates coherence by, in part, tapping a social, emotional, and moral infrastructure that reflects "prevailing intrapsychic and social models of the person as actor and sufferer." Narrative truth is vulnerable to social influence.[8]

In Anita's narrative, the experience of observing others in her therapy group influenced how she experienced infertility herself. In her example, we again see a phenomenon we explored in the last chapter: how a social group (here a self-help group) helps to solidify a person's evolving narrative and reinforces it through normalizing ideologies that are amended to take difference into account. In Anita's particular social group, the emphasis has been on resolution through other means besides conception to realize the goal of parenthood. The social group thus subscribes to normalizing ideologies about the importance of parenthood but amends these ideologies to include adoption and other alternatives.

This reworking of normalizing ideologies enhances their moral authority. Because the ideologies are reworked by the group to encompass the group's experience, the resulting alternative ideologies carry more weight. The social group's opinion may become more important than "society's" opinion. The social group may therefore become a buffer from social expectations, enabling people to find a workable solution to the disruption.

THE TRANSFORMATIVE NATURE OF METAPHOR

Notions of progress are embedded in U.S. values of activity, achievement, and focus on the future. These ideas inform a view of life as a continuous stream and are borne out in metaphor. When Don and Laurel, who discussed life with Don's chronic illness in chapter 7, adopted a child in their late thirties, fatherhood accentuated his concerns about the future.

> We've got this seventeen-month-old rascal in the other room that right now is getting recharged. His battery pack is nuclear. We can wake him up if you don't believe us. It has been a wonderful experience. Neither one of us would ever change that. And it's two things: it makes you feel really old and it makes you feel very young, too—it really does. Because you really do relive your childhood through them. And I think that's really great. He's made me appreciate a lot of aspects of my life. He makes me appreciate all the years we had before he came along.

As a resource that lends power and credence to life disruption, metaphor enables the creation of critical linkages between the past, the present, and the future. The transformative nature of metaphor in redefining a situation is illustrated clearly in this example. Here the baby metaphorically represents both limitless ("nuclear") energy and the future. The baby serves, all at once, as a metaphor of generation, regeneration, and replacement, as he gives promise to the future and thus gives his father a renewed reason to live. Don's child becomes a medium for looking at the passage of time. The baby represents continuities between the past, the present, and the future. The baby fosters Don's determination to persevere despite his illness (a determination that is underscored by the energy metaphor). The baby thus becomes an agent of transformation.

It is noteworthy that in talking about living with his chronic illness in chapter 7, Don did not use metaphors of transformation in the same way as he does here. His discussion of his chronic illness was laden with metaphors about endurance, perseverance, and fighting. Cultural understandings apparently lead people to associate specific metaphors with certain experiences and not with others. For example, metaphors of transformation are associated with babies but are not usually associated with illness.

Baby metaphors recur in the narratives of people dealing with disruptions at all stages of life. Babies represent life, death, hope, energy, transformation, productivity, and perseverance. Baby metaphors exemplify the techniques that men and women use to wrestle with symbols of the social order and, hence, with cultural notions of continuity. As guiding metaphors, baby metaphors are part of the cultural discourse on continuity.

Don's baby allows him not only to relive his childhood but also to remember his entire life. Memory is a substitute for something that is missing, and consequently memories often deal with a rupture or loss.[9] Pierre Nora suggests that memory should be seen not as retrospective continuity—people have conceived of it this way in the past—but as the illumination of discontinuity.[10] He calls attention to the "cult of continuity" in Western societies, which emphasizes origins and the veneration of the past.

Memory apparently both illuminates discontinuity and enables people to maintain the illusion of continuity. Because of memory, lives *appear* to have continuity.[11] Memory is not simply a personal, subjective experience. It is socially constructed and present oriented and thus reconfigures experience.[12] People filter memories according to what is meaningful, and through these meanings they interpret the events in their own lives.[13] Memories used to maintain a sense of continuity are apparently highly selective.[14] Past life influences the current moment in time through this selection process, enabling the illusion of consistency to be maintained amid the facts of change.[15]

Symbols that keep a sense of continuity alive may stay the same but be expressed differently over time. The journey of life metaphor and transformation metaphors are examples of guiding metaphors that people used in these studies in culturally specific ways. Don illustrates this phenomenon.

> I come home and walk up to the front door, and he'll see me coming and he'll start screaming. He's got this huge smile on his face. There is nothing like that to come home to. I want to grow up with him, I want to be able to play with him, I want to throw the ball and do the things that my father was unable to do with me because of his time schedule. I would love to teach him how to ski and do all the things that I would really like to do. I think that's one of the things that keeps me fighting against my disease. I probably want to do it more for my benefit than for his at this particular time.

Don looks into the future as he shifts back and forth between continuities and losses. This openness toward the future—the phenomenological notion of protention—is an important component of biographical
narratives in the United States. Temporal experience has a crucial component, a forward reference in which past and present are experienced
as a function of what will be.[16] A future-orientation is a central value in
U.S. society, and this orientation shapes Don's narrative. His story, like
others in this book, has a particular fluidity as he moves back and forth
between past, present, and future. Don shifts from a focus on his illness
to a focus on the future, from a focus on the problems caused by his
illness to a focus on his life-affirming child.

In addressing the many things he wants to do with his son, Don looks
toward the future with both uncertainty and hope. Although he hopes to
do these things, he may not be able to do them all because of his illness.
Nevertheless, the desire to do things with his son and the desire to pass
on his own knowledge to his son contribute to his efforts to persevere.
He acknowledges that he wants these things more for himself than for
his son. They constitute continuity.

In Don's story, we see the cultural foundations behind metaphor; we
see how images of transformation are linked, in his story, to cultural values such as progress, activity, and the future. Whereas in chapter 7, we
saw how Don wrestled with ideologies of normalcy as he lived with his
chronic illness, here we see how the child is an agent of transformation
who embodies ideologies of progress and represents continuity.

EMPLOTTING TRANSFORMATION IN LIFE STORIES

Deeply embedded in both religious and secular explanations of how the
world works, the notion of transformation is emplotted in narratives of
people's lives. As noted in chapter 2, narrative is a way of expressing
development over time, and emplotment, a key component of narrative,
actively mediates between time and narrative by drawing a configuration out of a simple succession.[17] Biographical narratives are *culturally*
emplotted; that is, emplotment captures the various elements of time,
memory, and relationships to others in a manner that is cultural in na-

ture. Such narratives thus capture the person's conception of the cultural life course, cultural mores, and cultural constraints, placing them within a biographical container. When we think of memory as the representation and embodiment of loss rather than as simply retrospective continuity, it becomes clearer how memory is utilized in a cultural way.

Because continuity is mediated, in the United States, primarily through people rather than through external social structures,[18] the temporal dimensions of lives and the individually constructed histories of those lives are apparently critical elements in efforts to create and mediate a sense of continuity. In the United States, people manage discontinuities and disruptions primarily through memories that have cultural salience, beginning with memories that are embodied.

In the following story, Michael, a sixty-year-old Jewish man in the midlife study, transforms his life-story narrative through emplotment. Michael is trying to maintain a sense of coherence in the face of disruptive change. He examines the events in his life retrospectively as he talks about the most recent changes in his life.

> I think the real changes started three years ago when I separated from my wife. That was something I'd been thinking about for a long time. I was miserable in the marriage. I just felt very, very isolated and very lonesome. I was afraid to leave for all kinds of reasons—my friends were going to abandon me, my children, financial stuff. And just going through it. I was just terrified.

When people must choose between maintaining the status quo and initiating change, they usually attempt to do the former, at least until doing so becomes unbearable and threatens their sense of coherence. Disruptive change, whether people initiate it themselves or have it thrust unwanted on them, entails some losses: for example, abandonment by kin and friends. Fear of these losses can compel people to stay in an untenable situation. Michael had stayed in an unhappy marriage for over thirty years because he was trying to adhere to cultural expectations about the normal family. Michael feared both financial and social losses: he feared abandonment by children and friends, as well as financial losses.

Leaving his wife was the first in a series of events that propelled Michael into an extended period of disruption. Thinking about what actually happened the day he left his wife, he said,

> But the actual separation . . . On the day that I told her I was going to leave . . . Well, I had no idea it was going to happen that day. I was just sort of unhappy. I was seeing a therapist that day, and it just sort of came out. I had no idea that that was the day I was going to decide to leave. So I don't know . . . Something deep down inside of me took over. It was sort of funny in a way. That was the biggest change, and I think everything has stemmed from that. The next day I went to a convention with my thirty-eight-year-old business partner. We had drinks together, then he went off and had dinner with friends. In the morning I called my office, and my secretary said, "I'm sorry to hear about Jim," and I said, "What are you talking about?" She said, "Jim died," and I said, "That's crazy—I was with him at five o'clock yesterday. She said no, he'd gone on to dinner, apparently had an allergic reaction and an asthma attack and died in an emergency room. Within twelve hours these two major changes turned my life inside out.

Michael had himself been diagnosed with asthma approximately one year before his business partner died. Until that time he had experienced robust good health. Since his diagnosis, Michael has been to emergency rooms for asthma episodes many times and has been hospitalized, as well. These experiences have affected his former view of himself as healthy, so that he now feels vulnerable.

When Michael was in his fifties, changes in his identity triggered a search to find meaning in his life. Michael's search for meaning was intensified when his partner, who was twenty years younger than Michael, died unexpectedly; his partner's death underlined his awareness of his own mortality, the nearness of death, and the ephemeral quality of life. Making the most of life became a conscious, purposeful effort—the goal he gave his full attention to. As his identity continued to change in this quest, so did his view of the past.

Having rethought the past, he faced the future with single-minded purpose: to find himself, the other parts of himself that he thought he had ignored, and almost lost, for so many years.

What I'm doing now is getting in touch with who I really am.

In describing his efforts to locate who he really is, he identifies a further means of reestablishing a sense of coherence through a search for himself.

> I really took a wrong turn in the road forty years ago. I should have let that creative side of myself in. I was dying in that relationship. It was a horror. And the way we lived . . . I'm not that wealthy guy, I don't care about that stuff. None of it means anything to me.

In his efforts to reconcile changes in his identity and the disruptions he experienced in his life, Michael resorts to metaphor. In order to begin life anew yet give his life a sense of consistency, he characterizes his marriage as "a wrong turn in the road." He uses images of death (he was "dying in that relationship") and rebirth. Michael introduces into his story two organizing metaphors in Western thought: the journey of life metaphor and the transformation metaphor of death and rebirth. The portrayal of his marriage as a wrong turn serves an important function in the creation of a sense of continuity: the marriage is metaphorically transformed into a temporary disruption in a lifelong stream of continuity.

A sense of failure to live up to cultural norms of the idealized life may be especially pronounced during times of transition. In describing his past life, Michael emphasizes order and family expectations. From a close-knit Jewish family, he identifies family values as pivotal in connecting the present to the past.

> My parents were very poor. They lived in the slums. But my father was a very brilliant man. He became an attorney. He was very tough, very demanding on himself and on me. I thought I was supposed to follow a certain path. He wanted me to go to law school, and I dreaded the idea. The only way I knew to avoid it but still have his approval was to go to an acclaimed business school. You couldn't be too unhappy with a son who did that. So I did, and I've been in stocks and bonds all my life.

Michael further bolsters his sense of coherence by depicting family successes. This rags to riches story, like the mythic fables of Horatio Alger, is a metaphor for success. Michael explores the success metaphor, which he has lived out so fully, in his efforts to maintain a sense of coherence.

Once embarked in a certain direction as a result of his family's expectations, Michael had found it hard to change course. He lived the American rags to riches story, but doing so created conflict between the values he had been raised with and his identity.

> About ten years later he[father] made an investment for me that made me a huge amount of money. So I've always been quite wealthy. And I've always lived up to that role . . . But I don't think that's who I really am.

During the tumult of the recent past, Michael's identity has been changing. Here he begins to outline a shift in who he sees himself to be, a shift from his former view of himself as a wealthy man to a view of himself as a more ordinary person. To create a sense of coherence, however, Michael must reframe the success metaphor. Michael describes the complexities of this metaphor in his life story. He did not know how to deal with his unexpected wealth, especially in the face of disruption.

> The same weekend they called me to come get the check, my wife was hospitalized for the first time. They said they didn't know how long she would be there—it might be a very long time. They didn't know what was going to happen. I went from the hospital to the East Coast to get this check that made me wealthy. And then I went home, and there I was, just sitting there by myself with all this money and no one to share it with.

In discussing his loneliness, Michael calls attention to the lack of meaning he experienced. Being wealthy only underscores his loneliness. Although his life became one of privilege, he was never completely comfortable. He said,

> When she came home, we lived in this very grand house, but we both felt like we were impostors living in that house. It was really grander than we were.

When he subsequently lost his wealth in a business fiasco, he returned to habits that were closer to the way he was raised. In describing everyday life as he now lives it, he juxtaposes two versions of success, and indeed, two lives.

> Now I do the dishes and I cook. The other night I sat down and picked up a book and read. I never did that in my former life. Partly, I was intimidated by my wife, but partly, it just wasn't what I was supposed to do.

Here Michael conveys his sense that he has lived two lives, and that he had not been true to himself in his former life. He indicates social rules for behavior dictated his actions rather than his own ideas of what encompassed a life. He comes to see his former life as a "false" life, which enables him to reshape the success metaphor and use it as a means of creating continuity. The success metaphor is constituted by what he is doing now. The old version thus becomes the "false" metaphor for success, which enables him to rationalize a sudden change of fortune.

Loss of his wealth caused an abrupt about-face for Michael. Having lost his fortune and his business through a series of calamities, Michael is philosophical. He observes that he was his own undoing.

> I got into this business deal. It's my form of craziness. Some people gamble, some people smoke dope. I didn't need to do it financially. I had enough money to live on for the rest of my life. I didn't need to take this huge risk. I did it to prove my masculinity or my virility, or find a place to put my energy. Something like that.

Michael is trying to create a sense of coherence into which he can fit his notions about the meaning of success and the changed self. In doing so, he introduces two new themes: his weak spot and his masculinity, indicating the association between masculinity and the work ethic for men in the United States. Michael's story depicts how he has struggled to give himself a sense of coherence by manipulating cultural notions of success to fit his own set of life circumstances.

Michael combines metaphors as he wrestles with changes in his life that affect his sense of self. Looking back, he said of this experience,

> I suffer from terminal optimism. I bought a business that had been a failure. I thought I understood why and that I could overcome the prob-

lems—that was real optimism on my part. I also think optimism was the reason I stayed in my marriage for twenty years too long. I kept thinking it was going to be okay, it was going to get better. My optimism may kill me, I don't know.

In this statement Michael uses the metaphor "terminal optimism" both as a rationale for his actions and as a frame for his life experience. This metaphor is an important component of the organizing metaphors of transformation and life journey that Michael has invoked. Metaphors such as this lend credence to his struggle to explain the recent misfortunes that have plunged him, for a time, into chaos. As an explanation, the notion of terminal optimism facilitates Michael's efforts to create a sense of continuity in his life. By indicating that his optimism may kill him, however, he also conveys the depth of his emotions about the changes he has undergone. His optimism is thus embodied. As Michael seeks to bring this period of turbulence in his life to a close, his narrative encompasses the depth of his feelings and his philosophy of life.

To renegotiate his identity, Michael must rework several levels of understanding. First, he must rework his embodied knowledge, specifically with respect to his experience of having asthma. Second, he must rethink his identity and how he presents himself to the world. His new understanding of himself as having an ordinary life informs his identity. Personhood is intimately tied, for Michael, to financial and social success. Thus, the experiences, such as divorce, that indicated failure to him must be integrated into Michael's views of himself as a person.

Michael is engaged in reviewing his life, a phenomenon that occurs increasingly from midlife on.[19] Midlife has been characterized as a time of mastery and personal power, a time of consolidation of personal gains, and a time of shifts in perceptions of time and mortality, from consideration of time since birth to consideration of time left to live.[20] As people look to the future while simultaneously reflecting upon the past, they continuously reformulate their identities to be compatible with their experience of life.[21] Narrative and metaphor facilitate this integrative process.

The cultural life course provides the basis for a cultural discourse on how life itself is conceptualized. Thus, in Michael's story we see the metaphoric unfolding of his life in a narrative that is organized to present events in his life in a linear manner. We see how his story is emplotted. He divides his story into several key areas: his relationship with his former wife and his successful and unsuccessful business deals.

To create a sense of continuity, Michael emplots his narrative around the notion of terminal optimism as well as around specific memories: memories of his family, especially his father, memories of his former life, memories about his expectations, memories of past business deals. Wedded to these memories are fears. His memories are mediated by the losses he has experienced.

In the telling of these chapters in his life, Michael uses a variety of metaphors. Because Michael's story is not new to him, it is unlikely that these metaphors came to his mind for the first time as he was narrating his story to me, but it may be that he articulated them fully for the first time in the telling of his story. These events occurred over a period of years, during which time he has been refining his narrative and searching for metaphors to help him understand his whole life.

Metaphors give shape and form to life stories. They are tools for working with experience, as they embody the situational knowledge that constitutes culture.[22] People integrate explicit metaphors and more implicit images that encompass their whole life into their frameworks for understanding their lives.[23] When life begins to return to normal and people attempt to bring closure to a period of disruption, the role of metaphor, noted in chapter 2, becomes most apparent: metaphor represents a synthesis of interpretation and creation, in which previous interpretations yield to new ones.

In Michael's story, we see how he engages various cultural discourses that concern him, such as the discourse on the family and the discourse on components of power in U.S. society: success and status. Family, success, and status were the stakes at risk as he tried to deal with the disruptions to his life; that is, he was fearful about how others would view the changes in his family life and about his status and success as others saw them. Divorce has now been normalized, and consequently he brought a broadened view of this event into his narrative and related it to expanded discourses on the family.

Michael's story is thus a good example of how metaphor is creatively used to create linkages between past and future when disruption occurs, and how those metaphors may reflect normalizing ideologies. The metaphors Michael uses enable him to create bridges back to normalizing ideologies to which he subscribes despite his temporary divergence from them because of divorce. Michael has also used the process of narrative smoothing to align his story with normalizing ideologies, and that process has also enabled him to present a picture of wholeness and completion in the end.[24]

11 Disruption and the Creation of Continuity

When I began these studies of disruption many years ago, I was heavily invested in creating continuity for myself, in learning how others experience continuity, and in understanding how continuity is culturally mediated. At some midpoint, however, I found that I was really studying not continuity but disruption. Continuity is an illusion. Disruption to life is a constant in human experience. The only continuity that has staying power is the continuity of the body, and even that is vulnerable. But that reality is too unsettling for people to live with. Faith in continuity of the body may preserve the illusion of a more sweeping kind of continuity.

The study of disrupted lives enables us to look closely at the disparity between cultural notions of how things are supposed to be and how they are, a disparity that is highlighted by disruption. In the United States, people subscribe to a complex ethos that posits an orderly, predictable life. This ethos shields people from an alternative view of life as unpredictable and chaotic. Although continuity in life is an illusion, it is an effective one: it organizes people's plans for and expectations about life, as well as the ways in which they understand who they are and what they do.

Throughout this book, I have tried to demonstrate that the construct of continuity is so deeply embedded in U.S. life at every level that it amounts to a cultural ideology. The sheer number of ways in which people strive to create continuity underscores the centrality of the construct. In these pages we have heard from people with little education and from people with considerable education, from people who have experienced almost fatal neglect based in racism and from people who have had every opportunity in life. What is remarkable is that, despite the diversity of their backgrounds and life experiences, these people use similar ways to attempt to create continuity out of disruption.

The ideology of continuity is built on an array of disparate cultural components that operate at various levels of society. I have discussed these components, and they include (1) embodied knowledge and all that it generates and comprises, including bodily order and memory; (2) a view of a linear cultural life course that draws on notions of development, adaptation, and transformation; (3) a binary view of order and chaos; (4) the values of personal responsibility, perseverance, control over the environment, and an orientation toward the future; and 5) the way order is embedded in daily life by means of, for example, the ordering of narrative and the ordering of the very experience of disruption. In exploring these components, I have emphasized two particular conduits for shaping how people understand continuity: the moral force of normalizing ideologies and the cultural foundations of metaphor.

In this book, I have continually drawn attention to people's sense of difference from others. By spending so much time focusing on the experience of difference, I realize that I have set up a diametric opposition between difference and normalcy. I have chosen to highlight this opposition in order to illustrate the ways in which the experience of difference affects people's immersion in cultural processes. We must recognize, however, that through bodily experience and its extension into practice in daily life, difference and normalcy collapse into each other at every turn.

Reading these stories as a whole, we find that the concerns of young and old are not decidedly different—they are human concerns that reflect the issues people face at different phases of life. Age, although an important contextual factor, has little relevance for embodied knowledge.[1]

How people use cultural resources to make sense of their lives when a disruption occurs has been a recurrent theme in this book. We have seen how people in the United States work creatively with core categories, such as the family, manhood, womanhood, health, and aging. Each of these categories provides both a window on the assumptions people make about themselves and insights about specific types of disruptions. We have seen how people amend ideas associated with these categories to encompass their experiences. That is, they find antidotes to the moral force of normalizing ideologies associated with such constructs. For example, new ways of understanding family, womanhood, and manhood have emerged in the narratives in this book. In this continual process of elaboration of and amendment to existing cultural ideologies, we see human agency at work in everyday life.

Resistance to the moral force of normalizing ideologies is part of this process. Social scientists have largely overlooked such everyday forms of resistance in their preoccupation with large-scale social phenomena.[2] In doing so, they have ignored the politics of everyday life and its primary role in the shaping of cultural themes. Not only is the performance of embodied actions political, but also those actions, whether they be of individuals or social groups, have much to tell us about the uses of power. In this book, we have seen how disruption and efforts to create continuity lead, ultimately, to issues of agency, resistance, and power.

CONTINUITY OF THE BODY

I have tried to show that although we must attend to all the facets of disruption to understand it, we must start with embodiment.[3] Regaining a sense of continuity is a long and laborious process that is mediated, first and foremost, through bodily experience. We have seen how the creation of meaning begins with the body. We have seen how bodily knowledge is disrupted when the unexpected occurs and how the restoration of a semblance of normalcy in everyday life brings about a resurgence of embodied knowledge. Although we have seen repeatedly how illness wreaks havoc with bodily knowledge, we have also seen how events that are external to the body disrupt meaning and challenge bodily knowledge. We have seen how bodily knowledge is extended through sensory processes and how body parts continue to be embodied even when they are no longer present.

The body remembers. Embodied knowledge is shaped by memories that are social. People may attempt to erase unpleasant bodily memories, such as the fears caused by symptoms of a life-threatening illness. They may attempt to shut out memories; for example, people who can no longer walk may shut out the memory of being able to walk. But these efforts are, by and large, futile because bodily memories persist. Long after bodily changes have occurred, people continue to experience their bodies as they used to be. People who can no longer walk may attempt to get up out of a wheelchair and walk, or they may say "I'm fine just sitting here" and see themselves as unimpaired. This notion of bodily continuity, which, as I have said, may be the only enduring continuity, enables people to create a sense of continuity that extends beyond the body. It follows that when bodily changes are so profound as to destroy bodily continuity, people's ability to find meaning in life may be completely thwarted.

The reestablishment of embodied knowledge after a disruption and the enactment of that knowledge through narrative are cultural processes. Body and voice cannot be teased apart. The interior, unspoken voice is embodied. These embodied thoughts may be incompletely formed. The exterior voice—that is, spoken narrative—is a carefully crafted and finely honed reflection of this inner voice. Narrative serves as a medium through which somatic acts are communicated, and it thereby affirms and reinforces embodied knowledge.

The intersection of body and voice is an intimate process that cannot be fully known by others. What *can* be known and is accessible is the way in which culture is manifested in this process. That is, we can understand the permeability of culture through bodily experience as well as through narrative. Cultural processes are mediated at their most elemental level through subjective experience, which enables people to take in and reformulate the external world.

One of the complexities of disruption to life is the experience of oneself as "the other." When disruption occurs, people experience the body as if it belongs to a stranger, and there is a deep discomfort, indeed an agony, in this experience. The stories in this book attest to people's efforts to bring their bodies back into themselves. The process of re-merging body and self is a lengthy and complex one, entailing the reworking of embodied knowledge.

Another disquieting experience is seeing oneself as different from others. Seeing oneself as different, and sharing society's opinions and attitudes about people who are different, underscore the agony of identifying one's body as unknown. Moving from identifying others as crippled, infertile, or old, for example, to seeing oneself in this way, creates a sense of disruption in itself. The process of redefining difference and where one stands in relation to others is, as we have seen, enormously challenging, lengthy, and complex. It occurs in tandem with the reestablishment of embodied knowledge. Identity may be amended to encompass the changes that have occurred. Ultimately, people may adopt a new stance in how they present themselves to the world.

THE CULTURAL FOUNDATIONS
OF NARRATIVE AND METAPHOR

Although I have relied heavily on narratives in this book, I have done so primarily as a means to gain access to embodied distress. I have treated narrative as the enactment of bodily experience. In studying U.S. society, where verbal self-expression is highly valued, narrative becomes a medium for understanding embodied distress and action. Postmodern theorists have focused on text to the exclusion of phenomenological perspectives,[4] and certainly textuality has played an important role in anthropology. Focusing on the text, however, reveals only part of the picture and may lead to faulty theorizing.[5]

As we have examined people's stories, we have seen how embodied distress reshapes these narratives. We have seen how narratives follow certain cultural conventions; that is, how the story form itself is cultural. In the United States, stories have beginnings, middles, and endings, even if the end is not yet known. Moreover, stories are usually told in a linear way. At least, they usually start out in a linear manner,[6] but we have also seen how quickly linearity can break down once people become engaged with the story they are narrating. Thus, the order of the text gives way as the story moves from the disruptive event and people are plunged deeper and deeper into chaos. It is usually at this point in the narrative that the body is engaged in the discussion because the effects of disruption are increasingly felt at the bodily level.

We have seen that people emplot their narratives in a culturally meaningful way so as to draw a configuration out of a simple succession of events. In the process of emplotment, they reshape events and memories to draw on culturally salient images. We have seen many examples of how the body itself is emplotted within the plot. Emplotment has also been reflected in people's efforts to adhere to ideologies of normalcy and their resulting sense of difference when those efforts fail. For example, people undergoing infertility emplot their stories around images of womanhood, manhood, and the meaning of family, whereas people who are chronically ill emplot their stories around images of impairment, recovery, and death.

Stories are also emplotted around the narrator's evolving political beliefs. We see this type of emplotment most often in narratives of resistance to normalizing ideologies when people—for example, women who have abandoned an effort to become mothers or older people who refuse to put themselves into a dependent role—state their refusal or inability to comply with normalizing ideologies. Such stories are usually emplotted around an alternative ideology or value, for example, independence or autonomy. By replacing the rejected ideology with another, the narrator pulls the story back into some semblance of conformity with the social order.

Because most of the stories in this book are incomplete, in the sense that closure on the disruption that occurred has not yet been reached, they are full of subjunctivizing elements. People try out the possibilities in order to bring satisfactory closure to their stories. At the same time, they anticipate or wish for closure that embraces normalizing ideologies. In doing so, people draw on key constructs such as order, personal responsibility, control over the environment, continuity, and transformation. When living up to normalizing ideologies appears to be out of reach, or when the story has a strong contrapuntal element of resistance to those ideologies, people explore alternative endings through subjunctivity.

The metaphors used by people in this book are linked, sometimes clearly and sometimes not, to normalizing ideologies. Metaphor has served as a window on the cultural foundations of U.S. society and, beyond that, of Western societies more generally. For Western societies we have seen metaphors that espouse, for example, mind-body dualism, transformation, and transcendence, and for U.S. society we have seen metaphors of rational determinism, personal responsibility, hope, perseverance, and control over the environment. We have seen an elaboration of metaphors on certain concepts that are pervasive in the United States, such as the importance of personal autonomy and independence, and we have been able to identify some of the desired qualities that people use again and again to describe themselves. We have also been able to identify some of the changes, reflected in the metaphors that people use, that are taking place in how people address issues of order and chaos and how technological development is changing definitions of what is normal, both among the general public and in social institutions such as biomedicine. We have seen how metaphor facilitates people's efforts to puzzle out their sense of difference, to make sense of the dissolution of order in their lives, to align themselves with normalizing discourses, and to resist those discourses in favor of alternatives. Working with metaphor can thus be seen as a cultural process.

Personal disruption prompts an effort to make sense of experience and transform it through metaphor. Metaphors are used not only to integrate knowledge but also to create new understandings of the phenomena people experience. The process whereby metaphor makes sense of chaos and creates coherence mirrors the process of trying to create continuity after a disruption. Because of this mirroring, metaphor may lend power and credence to the experience of disruption. We have observed both body metaphors and textual metaphors. Body metaphors facilitate a resurgence of embodied knowledge, while textual metaphors allow new ways of seeing. This is not to suggest that they can, or should, be separated from each other. Indeed, the academic exercise of separating them creates, to some extent, a false dichotomy, as these types of metaphor engage each other and both lend a sense of the whole to people's experience.

In this book, we have seen how people's efforts to reintegrate the unfathomable, to make the unfathomable concrete, begin with the body. By means of body metaphors, efforts at reintegration extend outward from the body to complex and interrelated cultural processes. For example, we have seen how, in the United States, oppositional body metaphors—metaphors of life and death, order and chaos, productivity and uselessness—function as a kind of sorting-out mechanism that enables people to make sense of their experience in terms of both Western structures of thought and a specific cultural ethos.

People use everyday metaphors. It is the elaboration of these metaphors through a phenomenological process that embues them with cultural relevance. Throughout this book we have seen commonplace metaphors of everyday life being used to transform embodiment and experience. A metaphor can act as a dynamo, providing new energy for the project of reworking experience. As we have seen, commonplace metaphors can be expressed through the body, through practice, and through the spoken word. Moreover, metaphors have emotional valence. Those qualities of metaphor enable people to create a new way of understanding their experience, no matter how commonplace a given metaphor may be.

We have seen that metaphors provide a way of integrating out-of-the-ordinary life experiences into identity. In using metaphor, people work simultaneously on changes in their identities and on changes in their lives. Identity reformulation is tied to transformation of the body; one woman, for example, moves from hating her body to cherishing it and talking to it directly. People address identity issues directly (one man says his identity is in "a constant process of revision or editing") as well as indirectly (one mans says he is "starting to lose [his] life," an image that stands for the danger of an ignominious end, the opposite of transformation). By using metaphor as a tool to address identity, people can rework cultural notions about how life is supposed to be and create the potential to reestablish a sense of continuity. Metaphoric shifts facilitate the ability to amend and reframe personal conceptions of cultural discourses.

Metaphors not only serve as tools for working with experience and simplifying the process of creating meaning but also suggest new meanings.[7] The notion of hope was used metaphorically, for example, to articulate cultural values and worldview, to articulate the meaning of loss, and to reframe hope through transformation; one woman said, "What has to change—what needs to be transformed—is what you hope for." People also applied this continuous process of metaphoric reframing to the way that they identified themselves, raising questions such as, what is a woman, a man, a mother, a baby? Metaphor thus serves as a mediator for change, enabling individuals to reestablish a sense of connection with the social order, while obscuring cultural paradoxes and unresolvable dilemmas.

What must be patently obvious are the myriad ways in which people resort to culture work to make sense of disruption and distress and to reinforce experience and action. In resorting to culture work, they rework their personalized versions of normalizing ideologies by creating new or altered images. Those images derive their power, as well as their meaning, from their ability to mobilize human energy by eliciting people's desires and motives.[8] In doing so, those images can act as agents of transformation, redirecting energy back toward people themselves so that people feel moved to act in accord with the social order embodied in the symbols. As we have seen, redirecting energy is a complex process that may require people to rework their understandings of the world through narrative and metaphor, and may ultimately involve working around culture when normalizing ideologies cannot be met in a straightforward way.

NORMALCY AND MORAL DISCOURSES

In this book I have emphasized a phenomenological perspective and the lived experience of people struggling with disruption to their lives. As noted at the outset, the body generates categories of social analysis, a process we have observed throughout this book. The examination of disruption from a cultural phenomenology perspective enables us to gain insights into how disruption is mediated by people themselves, that is, how agency mediates power relationships.[9] Lived experience speaks for itself and informs other levels of analysis. Cultural phenomenology enables us to tap communal life through embodied experience.

The profundity of the disruption people in this book experienced underscores the heavy weight that cultural notions of continuity carry in their lives. Their views of cultural notions of continuity did not encompass the disruptions to life that befell them, and consequently, a protracted search for answers to their dilemmas ensued. Although people sought to continue to act in accord with the social order, they often had to relinquish that goal. In grappling with this dilemma, they struggled with the symbols associated with the cultural discourse, attempting to reshape their personal frameworks of understanding to encompass their experience.

In this book, I have tried to show the moral force of normalizing ideologies for those who experience disruption, and thus difference, from others. In the accounts in this book, we have seen the conflict between the desire for normalcy and the acknowledgment of difference being enacted over and over again. What people struggle with repeatedly in their efforts to transform experience is the attempt to be both normal and different.[10] Those who interpret their efforts as reflecting normalcy and at the same time acknowledge difference are the ones who view the disruption as transformed and the task of recreating order as nearing completion.

We thus saw people looking for disparities in discourses on normalcy. Invariably, they were able to identify some disparities but not others. Cultural blinders to certain disparities in a discourse persisted, despite a heightened clarity of vision about the discourse in question, because tearing apart a discourse completely always carries the danger that the process of deconstruction might lead to complete loss of meaning. This fear was voiced by some people in this book—for example, when people indicated that certain avenues of inquiry held no meaning, or when people indicated they were not able to see the entire picture yet.

The total deconstruction of a discourse in a story occurred only if the narrator had an alternative discourse that provided acceptable explanations for the disruption. People sometimes rethought this alternative discourse as well to provide a personal fit. Their growing ability to recognize the sweeping nature of moral discourse and to recognize its failure to fit with their own personal concerns was one response to being forced to grapple with personal difference. It is apparent, however, that the ability to say "that [cultural expectation] doesn't apply to me" is quite variable. For some, the internal dialogue about meeting cultural expectations is one with which they will never be done.

As I have said, part of the struggle to come to terms with discourses on normalcy involves the reshaping of personal notions of what is normal. This was especially apparent when people qualified the meaning of normal by using phrases such as "what's normal for me" in the course of their stories. People rethink moral discourses on normalcy not simply in terms of the particulars of their life situation, such as a serious health problem or a family crisis, but also in terms of their age, ethnicity, gender, and class. We saw how the way people modified the discourse on the family depended on gender and ethnicity, and how the way people addressed the discourse on age depended on their own age.

The way in which the cultural ethos of rational determinism interfaced with moral discourses at the personal level was central to people's ability to come to terms with those discourses. For example, belief in the ability to control the environment was a key factor in people's determination to bring their stories into some semblance of unity with a moral discourse. This belief, coupled with the cultural emphasis on perseverance, for example, led women and men to pursue parenthood in the face of infertility for inordinate periods of time. They struggled with moral discourses about parenthood and gender roles, often without resolution. Likewise, the cultural emphasis on self-determination and autonomy interacted with moral discourses on age and personal responsibility for health, to affect the views and actions of people in middle and later life who had chronic illnesses.

This book has emphasized the effects of core cultural discourses on people's narratives of disruption, and consequently I have given little attention to the effects of these discourses within the broader social domain. Clearly, however, social institutions may shape discourses on normalcy, and those institutions not only expand such discourses in certain directions but also affect the translation of those discourses into practice. In one case, for example, we saw how proposed surgery had the potential to transform the meaning of normalcy: having a kidney removed, and living with only one kidney, were framed by physicians as normal. In this example biomedicine redefined normalcy in the human body. Discourses on normalcy may thus enable certain kinds of narratives but not others.

Discourses on normalcy mediated by social institutions play a major role in shaping the personal experience of disruption. They are not simply layered onto the experience of disruption, however; they are part of it. It is not possible to tease apart the experience of disruption and the discourses on normalcy. They form an ongoing dialogue, one that is continuously transformed in people's experiences.

Cultural discourses change as society changes. Throughout this book we have seen intimations of this process. For example, despite the persistence of cultural discourses that emphasize the importance of motherhood, expanded reproductive technologies have altered the discourse by introducing new possibilities. People have, in turn, further amended the discourse. The discourse on motherhood is but one example of a discourse on normalcy into which science-based models have filtered over time. The discourse on order has been altered over time by the introduction of chaos theory into everyday life, a shift that may have both widespread and profound consequences.

FROM PERSONAL PROCESS TO GROUP PROCESS

I began this book by talking about disruption to life, but I end by talking about agency and resistance.[11] The effort to create a sense of continuity after a disruption, by its very nature, engages issues of power. People's initial concerns after a disruption are about the loss of personal power and how to regain that power, that control over their lives. But these concerns often lead people to consider power and powerlessness in a broader context. Whether the struggle with issues of power and resistance was lifelong, as it was for people who experienced a lifetime of racism and discrimination, or whether the experiences of difference and not getting what they wanted were new, people nevertheless enacted their narratives and took other actions within the context of normalizing ideologies.[12] In doing so, they transformed the disruptions in their lives.[13] As we have seen, this was not a straightforward process. Individual acts of resistance, as well as large-scale resistance movements are often conflicted, internally contradictory, and ambivalent.[14] Nevertheless, resistance to normalizing ideologies was both deep and pervasive, and people expressed this resistance in a great variety of ways: by refusing to use a wheelchair, joining a self-help group, or subscribing to alternative ideologies. Resistance can be more than opposition—it can be truly creative and transformative.[15] We have seen many examples of it being so in this book.

The enactment of new cultural themes that emerge from efforts to mediate disruption has significant implications for group processes and, ultimately, for culture. People talk to other people, informally to friends and family and more formally to people in groups, such as self-help groups. As they talk, their narratives develop and change. New cultural themes are introduced, and old ones are amended. Embodied knowledge is collectively reinforced in social groups through memory, and this process is empowering. As we have seen, individual views of normalcy are reshaped in groups. Groups amend normalizing ideologies to reflect their particular views, and because these amended ideologies carry particular moral force for group members and buffer them from more generalized ideologies of normalcy, they facilitate agency.[16] This process can be observed in small groups, such as a group of stroke survivors discussing their everyday lives, and in large groups with overt political agendas.

Embodied actions such as the enactment of narrative inform this ongoing amending of ideologies. In their narratives, the people in this book made statements of resistance to cultural discourses on normalcy and the social institutions they represented at the same time that they made statements of empowerment. The indigenous organizations and community-specific activities they identified were sources of meaning for people who were intent on creating order out of disruption. These communities embodied people's experience at another level. Embodiment through social groups is known to be a potent source of reaffirmation, especially among persons who experience difference.[17] Moreover, people are members of more than one community. Communities reproduce some of the dynamics found in small-scale societies and reduce the negative effects of impersonal, industrialized societies and their associated discourses. These small-scale communities represent continuity by reinforcing the acceptability of narratives of difference and at the same time discussing and debating discourses of normalcy.

Over time, variations on dominant ideologies may be recognized by others and may take on increased weight in society, especially if large numbers of people hold these variant perspectives. For example, awareness of infertility among the general public has increased over the past twenty years, in part, because many women and men have told their stories through the media and have developed a national self-help group that attempts to influence policy and legislation. Because of the heterogeneity of the United States, multiple discourses and multiple ideologies exist. All of the various groups that I have mentioned contribute to this multivocality. Such groups reflect not a single voice but a plethora of voices and perspectives. It is through them that social change occurs.

POSTSCRIPT: STUDYING OURSELVES,
STUDYING OTHERS

Much has been said in anthropology, traditionally, about the importance of studying other cultures rather than one's own. Cross-cultural research continues to be more highly valued than research on one's own society, even though more and more anthropologists, at least in the United States, are now conducting research at home. Emphasizing cross-cultural research has the result that those studied are always the other; and this result has its attendant problems, from the positioning of colonizer and colonized to the lack of opportunity to see oneself as the other and the loss of the illumination that that opportunity might bring.[18]

I maintain that studying our own culture may enable us to see the theories we espouses more clearly. A better understanding of how people in our own culture construe their worlds has implications for how we study people in other cultures and may help to clarify what kinds of constructs we impose on the people we study. An examination of the overlapping cultural frameworks of U.S. society and the West can be a boon, not just to the understanding of cultural phenomena in the United States but also to the consideration of how cultural ideas specific to the United States and other Western societies may affect anthropological constructs and ways of thinking about culture. Examining issues of order in our own society, for example, may facilitate a better understanding of the need to create anthropological order.

While we can learn certain things by studying other cultures, we can learn other things by studying our own. For example, in this book I have tried to show how U.S. conceptions of the self amount to a cultural discourse on the self that is deeply embedded in many people's narratives and informs their frameworks for understanding their lives. The preoccupation with the self and the way in which cultural phenomena are psychologized by people have made it more difficult to sort out anthropological theorizing on the self and to determine the extent to which it reflects Western, or specifically U.S., perspectives. To give another example, the discourse on body and mind and the way that people conceive of the body as being accessible through the mind, are apparently pervasive in U.S. society. With this in mind, we can not only see the unfolding cultural discourse on the body in U.S. society more clearly but also better examine the discourse on the body in anthropology. Moreover, we can look beyond the body both to social institutions, such as biomedicine, and to newly emerging realms, and see more clearly how they reproduce underlying cultural discourses on the body.

Postmodern social theory has emphasized discontinuity rather than continuity, the former being echoed in the emerging science of chaos. Discontinuity is broadly echoed in both industrial and developing societies, and social traditions and social groups are becoming increasingly fragmented as societies undergo rapid social change. That disruption in postmodern times has become everyday fare does not make it more comfortable to live through but does make it a common experience that influences personal and collective action. Nevertheless, because disruption initiates the process of rethinking what is meaningful in life, it is unlikely that people will become more complacent about it despite the emergence of new forms of understanding disruption and chaos. The need to restore meaning to life necessitates creating order out of disarray. The multiple ways that people do this reflect the creative uses of culture.

Appendix

This book began to take shape when I was analyzing data on disruption in the infertility study. The research questions revolved around aspects of disruption in midlife, and consequently those data address disruption in great depth. As I considered writing a book using narratives about disruption from that study, I began to think about previous work I had done on disruption—the studies of stroke, late-life transitions, and midlife change—and how great were the commonalities in people's assumptions about continuity in life. Although the data for each of these studies had been analyzed in depth, little work had been done on studying the narratives as narratives. This part of the work felt unfinished. Meanwhile, the ethnic minorities study—on disruption caused by chronic illness—had gotten underway, and the same overall topics began to emerge. Gradually, the book I was planning began to encompass all five studies. The narrative analysis that I undertook for this book is a reanalysis of data from those studies.

As I have mentioned, the five studies comprise two ethnographies, one on the experience of the discovery of infertility and related disruptions in midlife and the other on living with a chronic illness in later life. One might expect that these two ethnographies would present methodological differences. In fact, the differences were minor: (1) the interviews occurred at different times of the day (people who were retired preferred to be interviewed during the day, whereas people who worked during the day needed to be interviewed at night), (2) the interviews differed in length (very old people or those who were infirm required shorter, more frequent interviews because of their reduced stamina), and (3) the age gap between interviewee and interviewer was, obviously, different in the two ethnographies.

Despite these differences, there were marked methodological consistencies across data sets. First, all the studies followed a similar process in conceptualization, data collection, and data analysis. Second, I have used my own interviews in the majority of cases, and, all but one of the other interviewers interviewed people in both younger and older age groups.

APPROACH OF THE RESEARCH

I will outline key factors in research design first, as they reflect my overall approach to research. The primary approach I take in designing a research study is to build the study around research questions. Research questions guide the overall approach to be used, such as the methods, the nature of the questions to be asked in interviews, and the number of times a person will be interviewed. Research questions developed at the outset of a study are purposely not exhaustive. I anticipate in every study that some of them will change during the course of the work and will be replaced by more finely honed questions as a greater understanding of the topic under study evolves. The research questions for all these studies addressed disruption and were contextualized to the specific type of disruption being studied.

A chief consideration is whether the research should be considered longitudinal. That is, I ask if the research questions address change over time. Each of these studies addressed change over time, as how people's stories and their lives change with the passage of time is another of my abiding interests.

The thrust of the interviews in all studies was on the collection of richly textured data on the meanings and interpretations people placed on the disruption in their life. Within the structure provided by the interview itself, the respondent's narration of the experience gives structure not only to the experience but also to the research encounter. While research questions may be used to guide the research overall, too much structure would not allow the respondent to speak of those matters that most concern her or him. A careful balance is therefore necessary. Respondents must be given freedom to discuss their experiences and ideas in their own terms and an interviewer must listen with great care. To accomplish these ends, ethnographic interviewing methods include both directive and nondirective strategies.[1] The exact wording of interview questions and the sequence of the questions emerge during each interview so that questions are relevant, tactful, and appropriate for each situation. Interviewers make extensive use of probes to explain unclear responses and to supplement sparse comments. All interviews are tape recorded and are transcribed verbatim shortly after the interview takes place.

The interviewer "reframes" a respondent's statements as further questions in the interview, thus following the respondent's line of thinking and following the respondent's lead in developing the content of the interview. It has been suggested that it is inaccurate to think of ethnographic interviewing as unstructured and survey interviewing as structured, and that a more appropriate way of viewing these practices is as "reflexive" interviewing and "standardized" practices.[2] For example, interviews for these studies were structured so that respondents could, by telling their story in their own words, develop their own structure of the process in their narration. Once the interviewee begins, the interviewer appears to do little more than insert probes to elicit additional data about topics the interviewee raises, but, in fact, the interviewer is actively engaged in the reframing process. This process directly relates to the issue of cultural meaning. By turning back the respondent's statements for ever greater elucidation, the researcher allows the respondent to develop ideas, thus facilitating the emergence of underlying cultural notions in the interviewing process.

Because people in these studies experienced disruption to bodily functioning or bodily expectations, the interview questions encompassed many queries that led to responses about bodily perceptions. For example, frequently used questions included "How has the illness affected you?" and "How do you see yourself?" The most frequently used probe, "Can you tell me more about that?" often elicited detailed responses about bodily perceptions. In all the studies, people volunteered statements about their bodily functioning and perceptions without being asked. I conclude this is because bodily distress was at the root of the disruption in almost all cases.

Although in-depth interviewing has been the primary means of data collection in all these studies, participant-observation has been a secondary means of data collection. Participant-observation was used in four of the five studies on which this book is based. In the stroke study, for example, Sharon Kaufman and I spent the first year of the research on an inpatient rehabilitation unit, alternating months,[3] and in a later phase of the research we observed people in their homes and with rehabilitation therapists. In the late-life transitions study and the ethnic minorities study, participant-observation was and continues to be carried out in health clinics serving older adults.[4] In the infertility study participant-observation occurred primarily in attendance at public meetings and lectures of Northern California Resolve. In all studies, participant-observation data have been analyzed separately from interview data and support the findings from interview data. Analysis of participant-observation data may provide a different perspective from analysis of interviews with the same population, however.[5]

In each of the studies a qualitative data analysis was undertaken prior to the narrative analysis. The same overall procedures were followed in each study. The development of core categories was the first step in data analysis. A core category not only reappears often but also is continually analyzed for its implications for theory, its room for variation, and its linkages with other emergent core categories.[6] Core and emergent categories are developed through ongoing reading and analysis of transcripts and development of codes. Coding categories are generated from meanings inherent in the data themselves.[7]

Paradigm cases were used to develop the analysis in terms of range and variation in the data.[8] A paradigm case is a case that is a strong instance of something, that appears to be prototypical in the early stages of data analysis, before it can be categorized. I consider many narratives that I used in this book to be paradigm cases.

A case-by-case analysis was carried out, as well. The process begins with a close reading of each case for (1) repetition of specific words, phrases, and general thought patterns, (2) the structure of the overall case, and (3) the topics that dominated respondents' reports as well as topics that were not raised at all.[9] In addition to these analyses, which were common to all the studies, additional analyses that were specific to each study were also conducted (for example, people were grouped by level of impairment in the studies of chronic illness in later life or by type of medical treatment pathway in the infertility study and then compared across groups).

SELECTING NARRATIVES FOR THIS BOOK

Selecting narratives for this book was a difficult task, not because it was hard to find appropriate cases but because of an overabundance of such data. I wanted to include many more narratives than was possible and longer excerpts from the narratives that I did include. Ultimately, inclusion of the narratives in this book depended on (1) whether the story reflected core issues in the experience of disruption, 2) whether the narrators contributed to a good cross section of respondents with respect to type of disruption, gender, age, ethnic background, and social class, (3) whether the story addressed different aspects of disruption, and (4) whether the story informed an understanding of disruption as a process.

All these studies emphasized the analysis of complex cultural matrices, not only for what they may tell us about the subject at hand but also because they will likely lead to an understanding of people's experience, broadly contextualized. Reanalysis of the data has thus revealed how discontinuity is processed subjectively, the cultural meanings it calls forth, how it is mediated, and how people attempt to create continuity.

Some cases were chosen because they were especially representative of the experience of a large number of people. In a number of cases, I chose a narrative because it was a paradigm case and thus had all or most of the major elements of a story of disruption in a particular study. In selecting narratives, I struggled with an overabundance of eloquence rather than a lack of it; almost everyone had a great deal to say on the subject of disruption to life. Eloquence alone was not enough, however. I asked questions of each story: Is this case unusual? Is it an outlier, and thus a marked exception from the study in which it is situated? While the particulars shaping a person's experience of disruption might be infrequent in a given study (such as the experience of being adopted), the overarching issues with which they grappled were not.

With respect to the use of metaphor, I would occasionally remember an interview that contained memorable metaphors and look up that case, but more often I discovered metaphors that I had not remembered in the text. In the process of studying people's narratives, metaphors emerged as a commonplace phenomenon; they could not be avoided.

As the book began to take shape, I realized that there would not be enough room to carry out one of my original goals, which was to explore in depth how narratives of specific people changed over time as the process of living with disruption changed for them. Because I did not have room to illustrate longitudinal change for everyone, I opted to illustrate this phenomenon with the stories of a few people. In some cases those stories are told in one place, while in several instances people's stories span more than one chapter. This approach was taken in an attempt to illustrate change in narratives over time, to give depth to people's stories, and to give the reader a sense of continuity in the stories, given the limitations of this book. The irony that I am trying to provide the reader with continuity in narratives even while I write of continuity as an illusion speaks to a point I made in the text: that efforts to create continuity are pervasive. The format of a book is an obvious place for the task of creating continuity to take place!

The process by which I analyzed narratives for this book extended the previously mentioned case-study approach. I built on this approach in my subsequent analysis, scrutinizing clues to embodied distress, examining all statements about the body and bodily distress, scrutinizing all episodes of health problems and medical interventions, and all expressions of emotion for their relation to bodily concerns. I also scrutinized narratives for linkages between bodily distress and social concerns, such as social issues that emerged in the management of symptoms of illness. I then examined each case for narrative elements such as plot, emplotment, and subjunctivity described in chapter 2. I examined the use of metaphors according to approaches to metaphor described in chapter 4.

The Infertility Study

Respondents were recruited from four sources: (1) 42 percent volunteered after seeing a printed flyer placed in the offices of physicians in private practice, health maintenance organizations, and low-income clinics; (2) 26 percent responded to a request for volunteers that appeared in a Resolve newsletter or flyer at Resolve workshops; (3) 25 percent were recruited by persons already in the study; and (4) 7 percent volunteered after hearing about the study from adoption counseling services.

The sample is composed of 134 couples and 9 women who were interviewed without their partners. Demographic characteristics are available for 118 couples. The majority of respondents lived in the greater San Francisco Bay Area, a five-county urban and suburban area, but 44 persons lived in rural areas of the state. The age range for women was 25 to 52 years (mean = 36.13). For men the age range was 27 to 71 years (mean = 38.04). The sample was predominantly middle class and college educated. This geographic locale has one of the highest cost-of-living levels in the United States, which is reflected in people's salaries. The majority had yearly family incomes of $60,000 or more and owned their own homes; but 35 couples had family incomes below $60,000, and 4 families had incomes below $20,000. Eighty percent of couples had some form of health insurance, but less than half of those who were insured had any coverage for the medical treatment of infertility. Respondents were primarily in professional, management, and white-collar employment; 97 women were employed outside the home and 21 were not employed; 114 men were employed and 4 were not employed. Forty persons (15 percent of the sample) were nonwhite or Latino (4 Native Americans, 14 Asian Americans, 12 African Americans, 6 Latinos, 2 East Indians, and 2 Pacific Islanders). With regard to religion, 43 were Catholic, 48 were Jewish, 55 were Protestant, 35 were members of other religions, 40 reported they had no religion, and 15 did not respond.

Partners were first interviewed together in detailed interviews lasting two hours or more; follow-up individual interviews took place approximately 6 to 12 months later, with final follow-up interviews with both partners taking place 12 to 24 months later. Data were collected by five interviewers, and I was responsible for collecting half the data. We conducted interviews in English, with the exception of interviews with one couple in Spanish. Interviews addressed the events that led up to medical treatment, each person's experience of infertility, feelings, and related experiences, such as familial and work-related changes. To study the process that individuals undergo after infertility is discovered, we included closed- and open-ended questions, so that respondents could describe their experience in their own words. The exact wording of each question and the sequence of the questions was decided in the interview setting so that questions were relevant, tactful, and appropriate for each situation. Interviewers used probes during the narrative to elicit specific information about emotional reactions to infertility, attitudes about adoption, effect of infertility on the marital relationship, and related topics.

The Midlife Study

People were recruited for this study using a snowball sampling technique.[10] The object of the study was to interview people who were experiencing a variety of disruptions, including marital difficulties or recent divorce, other kinds of family upheaval, financial difficulties, job and career changes, including job loss, the onset or exacerbation of chronic illness, and worsening health. There were 20 people, 12 women and 8 men between the ages of 35 and 65. The majority of people were middle-income white-collar workers and professionals. Three-quarters had college educations. The majority were white/non-Hispanic, and 3 were African American or Latino/Hispanic. All interviews were conducted in English.

Open-ended interviews of up to 3 or 4 hours elicited details of the disruption to life in the context of people's life histories. Topics included the disruption itself, the effects of the disruption on the respondent's life, self-portrayal and alterations to sense of self, everyday life, perceptions of bodily changes and the aging process, philosophy of life, and health beliefs and practices.

The Stroke Study

The stroke study was a two-part study, and people in both parts were recruited at the same inner-city community hospital. In the first study, Sharon

Kaufman and I identified several types of stroke trajectories, and in the second study we focused on them in the context of life reorganization. In this book, I draw specifically on interviews with 36 respondents that either I or a research assistant was able to interview 3 times (many people could not be interviewed longitudinally because of steadily worsening health): 23 women and 13 men, ranging in age from 48 to 105, with over one-half between 65 and 80 years of age. The group included 24 whites, 7 African Americans, and 5 Asian Americans. Most respondents had at least 2 other chronic medical conditions at the time of the stroke.

The majority of respondents had a low income; one-third were Medicaid recipients, and another one-third had incomes slightly above the cut-off that qualified people for Medicaid reimbursement. The remaining one-third had moderate incomes. The majority had a high school education or less. The majority of people were single and lived alone in rental apartments, including low-income housing, in the neighborhoods surrounding the hospital. One-quarter owned their own homes in middle-class and working-class neighborhoods, and most of these persons were married. Living arrangements were altered after a stroke in a number of cases, either temporarily or permanently, when respondents found it necessary to seek the help of others such as adult children or paid help.

Semistructured interviews with open-ended questions elicited respondents' perceptions of the details of the stroke: how and when it occurred; its magnitude; responses to inpatient and outpatient rehabilitation therapies; feelings about disability, recovery, loss, and disruption; opinions about medical care and social services; caregiving and social support; and plans for and fears about the future. All interviews were conducted in English. Each interview lasted approximately 1 to 2 hours.

The Late-Life Transitions Study

Persons in this sample were selected because they were undergoing a transition that affected their independence or were viewed as being vulnerable to such a transition. The sample was drawn from several sources: practitioners who identified and referred persons to the study in a community-based outpatient health-care program for elders, an acute care community hospital, and persons who had been discharged from the same acute care hospital several years previously following a stroke and had participated in the stroke study. For this study, 44 respondents were interviewed at least twice during a one-year period, and some were followed much more often, depending on the nature of the changes occurring in their lives (such as transitions from home to acute care to long-term care). There were 27 women and 17 men ranging in age from 80 to 98. At the time they were last interviewed, all but 6 persons were living in their own homes: of these 6, 4 were living in a long-term care facility and 2 were followed from acute care to a long-term care institution. Of the total, 4 people were African American, and 2 were Latino/Hispanic. The sample was composed of people in the low- to mid-income range, evenly distributed across the sample.

With one exception, interviews were conducted in English. Interviews were semistructured with many open-ended questions, lasted for approximately 1 to 2 hours, and focused on people's daily lives and routines, mobility, health, illness management, family and friends, interests, concerns, avocations, philosophy of life, and the aging process.

The Ethnic Minorities Study

African Americans in this study were recruited from home care services and from neighborhood health clinics. Data analysis was conducted on interviews with the first 24 persons recruited into the study. The age range was 49–91, although the majority were between the ages of 65 and 75. There were 13 women and 11 men. The majority had a high school education or less. The majority of respondents had a low income, although one-quarter had a moderate income. One-third of the respondents lived alone. They had between 2 and 6 chronic illnesses. The majority lived independently, without help from spouses, adult children, or paid help.

Semistructured interviews with open-ended questions elicited information about people's illnesses, their view of themselves and the aging process, their everyday life, their patterns of illness management and self-care their religious beliefs and philosophy of life, their access to and use of health care services. Each interview was in English and lasted approximately 2 hours.

WHO WAS LEFT OUT?

Who has not been included? The answer depends on the study in question. For the studies involving older people, the main issue is cognitive impairment. Cognitive impairment and depression were widespread in the stroke study, and the narratives of some people who suffered from these problems in a mild form are included here; but this group may be underrepresented in this work. In the late-life transitions study and the ethnic minorities study, we screened people out for cognitive impairment and severe depression because we wanted people to be able to talk with us in depth. Nevertheless, we included people who had mild cognitive impairment, and again, some of those stories are included here. If people's cognitive impairments are too great, they cannot easily participate in an in-depth interview, and this quickly becomes apparent.

The underrepresentation of cognitively impaired people raises a thorny question for social scientists who study the aging process, namely, how much cognitive impairment is too much? That is, should there be an arbitrary cut-off line for treating narratives of cognitively impaired people as valid data? The answer depends on the goals of the research, in my view. From my perspective, people who are cognitively impaired have a story to tell, and if they are able to tell it, it is worth listening to. Whether the story is "reliable" or not is another question. Talking to caregivers and health care providers provides additional data that can be compared with respondents' narratives.

The answer to who has not been included in the infertility study is more straightforward. Since over two hundred people were interviewed two or three times, almost everyone has been left out. There simply wasn't room to include more than a handful of their stories.

Notes

CHAPTER I: MEDIATING DISRUPTION

1. All names have been changed to protect the anonymity of the interviewees. In this book, I refer to people by the manner of address used in the interviews. Generally speaking, older people (usually over the age of sixty) were addressed as Mr., Mrs., or Miss as a mark of respect, according to the custom they were used to, whereas younger people, accustomed to informality, were addressed by their first names.

2. Sahlins, *Islands of History;* Kiefer, *Changing Cultures;* Neugarten, "Time, Age, and the Life Cycle."

3. In her research on everyday life in Bali, Unni Wikan addresses the importance of daily routine when she observes, "It was by following people as they moved, bridging scenes and encounters, that I became aware of how they cast their compelling concerns and the continuities in their day-to-day experience." Wikan, "Managing the Heart," 296.

4. For a discussion of the importance of order in people's lives, see, for ex-

ample, Hallowell, "The Self and Its Behavioral Context"; Kiefer, *Changing Cultures;* Lyon, "Order and Healing."

5.   M. Jackson, *Paths toward a Clearing,* 20.

6.   Harris, "Concepts of Individual," 602.

7.   Baltes, "Theoretical Propositions"; Schroots, "Metaphors of Aging and Complexity."

8.   This is John Meyer's observation; see Meyer, "The Self and the Life Course," 200.

9.   These disruptions include chronic illness and disability (Ablon, "The Elephant Man"; G. Becker, *Growing Old in Silence* and "Continuity after a Stroke"; Kaufman, "Illness, Biography"; Scheer and Luborsky, "Polio Biographies"), old age (Clark and Anderson, *Culture and Aging;* Myerhoff, *Number Our Day*), late-life childlessness (Alexander et al., "Generativity"; Rubinstein et al., "Key Relationships"), intergenerational relations (Kiefer, *Changing Cultures*), retirement (Luborsky, "Analysis" and "Alchemists' Visions"), and widowhood (Luborsky and Rubinstein, "Ethnicity and Lifetimes" and "Ethnic Identity").

10.   This is Cohler's observation; see Cohler, "The Life Story," 195.

11.   In contrast, Michael Jackson has observed that in Kuranko there is no word for life story, no genre of autobiography, and no emphasis on the self as autonomous in relation to others. That is not to say that people do not experience disruptions in such societies. They do, but their experience and expression of disruption may be very different. Jackson, *Paths toward a Clearing.*

12.   This is Catherine Hayles's observation. She notes that cultural attitudes marking the word chaos can be read in its etymology: the word derives from a Greek word stem meaning "to yawn" or "to gape." Hayles, "Chaos," 1–8.

13.   Hayles (ibid., 7) defines "chaotics" as signifying "certain attitudes toward chaos that are manifest at diverse sites within the culture, among them poststructuralism and the science of chaos."

14.   The science of chaos has not initiated this shift; instead, the growth of this new science has been catalyzed by the postmodern context, which provided a cultural and technological milieu in which it could flower. Hayles observes that the science of chaos thus represents "one site within the culture where the premises characteristic of postmodernism are inscribed" (ibid., 5).

15.   Fry and Keith, "Life Course as a Cultural Unit"; Fry, "Life Course in Context"; Meyer, "Levels of Analysis"; Rubinstein, "Nature, Culture, Gender, Age."

16.   Luborsky, "Romance with Personal Meaning," 450.

17.   Fernandez, "Persuasions and Performances"; Ortner, "On Key Symbols"; V. Turner, *Dramas, Fields, and Metaphors.*

18.   Kohli, "The World We Forgot."

19.   Kohli, ibid; Arney and Bergen, *Medicine and the Management of Living;* Meyer, "Levels of Analysis."

20.   Social scientists (Cohler, "Life Story"; Manheimer, "Narrative Quest") have questioned whether the social science preoccupation with coherence and continuity reflects the bias of Western values. Lila Abu-Lughod ("Writing against Culture," 146) suggests that culture theories overemphasize coherence, while Bernice Neugarten ("Continuities and Discontinuities") observes that social science studies focus excessively on continuity rather than change. There is another possible explanation for this emphasis, however: that those being studied attempt to maintain a sense of continuity amid facts of change. See Kiefer, *Changing Cultures*; Luborsky, "Process of Self-Report"; Wikan, *Managing Turbulent Hearts*.

21.   This cultural ethos contrasts with the characterization of Brazilian society as a "somatic culture." See Scheper-Hughes, *Death without Weeping*.

22.   Thomas Csordas ("Somatic Modes of Attention," 138) refers to such embodied distress as "somatic modes of attention." My own case is one example of this intersubjective phenomenon.

23.   This is Hayden White's suggestion; see White, "Value of Narrativity," 23.

24.   For examples of how issues of continuity can be traced in life-story narratives, see Clark and Anderson, *Culture and Aging*; Kaufman, *Ageless Self*; Kiefer, *Changing Cultures*; Luborsky, "Analysis," "Alchemists' Vision," and "Romance with Personal Meaning"; Myerhoff, *Number Our Days*. For discussions of how coherence is created and continuity is sustained, see Peacock and Holland, "Narrated Self"; Mishler, *Research Interviewing*; Agar and Hobbs, "Interpreting Discourse"; and Linde, *Life Stories*. George Rosenwald and Richard Ochberg (*Storied Lives*, 6) observe that, although people strive for coherence in their narratives, coherence is an illusion.

25.   This also is Hayden White's suggestion; see ibid., 23.

26.   Merleau-Ponty, *The Visible and the Invisible*.

27.   Connerton, *How Societies Remember*, 72. Embodiment, as one aspect of phenomenology, can be construed not only as a method but also as an emerging theoretical perspective in anthropology. Maurice Merleau-Ponty (*Phenomenology of Perception*) viewed phenomenology as a method, with embodiment as one aspect of that method. Embodiment refers to being, to living through the body, to the state of being embodied. Throughout the book I use the terms bodily experience and embodiment interchangeably.

28.   Bryan Turner (*Regulating Bodies*, 43) observes that anthropologists have been primarily concerned with using the body as part of a social classificatory scheme rather than with understanding the phenomenology of the lived body. The now voluminous literature on the anthropology of the body has tended to emphasize how the body is represented and how culture is "inscribed" on the body rather than focus on the lived body. For reviews of this literature, see A. Frank, "Bringing Bodies Back In"; Lock, "Cultivating the Body"; Lock and Scheper-Hughes, "A Critical-Interpretive Approach"; Scheper-Hughes and Lock, "The Mindful

Body"; B. Turner, *Body and Society*, "Missing Bodies," and *Regulating Bodies*. Recently, a growing number of anthropologists have turned to embodiment as a theoretical framework for the study of experience. See, for example, A. Becker, *Body, Self, and Society*; Csordas, "Embodiment as a Paradigm," "Somatic Modes," and *Sacred Self*; Csordas, ed., *Embodiment and Experience*; Desjarlais, *Body and Emotion*; G. Frank, "On Embodiment"; Gordon, "Embodying Illness, Embodying Cancer" and "Ethics of Ambiguity"; Jackson, *Paths toward a Clearing*; Pandolfi, "Boundaries inside the Body"; Stoller, *Taste of Ethnographic Things*; Watson and Watson-Franke, *Interpreting Life Histories*.

29.   More information about the research my colleagues and I have conducted on asthma can be found in Becker et al., "Dilemma of Seeking Urgent Care"; Janson-Bjerklie et al., "Clinical Markers"; Benner et al., "Moral Dimensions."

30.   This is an example of what Leder (*Absent Body*) refers to as the absent or taken-for-granted body.

31.   Merleau-Ponty (*Phenomenology of Perception*) refers to automatic bodily functioning as the preobjective self, a culturally constituted way of being-in-the-world.

32.   Merleau-Ponty (*The Visible and the Invisible*) attributes a transcendental function to the body-subject: the body is the basis of the constitution of the human world.

33.   Merleau-Ponty, *Phenomenology of Perception*, 146. In interpreting Merleau-Ponty's work, Martin Dillon ("Preface," xv) observes, "The body contributes to the world we live in but the reverse is also true: the world contributes to the constitution of our body."

34.   Dillon ("Preface," xvi) notes that in Merleau-Ponty's critique of the transcendental subject, both the subject and its transcendent function, though preserved, are transfigured to be responsive to worldly conditions.

35.   Becker et al., "Dilemma of Seeking Urgent Care"; Benner et al., "Moral Dimensions."

36.   Janson-Bjerklie et al., "Clinical Markers"; Becker et al., "Dilemma of Seeking Urgent Care."

37.   Dillon ("Preface," xvi) notes that in *The Visible and the Invisible*, Merleau-Ponty develops the thesis of reversibility of the flesh, a circular process in which body learns to come to terms with its environment and then returns to the world by acquiring that environment in a sedimented form that structures the world with a habitus derived from body. David Michael Levin ("Visions of Narcissism," 74) observes that "Intercorporeality and reversibility are categories derived from the flesh of our experience; and they bespeak a social order that calls into question all social systems where domination prevails over principles of mutual recognition and participatory justice." Pierre Bourdieu's work (*Outline; Distinction; Logic of Practice*) represents a shift from a focus on the body as a source of sym-

bolism to an awareness of the body as the locus of social practice. Recent work in anthropology examines embodiment and social practice. See, for example, Csordas, "Embodiment as a Paradigm," "Somatic Modes," and *Sacred Self*.

38.   Levin ("Visions of Narcissism") argues that the body is already prosocial and that, contrary to what Michel Foucault suggests, the body's behavior does not need to be totally introduced by the work of society.

39.   Becker et al., "Dilemma of Seeking Urgent Care."

40.   See, for example, Dillon, "Preface, xvi"; Levin, "Visions of Narcissism," 77–79.

41.   Thomas Csordas ("Somatic Modes" and "Introduction," 12) and Paul Stoller ("Embodying Colonial Memories") suggest that the body be placed in a paradigmatic position complementary to the text rather than subsumed under the text metaphor; doing so enables body and textuality to be viewed as corresponding methodological fields.

42.   According to Maurice Merleau-Ponty (*Phenomenology of Perception*), language is one way of disclosing the phenomenological essence of embodiment. For a discussion of how language gives access to experience, see Csordas, "Introduction," 11.

43.   For a discussion of how bodily practices enact the past, see Connerton, *How Societies Remember*, 72. Narrative is considered to be one aspect of performance in the anthropology of experience (E. Bruner, "Experience and Its Expressions"; V. Turner, *Anthropology of Performance)* and in linguistic anthropology (Hymes, *In Vain I Tried to Tell You*). Csordas ("Imaginal Performance") identifies four streams of research that contribute to a theory of performance. For examples of how performances constitute action, see E. Bruner, "Experience and Its Expressions"; Laderman and Roseman, eds., *"Introduction"*; Stoller, "Embodying Colonial Memories." See Schiefflin, "On Failure and Performance," for a discussion of this theoretical shift. For a discussion of how people project images of themselves and their world through performances, see Palmer and Jankowiak, "Performance and Imagination."

44.   Unni Wikan (*Managing Turbulent Hearts)* also addresses this issue in her work.

45.   Terms such as "cultural norms" and "values" may seem to reflect leveling, or totalizing, notions of culture.

46.   This is Wikan's observation; see ibid., 14.

47.   Luborsky ("Analysis" and "Alchemists' Visions") uses the term conceptual template to describe an overarching personal meaning, a conceptual framework that integrates narrative, including explicit metaphors or more implicit images that encompass a person's whole life. These meanings are constituted from lifelong experiences in a sociocultural world. We can thus differentiate between *cultural* discourses that are widely debated and individualized *conceptual* templates.

48.   Postmodern theorists such as Jean-François Lyotard celebrate difference and uncritically applaud it (Best and Kellner, *Postmodern Theory*). Doing so has called attention to diversity and broken down totalizing stereotypes. However, inadequate attention has been given to the experience of difference and how profoundly it affects people's lives.

49.   Honi Fern Haber (*Beyond Postmodern Politics*, 116–17) observes that normalcy suppresses difference, and that structure both creates and excludes otherness. Yet she also observes that, conversely, the law of difference, as postulated by postmodern theorists, "forecloses on the possibility of revitalizing the discourses of otherness, and so forecloses on the possibility of voicing marginalized concerns." In other words, just as structural views of normalcy can be totalizing, so too can the principle of difference.

50.   Discourses on normalcy have been referred to as "public narratives" (Somers and Gibson, "Reclaiming the Epistemological 'Other'"), "traditions" (MacIntyre, *After Virtue*), and "webs of interlocution" (Taylor, *Sources of the Self*).

51.   This is Hayden White's suggestion; see White, "Value of Narrativity," 22–23.

52.   Sherry Ortner ("Resistance and the Problem," 175) raises the question of the ambiguity of the term resistance but notes that resistance is a useful category because it "highlights the presence and play of power in most forms of relationships and activities."

53.   This is Haber's observation; see Haber, *Beyond Postmodern Politics*.

54.   This is James Fernandez's observation; see Fernandez, "Introduction," 7.

55.   I use the word metaphor as a generic term for trope throughout this book (see Fernandez, ibid.). In drawing attention to metaphors as a tool in mediating disruption, I do not mean to suggest that metaphors should be examined to the exclusion of narrative content more generally. The examination of metaphor has its greatest relevance in the context of narrative, and that is how I approach it in this book. Examining metaphor in the context of people's narratives more generally reveals how people attempt to work around the constraints posed by culture at the same time that they strive to maintain a sense of normalcy.

56.   I do not utilize the observation material in this book. See the appendix for details about participant-observation for these studies.

57.   See G. Becker, *Healing the Infertile Family*; Becker and Nachtigall, "Ambiguous Responsibility"; Becker and Nachtigall, "Eager for Medicalization"; Nachtigall et al., "Effects of Gender-Specific Diagnosis."

58.   Although differences in income greatly affected the ability of women and men to pursue costly treatment, and the level of educational background further affected awareness of resources and access to treatment, these factors did not affect the richness of respondents' narratives in recounting the disruption caused by infertility or their interpretations of the meaning of infertility for their lives.

59.   For discussions of the disparity between elders' views of their health and

the views of health professionals, see George and Landerman, "Health and Subjective Well-Being"; LaRue et al., "Health in Old Age"; Okun et al., "Health and Subjective Well-Being"; Pearlman and Uhlmann, "Quality of Life in Chronic Diseases"; and Idler and Kasl, "Health Perceptions and Survival."

60.   Although the term Hispanic is widely used in the United States to refer to persons of Latin descent, Latino is the term commonly used in California, where the studies were conducted, and hence is used throughout this book.

61.   According to Bengston et al. ("Generations") a cohort can be defined as an aggregate of individuals born within a particular time interval, usually five or ten years. Each study, except the late-life transitions study, encompassed several cohorts. Corrine Nydegger ("Role and Age Transitions") observes that the concept of cohort provides the conceptual link between history and individual lives. Irving Rosow (*Socialization to Aging*) observes that finding a culturally meaningful definition of a cohort is problematic, while Christine Fry ("Life Course in Context," 132) notes the potential for the confounding of social time and life time.

62.   It is an academic conceit that a certain level of education is needed to communicate clearly. Michael Jackson has observed that these concerns have been raised for people in preliterate societies, as well, and refutes this concern, as I do. M. Jackson, *Paths toward a Clearing.*

CHAPTER 2: NARRATIVES
AS CULTURAL DOCUMENTS

1.   Narrative analysis has a long history in the social sciences. The variety of approaches to it and the influence on it of linguistics, history, philosophy, anthropology, sociology, psychology, and literature have resulted in different emphases in different disciplines. A range of approaches is reflected in the following work: Agar, "Stories, Background Knowledge, and Themes"; Bell, "Becoming a Political Woman"; Brody, *Stories of Sickness*; E. Bruner, "Experience"; J. Bruner, *Actual Minds*; Carr, *Time, Narrative, and History*; Mattingly and Garro, "Introduction"; Mishler, *Research Interviewing*; Riessman, "Strategic Uses" and *Divorce Talk*; Rosenwald and Ochberg, *Storied Lives*; Somers and Gibson, "Reclaiming the Epistemological 'Other.'" Social scientists have used narrative analysis to study a variety of disruptive events such as divorce (Riessman, "Strategic Uses" and *Divorce Talk*), pain (Garro, "Chronic Illness" and "Narrative Representations"; Good et al., *Pain as Human Experience*; J. Jackson, "Rashomon Approach"), illness (Estroff, "Identity, Disability, and Schizophrenia" and "Whose Story Is It?"; Kleinman, *Illness Narratives*; Mishler, *Research Interviewing*; Robinson, "Personal Narratives, Social Careers"), and the death of relatives (Luborsky and Rubinstein, "Ethnicity and Lifetimes" and "Ethnic Identity"; Rubinstein, "Narratives of Elder Parental Death").

2. For a discussion of healing biographical discontinuities through narrative, see V. Turner, "Social Dramas." For a discussion of how people organize and work through their experiences through narrative, see Rubinstein, "Narratives of Elder Parental Death," 259. See also Riessman, *Divorce Talk*.

3. Cheryl Mattingly and Linda Garro ("Introduction," 771) note that narrative is used to understand concrete events that require relating the inner world of desire and motive to the outer world of observable actions.

4. Elliot Mishler (*Research Interviewing*) discusses the empowering capacity of narrative and points out the interviewer's role in facilitating empowerment. See Carr, *Time, Narrative, and History,* for a discussion of how narration and action are intertwined.

5. See Linde (*Life Stories*). Anthropologists agree that a sense of coherence is culturally grounded, that it is through culture that people make sense of their worlds, while social science concepts developed by nonanthropologists, such as coherence (Antonovsky, *Health, Stress, and Coping*) and continuity theory (Atchley, "Continuity Theory"), all view continuity as mediated through the person rather than through culture. Charlotte Linde (*Life Stories,* 17) observes that creating coherence is a social obligation and a measure of cultural competence. For discussions of how concerns with meaning and coherence are reflected in how the person is conceived and portrayed, see Ewing, "Illusion of Wholeness"; Kaufman, *Ageless Self;* Linde, *Life Stories;* Luborsky, "Analysis" and "Alchemists' Visions."

6. Anthropologists have questioned whether narrative and experience are the same thing and asked why anthropologists so frequently assume that they are; see, for example, Wikan, "Self in a World of Urgency and Necessity." Narrative and experience are not equivalent. See B. Good, *Medicine, Rationality, and Experience;* Widdershoven, "Story of Life"; and Rosenwald and Ochberg, *Storied Lives,* for examples of the relationship betweeen experience and narrative. Anthropologists have methods of data collection other than narratives, observation, for example, and the data collected with these methods can be compared with narrative accounts.

7. M. Jackson, *Paths toward a Clearing;* Stoller, *Taste of Ethnographic Things.*

8. When an entire social group is disrupted, the uses of narrative at the cultural level become readily apparent. Moreover, disruptions experienced as part of a group will be experienced differently from those experienced individually. For example, Roger Keesing noted continuities in Kwaio resistance over decades as he listened to elders' retrospective portrayals of their lives. Continuities that had been shaped by a particular historical event recurred in people's interpretations of their personal tragedies through symbols of sovereignty and subjugation, opposition and capitulation. Keesing, *Custom and Confrontation,* 211. The analysis of narrative may elucidate complex social processes. See, for example, the relationship between narrative and shared cultural understandings (Farmer,

"AIDS-Talk"; Garro, "Narrative Representations"; Mathews et al., "Coming to Terms"); the role of narrative in mediating expectations between cultural models and individual experience (Garro, "Narrative Representations"); the role of narrative in the establishment of cultural models (Farmer, "AIDS-Talk"); the uses of metaphor in narrative accounts (Mathews et al., "Coming to Terms"); and the role of narrative in the interpretation of others' subjective experiences (Rubinstein, "Narratives of Elder Parental Death").

9.   Mark Freeman ("Ricoeur on Interpretation," 310) observes that "the story of our lives is not so much imposed upon the objective data of our experience as it is 'automatically' figured into the process of development itself."

10.   Ricoeur, "Can Fictional Narratives Be True?"; Ricoeur, "Narrative Time."

11.   E. Bruner, "Experience." Linda Hunt calls attention to Mexican oncologists' use of multiple narrative frameworks in efforts to maintain moral order; see Hunt, "Practicing Oncology."

12.   See Basso, "Stalking with Stories"; White, "Value of Narrativity." In analyzing illness narratives, Byron Good and Mary-Jo DelVecchio Good point out that they did not find one overarching voice of authority that transmitted a moralizing message. See Good and Good, "In the Subjunctive Mode."

13.   For discussions of the relationship of plot forms to coherence, see B. Good, *Medicine, Rationality and Experience*, 144–65; Ricoeur, "Can Fictional Narratives Be True?"; and Ricoeur, *Time and Narrative.*

14.   Ricoeur, ibid., 65–66.

15.   M. Good et al., "Oncology and Narrative Time"; B. Good, *Medicine, Rationality and Experience.* Cheryl Mattingly has developed the concept of emplotment as a means of understanding the work of health professionals and patients that takes place in clinical settings such as hospitals. Mattingly, "Concept of Therapeutic Emplotment."

16.   For example, Good and Good ("Subjunctive Mode," 841) observe that illness narratives are constituted intersubjectively and are positioned among power relations.

17.   Edward Bruner follows Dilthey in this suggestion; see E. Bruner, "Experience," 12.

18.   This is Ricoeur's observation; see Ricoeur, *Time and Narrative*, 65–68. Ricoeur (ibid., 67–68) observes that everyday praxis orders the present of the future and the present of the past, that is, how practice in the current moment in time orders one's view of past, present, and future.

19.   See Carr, *Time, Narrative, and History*; Heidegger, *History of the Concept of Time*; Ricoeur, *Time and Narrative*, 60–64.

20.   This is Gelya Frank's observation; see G. Frank, "Finding the Common Denominator."

21.   For discussions of the subjunctive element in narratives, see J. Bruner, *Ac-*

tual Minds), 26; B. Good, *Medicine, Rationality, and Experience*; Good and Good, "Subjunctive Mode."

22.   The analysis of themes has received considerable attention in anthropology. Mark Luborsky ("Identification and Analysis of Themes," 190–92) notes the appeals and pitfalls of searching for themes: on the one hand, themes are culturally laden, that is, they can provide insights into cultural beliefs and values that shape how people make sense of things; but, on the other hand, anthropologists need to recognize that "the search for themes is an activity and ideal we share with informants, one that is instilled early in life and reinforced in daily life." Luborsky identifies two types of thematic analysis: (1) identifying themes, which involves counting the most frequently occurring statements, that is, looking for repetition, and (2) discovering themes by examining the respondent's own view of what is important, that is, looking for what is meaningful at the word, clause, and story levels.

23.   Byron Good (*Medicine, Rationality, and Experience*, 164) suggests that new aspects of experiences are thematized, while other aspects of experience recede.

24.   Langness and G. Frank, *Lives*, 114.

25.   For some examples of phenomenological approaches, see G. Frank, "Finding the Common Denominator" and "On Embodiment"; Kaufman, "Toward a Phenomenology"; Watson, "Understanding a Life History"; Watson and Watson-Franke, *Interpreting Life Histories.* For discussion of bodily distress, see Csordas, "Embodiment as a Paradigm," "Somatic Modes," and *Sacred Self*; Csordas, ed., *Embodiment and Experience*; M. Good et al., *Pain as Human Experience*; Gordon, "Embodying Illness" and "Ethics of Ambiguity,"; Kleinman, *Illness Narratives*; Pandolfi, "Boundaries"; Scheper-Hughes, *Death without Weeping.*

26.   Mattingly, "Therapeutic Emplotment."

CHAPTER 3: ORDER AND CHAOS

1.   For discussion of the place of order in structures of meaning in human life, see Hallowell, *Culture and Experience*, 94–95; Lyon, "Order and Healing," 260. Unni Wikan observes that order is not to be denied, that it permeates social life, particularly in "public," but that we must see that despite cultural notions that order prevails, the reality of people's lives is in some intermediate zone between order and chaos, a zone that Renato Rosaldo calls "non-order": improvisation, muddling through, and contingent events. Wikan, "Managing the Heart," 35; Rosaldo, *Culture and Truth*, 103.

2.   Victor Turner outlined such a process for ritual, inspired by van Gennep's (*Rites of Passage*) concepts of separation, liminality, and reaggregation or reincorporation. However, Turner referred to the conclusion of the ritual process as

"communitas," to signify the communal nature of ritual; see V. Turner, *Ritual Process.*

3.   For extensive descriptions of how the body becomes disordered, see Murphy, *Body Silent.* In the social sciences there is a growing literature on chronic conditions. See, for example, Anderson and Bury, eds., *Living with Chronic Illness;* Becker et al., "Dilemma of Seeking Urgent Care"; Charmaz, *Good Days, Bad Days;* Estroff, "Identity, Disability" and "Whose Story Is It?"; Garro, "Explaining High Blood Pressure" and "Narrative Representations"; M. Good et al., *Pain as Human Experience;* Heurtin-Roberts, "High-Pertension"; Heurtin-Roberts and Becker, "Anthropological Perspectives on Chronic Illness"; Kagawa-Singer, "Redefining Health"; Kaufman, "Illness, Biography"; Kleinman, *Illness Narratives;* McLaughlin and Zeeberg, "Self-Care and Multiple Sclerosis"; Robinson, "Personal Narratives"; Strauss et al., *Chronic Illness and the Quality of Life.*

4.   The difficulty of putting suffering into words is especially well articulated in the literature on chronic pain. See, for example, Garro, "Narrative Representations"; M. Good et al., *Pain as Human Experience;* J. Jackson, "Rashomon Approach"; Kleinman, *Illness Narratives.*

5.   Kirmayer, "Body's Insistence on Meaning."

6.   Bury, "Chronic Illness."

7.   Although Kirk was not in my chronic illness study, his story fits with the many stories I have collected in studies specific to chronic illness about the discovery of a potentially life-threatening condition.

8.   Toombs, "Meaning of Illness."

9.   Becker et al., "Dilemma of Seeking Urgent Care," 305.

10.   In the United States, hope is used metaphorically in the fight against cancer; see M. Good et al., "American Oncology."

11.   Parsons, "Definitions of Health and Illness." Reaction to Parsons's theory pointed to how the application of the sick role to persons who were chronically ill made them appear to be deviant. See, for example, Gallagher, "Lines of Reconstruction"; Hingson et al., *In Sickness and in Health.*

12.   Luckmann, "Constitution of Human Life," 162.

13.   Kirmayer, "Mind and Body."

14.   Lowenberg, *Caring and Responsibility;* Reiser, "Responsibility for Personal Health."

15.   Strauss et al., *Chronic Illness;* Conrad, "Experience of Illness." Linda Pitcher ("Phenomenology") in reviewing the writings of Descartes and subsequent philosophers, observes, "Reading Descartes' original text, we see that mind-body distinction is far less dogmatic and less dialectic than the countless volumes of philosophical and scientific discourse following its proposal would have us believe . . . it is important to emphasize that Descartes' original treatise emphasizes the mind *and* body dualism, rather than the dialectical mind-body split so

often ascribed to it." Pitcher concludes that the modern-day scientific method is founded upon an interpretation of Cartesian dualism and seems to have stretched the text's meaning beyond the vision of Descartes himself.

16.   Corbin and Strauss, "Accompaniments in Chronic Illness."

17.   Lakoff and Johnson, *Metaphors We Live By.*

18.   Jackson, "Thinking through the Body" and *Paths toward a Clearing.*

19.   Lakoff, *Women, Fire, and Dangerous Things.* For anthropological discussions of embodied metaphors, see Kirmayer, "Body's Insistence on Meaning"; Low, "Embodied Metaphors."

20.   Murphy, *Body Silent.*

21.   Sontag, *Illness as Metaphor.*

22.   Quinn, "Cultural Basis of Metaphor"; Kirmayer, "Mind and Body."

23.   Bernice Neugarten ("Adult Personality," 143) contrasts on-time events, which occur during expected times of life, with off-time events, which occur when they are not expected to, such as dying before one's time.

24.   Becker and Kaufman, "Managing an Uncertain Illness Trajectory."

25.   The notion of life reorganization has been utilized by Robert Rubinstein and Mark Luborsky in their research on ethnicity and life reorganization by elderly widowers (Luborsky and Rubinstein, "Ethnicity and Lifetimes" and "Ethnic Identity") and by Gay Becker and Sharon Kaufman in their research on chronicity and life reorganization after a stroke (G. Becker, "Continuity"; Becker and Kaufman, "Managing an Uncertain Illness Trajectory"; Kaufman, "Illness, Biography" and "Toward a Phenomenology").

CHAPTER 4: METAPHORS AS MEDIATORS
IN DISRUPTED LIVES

1.   See Wagner (*Symbols*, 6). Metaphor and metonymy are intimately connected. Metonymy is the substitution of one word for another, and Michael and Marianne Shapiro have suggested that it precedes metaphor (Shapiro and Shapiro, *Hierarchy and the Structure of Tropes*). Deborah Durham and James Fernandez ("Tropical Dominions," 210) suggest that metonymy should be at least as important to anthropological research as metaphor because of anthropological attention to social order; metonyms reorder social order. For a discussion of extending a metaphor into a broader frame of cultural relevance, see Wagner, *Symbols,* 9. See V. Turner, *Dramas, Fields, and Metaphors,* 50–51, for a discussion of root metaphors, creative imagination, and the development of community. Within metaphor theory there are two levels of inquiry: (1) how to understand the relation of "poetic" metaphors to metaphors in ordinary speech and prose and (2) how metaphors are incorporated into more general theories of meaning. I am concerned with both levels: the examination of specific metaphors that are culturally laden provides many clues to how cultural meanings are trans-

formed; and the incorporation of metaphors informs our understanding of cultural processes.

2.   Fernandez, "The Mission of Metaphor"; Wagner, *Symbols.*

3.   This is Paul Ricoeur's suggestion; see Ricoeur, *Rule of Metaphor.*

4.   This is Mark Freeman's observation: see Freeman, "Ricoeur on Interpretation," 309. Paul Ricoeur refers to this process of invention as rapprochement, the creation of a new structure, whereby a literal or static view of reality is surpassed by one that refers both to the past and to the future. Ricoeur, "Metaphorical Process." Decenteredness, a central thesis of postmodernism, challenges the traditional Western view that the concept of structure implies a center (Haber, *Beyond Postmodern Politics,* 12). The metaphor of the center, a root metaphor of Western metaphysics, is at the heart of efforts to restore order and continuity to life when disruption occurs. Jacques Derrida ("Structure, Sign, and Play," 224–25) notes that "The concept of centered structure, although it represents coherence itself . . . is contradictorily coherent . . . the center is not the center." Inherent in this notion of decenteredness is "metaphorical displacement," to use Derrida's term, in which each successive metaphor replaces the one that precedes it.

5.   Freeman, "Ricoeur on Interpretation," 310.

6.   This view is akin to Michael Jackson's view of metaphor as praxis; see M. Jackson, "Thinking through the Body" and *Paths toward a Clearing.*

7.   Naomi Quinn ("Cultural Basis") observes that metaphors are highly constrained by cultural assumptions about the world and questions whether they reorganize thinking. She argues that in instances where metaphors reorganize thinking, they are the exception rather than the rule; it is her view that if metaphors do reorganize thinking, cultural models (cognitive templates of various aspects of culture) form the basis for such reorganization.

8.   This is James Fernandez's suggestion; see Fernandez, "Mission of Metaphor" and "Argument of Images."

9.   For other research that addresses the use of metaphors about infertility and reproductive technologies, see Feldman-Savelsberg, "Plundered Kitchens and Empty Wombs"; Ragone, *Surrogate Motherhood;* and Sandelowski, *With Child in Mind.*

10.   To some extent this discourse is submerged within other discourses, for example, the discourse on "family values," as it is popularly called.

11.   Office of Technology Assessment, *Infertility.*

12.   This shift has resulted in the medicalization of childlessness and in the common use of the medical term infertility by the lay public and in the social science literature. Becker and Nachtigall, "Eager for Medicalization."

13.   Becker and Nachtigall, "Ambiguous Responsibility" and "Born to Be a Mother"; Inhorn, "Interpreting Infertility."

14.   Becker and Nachtigall, "Eager for Medicalization" and "Born to be a Mother."

15.   Ibid.

16.   Fernandez, "Mission of Metaphor," 129.

17.   Kirmayer, "Body's Insistence on Meaning"; Quinn, "Cultural Basis."

18.   Beck, "Metaphor as a Mediator."

19.   Moore and Myerhoff, *Secular Ritual.*

20.   Luborsky, "Alchemists' Visions," 21.

21.   This is Laurence Kirmayer's observation; see Kirmayer, "Body's Insistence."

22.   Miller, *Drama of the Gifted Child.*

23.   This is David Schneider's analysis; see Schneider, *American Kinship: A Cultural Account* and *American Kinship.* In denaturalizing kinship and showing it to be culturally rather than naturally informed, Schneider identified the U.S. cultural model of kinship. See also Yanagisako and Delaney, "Naturalizing Power."

24.   Terrell and Modell, "Anthropology and Adoption."

25.   Adoption has been defined as a procedure which establishes the parent-child relationship between persons not related by nature; see Leavy and Weinberg, *Law of Adoption.* Judith Modell argues that adoption mirrors biology and upholds a cultural interpretation of biological, or genealogical, kinship. In her study she found that "blood" makes adoption problematic because "adoption is always self-conscious." She notes that adoptive kinship demystifies the traditional symbols of kinship: blood, birth, and nature.
See Modell, *Kinship with Strangers,* 4.

26.   Modell (ibid.) found that the "chosen child" story led people to feel they couldn't live up to their family's expectations.

CHAPTER 5: THE DISORDERED BODY

1.   Marcel Mauss maintained that bodily sensations and movements are affected by culture through "acquired habits and somatic tacts"; see Mauss, "Les Techniques du corps."

2.   This is Sally Gadow's observation; see Gadow, "Body and Self."

3.   Murphy, *Body Silent,* 10.

4.   Bury, "Chronic Illness."

5.   Weigle, *Creation and Procreation.*

6.   Luke, *Woman Earth and Spirit*; Teubel, *Sarah the Priestess.*

7.   Gilligan, *In a Different Voice.*

8.   See Jackson, *Paths toward a Clearing*; Kirmayer, "Body's Insistence on Meaning"; Lakoff, *Women, Fire, and Dangerous Things.* Setha Low ("Embodied Metaphors") suggests that metaphors of thought can be generated by the experience of the body as well as through culture more generally. Mark Johnson (*Body in the Mind*) contends that metaphor is the earliest vehicle for ordering bodily sensation

and action, while George Lakoff (*Women, Fire, and Dangerous Things*) asserts that reason is made possible by the body as it experiences the world.

9.   Foucault, *Discipline and Punish;* Low, "Embodied Metaphors"; B. Turner, *Body and Society.*

10.   Quinn and Holland, "Culture and Cognition."

11.   Laqueur, "Orgasm, Generation."

12.   Inhorn, *Quest for Conception.*

13.   Snowdon et al., *Artificial Reproduction;* Nachtigall et al., "Effects."

14.   Snowdon et al., *Artificial Reproduction.*

15.   See Riley and Bond, "Beyond Ageism"; Davidson, "Metaphors of Health and Aging." Such attitudes contribute to the devaluation of those who are old (Moss and Moss, "Death of the Very Old"), to a view of aging as synonymous with disease, disability, and decline (Minkler, "Aging and Disability"), and to ambiguous status in old age.

16.   For a discussion of the association of senescence with loss of control of the body, see Hennessy, "Culture in the Use, Care, and Control of the Aging Body," 42. For a discussion of the association of senescence with a series of losses, see Davidson, "Metaphors of Health and Aging." For a discussion of the view of senescence as a prelude to death, see Moss and Moss, "Death of the Very Old"; Sankar, "Living Dead."

17.   For some exceptions in which the notion of embodiment has been applied to the old, see G. Becker, "Oldest Old"; Doolittle, "Experience of Recovery" and "Clinical Ethnography"; Gadow, "Frailty and Strength."

18.   This is Mark Luborsky's suggestion; see Luborsky, "Process of Self-Report," 1457.

19.   Williams, "Genesis of Chronic Illness."

20.   See, for example, G. Becker, *Growing Old in Silence;* G. Frank, "On Embodiment"; Scheer and Luborsky, "Cultural Context of Polio Biographies."

21.   Hill et al., "Role of Anticipatory Bereavement."

22.   Moss and Moss, "Death of the Very Old."

23.   Scheer and Luborsky, "Cultural Context of Polio Biographies."

24.   Rhodes, "Studying Biomedicine."

25.   Foucault, *Birth of the Clinic.*

26.   Featherstone and Hepworth, "Mask of Ageing," 375.

CHAPTER 6: PERSONAL RESPONSIBILITY FOR CONTINUITY

1.   Alexander et al., "Generativity in Cultural Context," 425.

2.   This is Grace Gladys Harris's observation; see Harris, "Concepts of Individual," 607.

3.   A semantic question further clouds this discourse: what do the words "individual," "self," and "person" mean? They are often used interchangeably, yet associations with each have built up over time. Harris (ibid., 608) suggests that the term individual connotes a "psychobiological entity." She also suggests that to focus on the self is to formulate questions and to direct observation to posited intrapsychic structures and processes. She notes that focusing on persons as agents in society, however, brings properties of the social order and its cultural forms to the fore. Marcel Mauss ("Category of the Human Mind") contrasted the concept of the self, which he defined as *consciousness* of the self—the awareness of body and spirit—with the social concept of the person as a compound of jural rights and moral responsibility. Thomas Csordas differentiates between the preobjective self and a representation of self (Csordas, *Sacred Self*, 14–15). He identifies two analytic levels: the preobjective self (being-in-the-world) and the objectified self of personhood and representation. Referring to James Fernandez's ("Argument of Images") conceptualization of "the inchoate" as the ground of emotional meaning, moral imagination, identity, and self-objectification, Csordas notes that these are characteristics of persons, not of the preobjective self. Although we can differentiate the preobjective self from personhood for academic purposes, it is an artificial distinction at the level of experience, as the two merge into each other at every turn.

4.   Anthropological views of the self are apparently influenced by the thinking current in a given era. Two perspectives currently prevail within the social sciences: a "normative" perspective and an alternate view that suggests that the notion of a cohesive self is illusory. D. W. Murray ("What is the Western Concept of the Self?") characterizes these two views, respectively, as "transcendent" and "contingent" and notes that it is simplistic to link transcendent views to the West and contingent views to other cultures. The transcendent, or normative, self is viewed as cohesive, bounded, autonomous, continuous, and stable; see, for example, Dumont, "Modified View of Our Origins"; Geertz, "Making Experience"; Hallowell, *Culture and Experience*; Kaufman, *Ageless Self*; Marsella and White, *Cultural Conceptions*; Taylor, *Sources of the Self*. This view of the self has been related to Western traditions and values of autonomy and independence (Ewing, "Illusion of Wholeness"; Murray, "What is the Western Concept of the Self?"; Shweder and Bourne, "Does the Concept of the Person Vary?") and has been weighted towards the effects of social structure and individual agency. In contrast, the contingent self is viewed as culturally determined and has been most often linked to cross-cultural work (Murray, "What is the Western Concept of the Self?"). This view emphasizes contested and negotiated meanings, diversity, and inner experience; see, for example, Ewing, "Illusion of Wholeness"; Luborsky, "Cultural Adversity of Physical Disability"; Marsella et al., *Culture and Self*; Rosaldo, "Anthropology of Self and Feeling"; Shweder and Bourne, "Does the Concept of the Person Vary?"

5.   For examples of the perspective described in Ewing, "Illusion of Whole-ness," see Luborsky, "Romance with Personal Meaning," and Rosenwald and Ochberg, eds., *Storied Lives.*

6.   Grace's story of disruption illustrates various aspects of narrative theory. First, we see how emplotment brings together several interrelated stories in a complex relationship. We also see how emplotment builds over time. In the first interview the importance of social standing emerges; it is juxtaposed against Grace's sense that she doesn't know who she is. Several months later, these themes reemerge in the context of both work and family conflict. We also see the emergence of subjunctivizing elements—Grace wrestles with possibilities be-cause the future stretches out uncertainly.

7.   This is Margaret Clark and Barbara Anderson's view; see Clark and Ander-son, *Culture and Aging.*

8.   For a discussion of the relationship between values and culturally specific direction, see D'Andrade, "Cultural Meaning Systems." For a discussion of how values become the basis for commonsense construals of the world, see Quinn and Holland, "Culture and Cognition," 11.

9.   For discussions of the relationship of values to memories, life experiences, and social ideologies, see Quinn, "Motivational Force"; Holland, "How Cultural Systems Become Desire"; and C. Strauss, "What Makes Tony Run?"

10.   For a discussion of the ideology of individualism and rational determinism, see Rubinstein et al., "Key Relationships."

11.   For literature on the lives of African Americans, see Martin and Martin, *Black Extended Family;* Milligan, "Understanding Diversity." For work on the meaning of identity, see Smith and Thornton, "Identity and Consciousness."

CHAPTER 7: LIVING IN LIMBO

1.   For applications of the concept of liminality to disabled persons and per-sons experiencing difference from a physical norm, see Ablon, *Little People in America;* Murphy et al., "Physical Disability and Social Liminality."

2.   van Gennep, *Rites of Passage.*

3.   V. Turner, *Ritual Process.*

4.   Murphy et al., "Physical Disability," 237.

5.   DES was given to women thirty-five to forty-five years ago to prevent miscarriage. The daughters of those women often have reproductive health problems.

6.   Kirmayer, "Mind and Body."

7.   This is Marguerite Sandelowski's suggestion; see Sandelowski, "Com-pelled to Try."

8.   Tversky and Kahneman, "Framing of Decisions"; Tymstra, "Imperative Character."

9.   The disrupting effects of chronic and disabling illnesses on individual identity have been examined by social scientists (see, for example, Ablon, "The Elephant Man"; G. Becker, *Growing Old in Silence* and "Continuity"; Becker et al., "Dilemma of Seeking Urgent Care"; Bury, "Chronic Illness"; Corbin and Strauss, "Accompaniments in Chronic Illness"; Kaufman, "Illness, Biography"; Kleinman, *Illness Narratives;* Luborsky, "Cultural Adversity" and "Process of Self-Report"; Scheer and Luborsky, "Cultural Context of Polio Biographies"; Williams, "Genesis of Chronic Illness") and written about by those who have conditions considered to be chronic (Murphy, *Body Silent;* Register, *Living with Chronic Illness;* Sacks, *Leg to Stand On;* Zola, *Missing Pieces*).

10.   For discussions of illness trajectories, see Strauss et al., *Chronic Illness,* and Wiener and Dodd, "Coping amid Uncertainty."

11.   Kaufman, "Illness, Biography"; Kiefer, *Changing Cultures;* Williams, "Genesis of Chronic Illness." In an examination of the disruption caused by the loss of vision in late life, Ainlay found that vision loss exploded the taken-for-granted nature of individuals' understandings of their bodies and their ties to others; see Ainlay, *Day Brought Back My Night,* 115.

12.   See, for example, Corbin and Strauss, "Accompaniments in Chronic Illness"; Kaufman, "Illness, Biography"; Robinson, "Personal Narratives."

13.   Oleson et al., "Mundane Ailment," 451.

14.   Sacks, *Leg to Stand On;* Murphy, *Body Silent.*

15.   Before interviewing them myself, I followed a number of people in this study, for example, Miss Mintz, through a course I taught with other members of a clinical team. After a student followed the person from hospital to home or institution, completed the course, and concluded the encounter with the person, I sought permission from the person's physician to follow that person myself.

16.   A board and care home is an intermediate care facility between independent living and institutionalization. To be eligible to live in such a home in California, a person must be able to walk, although they may do so with the assistance of devices such as a walker or a cane.

CHAPTER 8: CREATING ORDER
OUT OF CHAOS

1.   A lengthy period of time is apparently needed to fully reconstruct a biography after the onset of a chronic, disabling illness. The longer the time from the original disruption, the more fully people appear to be able to create a sense of continuity. Biographical work to repair such disruptions may be incomplete, however, for those who experience the onset of chronic illness late in life. G. Becker, "Continuity after a Stroke," 148–50.

2.   See Becker and Kaufman, "Managing an Uncertain Illness Trajectory," for a discussion of hope and uncertain illness trajectories in stroke rehabilitation.

3.   See Kaufman, "Illness, Biography," and Becker and Kaufman, ibid., for a discussion of the meanings people who have had a stroke attach to recovery.

4.   Lifeline is an alert system, an alarm, that is worn on the body and is intended for emergencies in which the wearer is rendered immobile.

5.   See Rubinstein et al., *Elders Living Alone,* for an in-depth discussion of the meaning of home.

6.   Gerontological research has shown repeatedly that elderly individuals may be more vulnerable to discontinuities than are younger people; see, for example, Ainlay, *Day Brought Back My Night;* Clark and Anderson, *Culture and Aging;* Kaufman, *Ageless Self;* Luborsky, "Analysis" and "Alchemists' Visions"; Myerhoff, *Number Our Days;* Sankar, "It's Just Old Age."

CHAPTER 9: HEALING THE BODY
THROUGH THE MIND

1.   Laderman and Roseman, "Introduction."

2.   Lyon, "Order and Healing."

3.   Gerber, *Married to Their Careers.*

4.   Margery Fox (ibid., 113) observes that the role of the Christian Science practitioner offers a variety of challenging interpersonal relationships articulated within a higher order of meaning and that the practitioner operates under principles that endow her life and work with transcendence.

5.   In writing about Christian Science, I draw solely on my own experience of the religion. For a thorough analysis of the religion's ideology and practices, see Fox, ibid.

6.   See Fox, ibid., 101–102, 106–109, for a more thorough discussion of how Christian Scientists think about illness.

7.   The similarity to psychotherapy systems is obvious: people learn to think about life problems in certain ways in the course of treatment and then, ideally, are able to use those techniques on their own later.

8.   Christian Science does not recognize age and the aging process, for both are seen as reflections of the material world; see Fox, ibid.

9.   The theme of the "wounded healer" is common across cultures; see Halifax, *Shaman.*

10.   In the ethnic minorities study, open-ended questions have been developed to probe people's perspectives on their spiritual lives and the relationship of their spiritual lives to health.

11.   Although the data I collected in four of the five studies I report on in this

book focused on people's experiences of illness in a biomedical system of care, many of these people simultaneously used other forms of healing.

12.   Sharp, "Folk Medicine Practices."

13.   Achterberg, *Woman as Healer.*

14.   This is Michael Jackson's observation; see M. Jackson, *Paths toward a Clearing.*

15.   Desjarlais, *Body and Emotion.*

16.   I am indebted to Robert Rubinstein for this insight.

17.   On the group level, self-help techniques such as twelve-step programs have broad appeal in U.S. society, cutting across class lines. While individual groups may reflect class and color boundaries, their pervasive popularity suggests that a basic cultural ethos is embedded in their philosophy, and that they convey normalizing ideologies that facilitate life changes. Such groups may also facilitate upward social mobility, as they provide a philosophy, a vocabulary, and a rationale for transcending class-based limitations.

18.   See Garro, "Narrative Representations," for a discussion of how the body-mind relationship was depicted by respondents in a study of temporomandibular joint (TMJ) disorders.

CHAPTER 10: METAPHORS
OF TRANSFORMATION

1.   See, for example, Cohler, "Personal Narrative"; Manheimer, "Narrative Quest"; Ryff, "Subjective Construction of Self and Society."

2.   Vash, *Psychology of Disability;* Jung, *Modern Man in Search of a Soul.*

3.   G. Becker, *Healing the Infertile Family;* Luborsky, "Romance with Personal Meaning."

4.   Resolve, Inc., a national, nonprofit membership organization, has affiliated chapters that offer monthly programs, telephone counseling, formal support groups, and medical information to people experiencing infertility. Northern California Resolve, the local chapter that helped me to recruit people for this study, provides outreach programs on a regular basis and is well known to people in this geographic locale who are undergoing medical treatment for infertility.

5.   For discussions of how therapy can transform suffering by providing meaning and of therapy as a hermeneutic enterprise; see Kirmayer, "Improvisation and Authority." For a discussion of narrative truth, see Spence, *Narrative Truth and Historical Truth.*

6.   Hope, as a cultural expression of U.S. values, is addressed in M. Good et al., "American Oncology."

7.   Stoller, "Epistemology of Sorkotaray."

8. These are Laurence Kirmayer's observations; see Kirmayer, "Improvisation and Authority," 198–99.

9. Davis and Starn, "Introduction."

10. Nora, "Between Memory and History," 16.

11. Hallowell, *Culture and Experience,* 94; Neugarten, "Continuities" and "Time, Age, and the Life Cycle."

12. Halbwachs, *On Collective Memory.*

13. Neugarten, "Time, Age, and the Life Cycle."

14. Ewing, "Illusion of Wholeness."

15. This is Christie Kiefer's suggestion; see Kiefer, *Changing Cultures.*

16. This is David Carr's observation; see Carr, *Time, Narrative, and History,* 29.

17. Ricoeur, *Time and Narrative.*

18. Alexander et al., "Generativity in Cultural Context."

19. Lowenthal et al., *Four Stages of Life.*

20. Fiske, *Middle Age;* Tamir, "Men at Middle Age."

21. G. Becker, *Growing Old in Silence,* 39–50.

22. Kirmayer, "Body's Insistence on Meaning."

23. Luborsky, "Analysis" and "Alchemists' Visions."

24. The process of refining a narrative over time is called "narrative smoothing"; see Spence, "Narrative Smoothing."

CHAPTER II: DISRUPTION
AND THE CREATION OF CONTINUITY

1. Sharon Kaufman has made a similar point in *The Ageless Self.*

2. Dirks et al., eds., *Culture/Power/History.*

3. Thomas Csordas ("Somatic Modes" and *Sacred Self)* has coined the term *cultural phenomenology* to refer to the synthesis of embodied experience and cultural meanings. Using the perspective of cultural phenomenology as a starting point can yield new understandings about the everyday workings of culture.

4. Jacques Derrida (*Of Grammatology*) maintains that nothing matters but the text.

5. The preoccupation of postmodern theorists with textuality to the exclusion of other perspectives greatly limits the relevance of postmodernism and has, for a time, hamstrung theoretical development. For thoughtful critiques on postmodernism, see Haber, *Beyond Postmodern Politics,* and Best and Kellner, *Postmodern Theory.*

6. I acknowledge that this form of storytelling is reinforced by the questions asked in these studies. In the first interview, we asked people to tell us everything that happened leading up to and since the event.

7. Luborsky, "Romance with Personal Meaning"; Wagner, *Symbols.*

8. This is Robert Paul's suggestion; see Paul, "What Does Anybody Want?" 447.

9. David Michael Levin ("Visions of Narcissism," 73) argues that Foucault perpetuates the old metaphysics when he regards the body as the absolute other of reason. Foucault's conception of the body-as-object is self-limiting and is not balanced by a phenomenological understanding of the body-as-subject, thus denying that agency exists. To impose specific structuralist perspectives on phenomenological perspectives potentially does violence to the integrity of a phenomenological perspective by reducing the legitimacy of such a perspective and subsuming it under structure. Ruth Behar ("Introduction") suggests that person-centered approaches have been discounted and viewed as less important than structuralist approaches. Although structuralist and poststructuralist theories can be applicable to the analysis that proceeds from work that is primarily phenomenological, their application is secondary in a phenomenological account of the workings of culture.

10. This desire for duality affirms Michael Jackson's (*Paths toward a Clearing*) point that we are the other.

11. See Dirks et al., *Culture/Power/History*, for an in-depth discussion of power and resistance.

12. Faye Ginsburg and Rayna Rapp ("Introduction") also observe that people cannot develop oppositional positions independent of the categories of the dominant culture.

13. Leith Mullings ("Households Headed by Women") also uses the notion of transformation with respect to women's efforts to create continuity. She applies the notion of transformative work to (1) efforts to sustain continuity under transformed circumstances and (2) efforts to transform circumstances in order to maintain continuity.

14. This is Sherry Ortner's observation; see Ortner, "Resistance," 179.

15. This also is Ortner's suggestion; see ibid., 191.

16. Steven Best and Douglas Kellner (*Postmodern Theory*, 283, 289) suggest that postmodern theories lack an adequate theory of agency, that they deemphasize community and intersubjectivity in favor of highly individualized modes of being.

17. For a general discussion of embodiment through social groups as a source of reaffirmation, see Toch, *Social Psychology of Social Movements*. For discussions of how this idea applies to persons who experience difference, see Ablon, *Little People in America*; G. Becker, *Growing Old in Silence*; Becker and Arnold, "Stigma as a Social and Cultural Construct."

18. Abu-Lughod, "Writing against Culture."

APPENDIX: ABOUT THE RESEARCH

1.   Hammersley and Atkinson, *Ethnographic Principles in Practice.*
2.   Ibid.
3.   See G. Becker, "Age Bias in Stroke Rehabilitation"; Kaufman, "Toward a Phenomenology."
4.   G. Becker, "Oldest Old"; Kaufman, "Social Construction of Frailty."
5.   See, for example, G. Becker, ibid., and Kaufman, ibid.
6.   Wiener, *Politics of Alcoholism.*
7.   Mishler, *Research Interviewing.*
8.   Benner, *From Novice to Expert.*
9.   Kaufman, *Ageless Self.*
10. Goodman, "Snowball Sampling."

References

Ablon, Joan. 1984. *Little People in America*. New York: Praeger.
———. 1995. "'The Elephant Man' as 'Self' and 'Other': The Psychosocial Costs of a Misdiagnosis." *Social Science and Medicine* 40:1481–90.
Abu-Lughod, Lila. 1991. "Writing against Culture." In *Recapturing Anthropology: Working in the Present,* ed. Richard G. Fox, 137–62. Santa Fe, NM: School of American Research.
Achterberg, Jeanne. 1990. *Woman as Healer*. Boston: Shambala.
Agar, Michael. 1980. "Stories, Background Knowledge, and Themes: Problems in the Analysis of Life History Narrative." *American Ethnologist* 7:233–39.
Agar, Michael, and Jerry R. Hobbs. 1982. "Interpreting Discourse: Coherence and the Analysis of Ethnographic Interviews." *Discourse Processes* 5:1–32.
Ainlay, Stephen C. 1989. *Day Brought Back My Night: Aging and New Vision Loss*. London: Routledge.
Alexander, Baine, Robert Rubinstein, Marcene Goodman, and Mark Luborsky. 1991. "Generativity in Cultural Context: The Self, Death, and Immortality as Experienced by Older American Women." *Ageing and Society* 11:417–42.

Anderson, Robert, and Michael Bury, eds. 1988. *Living with Chronic Illness: The Experience of Patients and Their Families.* London: Unwin Hyman.

Antonovsky, Anton. 1979. *Health, Stress, and Coping.* San Francisco: Jossey Bass.

Arney, William Ray, and Bernard J. Bergen. 1984. *Medicine and the Management of Living.* Chicago: University of Chicago Press.

Atchley, Robert. 1989. "A Continuity Theory of Normal Aging." *The Gerontologist* 29:183–90.

Baltes, Paul. 1987. "Theoretical Propositions of Life-Span Developmental Psychology: On the Dynamics between Growth and Decline." *Developmental Psychology* 23:611–26.

Basso, Keith H. 1984. "'Stalking with Stories': Names, Places, and Moral Narratives among the Western Apache." In *Text, Play, and Story: The Construction and Reconstruction of Self and Society,* ed. Edward M. Bruner, 19–55. Washington, D.C.: American Anthropological Association.

Beck, Brenda. 1978. "The Metaphor as a Mediator between Semantic and Analogic Modes of Thought." *Current Anthropology* 19:83–97.

Becker, Ann. 1995. *Body, Self, and Society: The View from Fiji.* Philadelphia: University of Pennsylvania Press.

Becker, Gay. 1980. *Growing Old in Silence.* Berkeley: University of California Press.

———. 1997. *Healing the Infertile Family.* Updated edition. Berkeley: University of California Press.

———. 1993. "Continuity after a Stroke: Implications for Life-Course Disruption in Old Age." *The Gerontologist* 33:148–58.

———. 1994a. "Age Bias in Stroke Rehabilitation: Effects on Adult Status." *Journal of Aging Studies* 8:271–90.

———. 1994b. "Metaphors in Disrupted Lives: Infertility and Cultural Constructions of Continuity." *Medical Anthropology Quarterly* 8:383–410.

———. 1994c. "The Oldest Old: Autonomy in the Face of Frailty." *Journal of Aging Studies* 8:59–76.

Becker, Gay, and Regina Arnold. 1986. "Stigma as a Social and Cultural Construct." In *The Dilemma of Difference: A Multidisciplinary View of Stigma,* ed. Stephen C. Ainlay, Gay Becker, and Lerita M. Coleman, 39–57. New York: Plenum.

Becker, Gay, Susan Janson-Bjerklie, Patricia Benner, Kathleen Slobin, and Sandra Ferketich. 1993. "The Dilemma of Seeking Urgent Care: Asthma Episodes and Emergency Service Use." *Social Science and Medicine* 37:305–13.

Becker, Gay, and Sharon Kaufman. 1995. "Managing an Uncertain Illness Trajectory in Old Age: Patients' and Physicians' Views of Stroke." *Medical Anthropology Quarterly* 9:165–87.

Becker, Gay, and Robert D. Nachtigall. 1991. "Ambiguous Responsibility in the Doctor-Patient Relationship: The Case of Infertility." *Social Science and Medicine* 32:875–85.

———. 1992. "Eager for Medicalization: The Social Production of Infertility as a Disease." *Sociology of Health and Illness* 14:456–71.

———. 1994. " 'Born to Be a Mother': The Cultural Construction of Risk in Infertility Treatment." *Social Science and Medicine* 39:507–18.

Behar, Ruth. 1995. "Introduction: Out of Exile." In *Women Writing Culture,* ed. Ruth Behar and Deborah A. Gordon, 1–32. Berkeley: University of California Press.

Bell, Susan. 1988. "Becoming a Political Woman: The Reconstruction and Interpretation of Experience through Stories." In *Gender and Discourse: The Power of Talk,* ed. Alexandra Dundas Todd and Sue Fisher. Norwood, NJ: Ablex.

Bengston, Vern L., Neal E. Cutler, David J. Mangen, and Victor W. Marshall. 1985. "Generations, Cohorts, and Relations between Age Groups." In *Handbook of Aging and the Social Sciences,* 2d ed., ed. Vern Bengston and Ethel Shanas, 304–38. New York: Van Nostrand Reinhold.

Benner, Patricia. 1984. *From Novice to Expert.* Menlo Park, CA: Addison Wesley.

Benner, Patricia, Susan Janson-Bjerklie, Sandra Ferketich, and Gay Becker. 1994. "Moral Dimensions of Living with a Chronic Illness: Autonomy, Responsibility, and the Limits of Control." In *Interpretive Phenomenology: Embodiment, Caring, and Ethics in Health and Illness,* ed. Patricia Benner, 225–54. Thousand Oaks, CA: Sage.

Best, Steven, and Douglas Kellner. 1991. *Postmodern Theory: Critical Interrogations.* New York: Guilford.

Bourdieu, Pierre. 1977. *Outline of a Theory of Practice.* Translated by Richard Nice. Cambridge: Cambridge University Press.

———. 1984. *Distinction: A Social Critique of the Judgment of Taste.* Translated by Richard Nice. Cambridge: Harvard University Press.

———. 1990. *The Logic of Practice.* Translated by Richard Nice. Stanford: Stanford University Press.

Brody, Howard. 1987. *Stories of Sickness.* New Haven: Yale University Press.

Bruner, Edward M. 1986. "Experience and Its Expressions." In *The Anthropology of Experience,* ed. Victor W. Turner and Edward M. Bruner, 3–30. Urbana: University of Illinois Press.

Bruner, Jerome. 1986. *Actual Minds, Possible Worlds.* Cambridge: Harvard University Press.

Bury, Michael. 1982. "Chronic Illness as Biographical Disruption." *Sociology of Health and Illness* 4:167–82.

Carr, David. 1986. *Time, Narrative, and History.* Bloomington: Indiana University Press.

Charmaz, Kathy. 1992. *Good Days, Bad Days.* New Brunswick, NJ: Rutgers University Press.

Clark, M. Margaret, and Barbara Anderson. 1967. *Culture and Aging.* Springfield, IL: Charles C. Thomas.

Cohler, Bertram. 1982. "Personal Narrative and Life Course." In *Life Span Development and Behavior,* ed. Paul Baltes, 4:205–41. New York: Academic Press.

———. 1991. "The Life Story and the Study of Resilience and Response to Adversity." *Journal of Narrative and Life History* 1:169–200.

Connerton, Paul. 1989. *How Societies Remember.* New York: Cambridge University Press.

Conrad, Peter. 1987. "The Experience of Illness: Recent and New Directions." In *Research in the Sociology of Health Care,* ed. Julius A. Roth and Peter Conrad, 6:1–31. Greenwich, CT: JAI.

Corbin, Juliet, and Anselm Strauss. 1987. "Accompaniments in Chronic Illness: Changes in Body, Self, Biography, and Biographical Time." In *Research in the Sociology of Health Care,* ed. Julius A. Roth and Peter Conrad, 6:249–81. Greenwich, CT: JAI.

Csordas, Thomas. 1990. "Embodiment as a Paradigm for Anthropology." *Ethos* 18:5–47.

———. 1993. "Somatic Modes of Attention." *Cultural Anthropology* 8:135–56.

———. 1994a. "Introduction: The Body as Representation and Being-in-the-World." In *Embodiment and Experience: The Existential Ground of Culture and Self,* ed. Thomas Csordas, 1–24. Cambridge: Cambridge University Press.

———. 1994b. *The Sacred Self: A Cultural Phenomenology of Charismatic Healing.* Berkeley: University of California Press.

———. 1996. "Imaginal Performance and Memory in Ritual Healing." In *The Performance of Healing,* ed. Carol Laderman and Marina Roseman, 91–113. New York: Routledge.

Csordas, Thomas, ed. 1994. *Embodiment and Experience: The Existential Ground of Culture and Self.* Cambridge: Cambridge University Press.

D'Andrade, Roy. 1984. "Cultural Meaning Systems." In *Culture Theory: Mind, Self, and Emotion,* ed. Richard A. Shweder and Robert A. LeVine, 88–112. Cambridge: Cambridge University Press.

Davidson, Warren A. S. 1991. "Metaphors of Health and Aging: Geriatrics as Metaphor." In *Metaphors of Aging in Science and the Humanities,* ed. Gary M. Kenyon, James E. Birren, and Johannes J. F. Schroots, 173–84. New York: Springer.

Davis, Natalie Zemon, and Randolph Starn. 1989. "Introduction: Memory and Counter-Memory." *Representations* 26:1–6.

Derrida, Jacques. 1970. "Structure, Sign, and Play in the Discourse of the Human Sciences." In *Writing and Difference.* Translated by Alan Bass. Chicago: University of Chicago Press.

———. 1976. *Of Grammatology.* Translated by Gayatri Chakravorty Spivak. Baltimore: Johns Hopkins University Press.

Descartes, René. 1870. "Meditation 6: Of the Existence of Material Things, and of the Real Distinction between the Mind and Body of Man." *Discourse on the Method of Rightly Conducting the Reason and Seeking Truth in the Sciences*. London: Blackwell and Sons.

Desjarlais, Robert. 1992. *Body and Emotion: The Aesthetics of Illness and Healing in the Nepal Himalayas*. Philadelphia: University of Pennsylvania Press.

Dillon, Martin C. 1991. "Preface: Merleau-Ponty and Postmodernity." In *Merleau-Ponty Vivant*, ed. Martin C. Dillon, ix–xxxv. Albany: State University of New York Press.

Dirks, Nicholas B., Geoff Eley, and Sherry B. Ortner, eds. 1994. *Culture/Power/History: A Reader in Contemporary Social Theory*. Princeton, NJ: Princeton University Press.

Doolittle, Nancy. 1992. "The Experience of Recovery following Lacunar Stroke." *Rehabilitation Nursing* 17:122–25.

———. 1994. "A Clinical Ethnography of Stroke Recovery." In *Interpretive Phenomenology: Embodiment, Caring, and Ethics in Health and Illness*, ed. Patricia Benner. 211–24. Thousand Oaks, CA: Sage.

Dumont, Louis. 1985. "A Modified View of Our Origins: The Christian Beginnings of Modern Individualism." In *The Category of the Person*, ed. Michael Carrithers, Steven Collins, and Steven Lukes, 93–122. New York: Cambridge University Press.

Durham, Deborah, and James W. Fernandez. 1991. "Tropical Dominions: The Figurative Struggle over Domains of Belonging and Apartness in Africa." In *Beyond Metaphor: The Theory of Tropes in Anthropology*, ed. James W. Fernandez, 190–210. Stanford: Stanford University Press.

Estroff, Sue E. 1993. "Identity, Disability, and Schizophrenia: The Problem of Chronicity." In *Knowledge, Power, and Practice: The Anthropology of Medicine and Everyday Life*, ed. Shirley Lindenbaum and Margaret Lock, 247–86. Berkeley: University of California Press.

———. 1995. "Whose Story Is It Anyway? Authority, Voice, and Responsibility in Narratives of Chronic Illness." In *Chronic Illness: From Experience to Policy*, ed. S. Kay Toombs, David Barnard, and Ronald A. Carson, 77–102. Bloomington: Indiana University Press.

Ewing, Katherine. 1990. "The Illusion of Wholeness: Culture, Self, and the Experience of Inconsistency." *Ethos* 18:251–78.

Farmer, Paul. 1994. "AIDS-Talk and the Constitution of Cultural Models." *Social Science and Medicine* 38:801–10.

Featherstone, Mike, and Mike Hepworth. 1991. "The Mask of Ageing and the Postmodern Life Course." In *The Body: Social Process and Cultural Theory*, ed. Mike Featherstone, Mike Hepworth, and Bryan S. Turner, 371–89. London: Sage.

Feldman-Savelsberg, Pamela. 1994. "Plundered Kitchens and Empty Wombs:

Fear of Infertility in the Cameroonian Grassfields." *Social Science and Medicine* 39:463–74.

Fernandez, James. 1972. "Persuasions and Performances: Of the Beast in Every Body and the Metaphors of Everyman." *Daedalus* 101:39–80.

———. 1974. "The Mission of Metaphor in Expressive Culture." *Current Anthropology* 15:119–45.

———. 1986. "The Argument of Images and the Experience of Returning to the Whole." In *The Anthropology of Experience*, ed. Victor W. Turner and Edward M. Bruner, 159–87. Chicago: University of Chicago Press.

———. 1991. "Introduction: Confluents of Inquiry." In *Beyond Metaphor: The Theory of Tropes in Anthropology*, ed. James W. Fernandez, 1–13. Stanford: Stanford University Press.

Fiske, Marjorie. 1979. *Middle Age.* Willemstad, Netherlands: Multimedia Publications.

Foucault, Michel. 1973. *The Birth of the Clinic: An Archeology of Medical Perception.* Translated by A. M. Sheridan Smith. New York: Vintage.

———. 1979. *Discipline and Punish.* Translated by Alan Sheridan. New York: Vintage.

Fox, Margery. 1989. "The Socioreligious Role of the Christian Science Practitioner." In *Women as Healers: Cross-Cultural Perspectives*, ed. Carol S. McClain, 98–114. New Brunswick, NJ: Rutgers University Press.

Frank, Arthur W. 1990. "Bringing Bodies Back In: A Decade Review." *Theory, Culture, and Society* 7:131–62.

Frank, Gelya. 1979. "Finding the Common Denominator: A Phenomenological Critique of Life History Method." *Ethos* 7:68–94.

———. 1986. "On Embodiment: A Case Study of Congenital Limb Deficiency in American Culture." *Culture, Medicine, and Psychiatry* 10:189–219.

Freeman, Mark. 1985. "Ricoeur on Interpretation: The Model of the Text and the Idea of Development." *Human Development* 28:295–312.

Fry, Christine L. 1990. "The Life Course in Context: Implications of Comparative Research." In *Anthropology and Aging*, ed. Robert Rubinstein, 129–49. Dordrecht, Netherlands: Kluwer.

Fry, Christine L., and Jennie Keith. 1982. "The Life Course as a Cultural Unit." In *Aging from Birth to Death.* Vol. 2, *Sociotemporal Perspectives*, ed. by Matilda White Riley, Ronald Abeles, and M. S. Teitelbaum. Boulder, CO: Westview Press.

Gadow, Sally. 1982. "Body and Self: A Dialectic." In *The Humanity of the Ill: Phenomenological Perspectives*, ed. Victor Kastenbaum, 86–100. Knoxville: University of Tennessee Press.

———. 1986. "Frailty and Strength: The Dialectic of Aging." In *What Does It Mean to Grow Old?*, ed. Thomas R. Cole and Sally A. Gadow, 237–43. Durham: Duke University Press.

Gallagher, Eugene B. 1979. "Lines of Reconstruction and Extension in the Parsonian Sociology of Illness." In *Patients, Physicians, and Illness*, 3d ed., ed. E. Gartly Jaco, 162–83. New York: Free Press.

Garro, Linda. 1988. "Explaining High Blood Pressure: Variation in Knowledge about Illness." *American Ethnologist* 15:98–119.

———. 1992. "Chronic Illness and the Construction of Narratives." In *Pain as Human Experience: An Anthropological Perspective*, ed. Mary-Jo DelVecchio Good, Paul E. Brodwin, Byron J. Good, and Arthur Kleinman, 100–37. Berkeley: University of California Press.

———. 1994. "Narrative Representations of Chronic Illness Experience: Cultural Models of Illness, Mind, and Body in Stories concerning the Temporomandibular Joint (TMJ)." *Social Science and Medicine* 38:775–88.

Geertz, Clifford. 1986. "Making Experience, Authoring Selves." In *The Anthropology of Experience*, ed. Victor Turner and Edward Bruner, 373–80. Chicago: University of Illinois Press.

George, Linda K., and R. Landerman. 1984. "Health and Subjective Well-Being: A Replicated Secondary Data Analysis." *International Journal of Aging and Human Development* 19:133–56.

Gerber, Lane A. 1983. *Married to Their Careers: Career and Family Dilemmas in Doctors' Lives*. New York: Tavistock.

Gilligan, Carol. 1982. *In a Different Voice*. Cambridge: Harvard University Press.

Ginsburg, Faye D., and Rayna Rapp. 1995. "Introduction: Conceiving the New World Order." In *Conceiving the New World Order: The Global Politics of Reproduction*, ed. Faye D. Ginsburg and Rayna Rapp, 1–18. Berkeley: University of California Press.

Good, Byron. 1994. *Medicine, Rationality, and Experience*. New York: Cambridge University Press.

Good, Byron J., and Mary-Jo DelVecchio Good. 1994. "In the Subjunctive Mode: Epilepsy Narratives in Turkey." *Social Science and Medicine* 38:835–42.

Good, Mary-Jo DelVecchio, Byron J. Good, Cynthia Schaffer, and Stuart E. Lind. 1990. "American Oncology and the Discourse on Hope." *Culture, Medicine, and Psychiatry* 14:59–79.

Good, Mary-Jo DelVecchio, Tseunetsugu Munakata, Yasuki Kobayashi, Cheryl Mattingly, and Byron J. Good. 1994. "Oncology and Narrative Time." *Social Science and Medicine* 38:855–62.

Good, Mary-Jo DelVecchio, Paul E. Brodwin, Byron J. Good, and Arthur Kleinman, eds. 1992. *Pain as Human Experience: An Anthropological Perspective*. Berkeley: University of California Press.

Goodman, L. A. 1961. "Snowball Sampling." *Annals of Mathematics and Statistics* 32:148.

Gordon, Deborah R. 1990. "Embodying Illness, Embodying Cancer." *Culture, Medicine, and Psychiatry* 14:275–97.

———. 1994. "The Ethics of Ambiguity and Concealment around Cancer: Interpretations through a Local Italian World." In *Interpretive Phenomenology: Embodiment, Caring, and Ethics in Health and Illness*, ed. Patricia Benner, 279–322. Thousand Oaks, CA: Sage.

Haber, Honi Fern. 1994. *Beyond Postmodern Politics: Lyotard, Rorty, Foucault*. New York: Routledge.

Halbwachs, Maurice. 1992. *On Collective Memory*. Edited, translated, and with an introduction by Lewis Coser. Chicago: University of Chicago Press.

Halifax, Joan. 1982. *Shaman: The Wounded Healer*. New York: Thames and Hudson.

Hallowell, A. Irving. 1955. *Culture and Experience*. New York: Schocken.

———. 1955. "The Self and Its Behavioral Context." In *Culture and Experience*. New York: Schocken.

Hammersley, Martin, and Paul Atkinson. 1986. *Ethnographic Principles in Practice*. London: Tavistock.

Harris, Grace Gladys. 1989. "Concepts of Individual, Self, and Person in Description and Analysis." *American Anthropologist* 91:599–612.

Hayles, Catherine. 1991. "Chaos: More than Metaphor." In *Chaos and Order: Complex Dynamics in Literature and Science*, ed. Catherine Hayles, 1–33. Chicago: University of Chicago Press.

Heidegger, Martin. 1985. *History of the Concept of Time: Prolegomena*. Translated by Theodore Kisiel. Bloomington: University of Indiana Press.

Hennessy, Catherine Hagan. 1989. "Culture in the Use, Care, and Control of the Aging Body." *Journal of Aging Studies* 3:39–54.

Heurtin-Roberts, Suzanne. 1993. "'High-Pertension'—The Uses of a Chronic Folk Illness for Personal Adaptation." *Social Science and Medicine* 37:285–94.

Heurtin-Roberts, Suzanne, and Gay Becker. 1993. "Anthropological Perspectives on Chronic Illness." *Social Science and Medicine* 37:281–83.

Hill, Connie Dessonville, Larry W. Thompson, and Doris Gallagher. 1988. "The Role of Anticipatory Bereavement in Older Women's Adjustment to Widowhood." *The Gerontologist* 28:792–99.

Hingson, Ralph, Norman A. Scotch, James Sorenson, and Judith P. Swazey. 1981. *In Sickness and in Health: Social Dimensions of Medical Care*. St. Louis: C. V. Mosby.

Holland, Dorothy. 1992. "How Cultural Systems Become Desire." In *Human Motives and Cultural Models*, ed. Roy D'Andrade and Claudia Strauss, 61–89. Cambridge: Cambridge University Press.

Hunt, Linda M. 1994. "Practicing Oncology in Provincial Mexico: A Narrative Analysis." *Social Science and Medicine* 38:843–54.

Hymes, Dell. 1981. *In Vain I Tried to Tell You*. Philadelphia: University of Pennsylvania Press.

Idler, Eileen, and S. Kasl. 1991. "Health Perceptions and Survival: Do Global Evaluations of Health Status Really Predict Mortality?" *Journal of Gerontology* 46:S55-S65.

Inhorn, Marcia. 1994a. "Interpreting Infertility: Medical Anthropological Perspectives." *Social Science and Medicine* 39:459–61.

———. 1994b. *Quest for Conception: Gender, Infertility, and Egyptian Medical Traditions.* Philadelphia: University of Pennsylvania Press.

Jackson, Jean E. 1994. "The Rashomon Approach to Dealing with Chronic Pain." *Social Science and Medicine* 38:823–34.

Jackson, Michael. 1983. "Thinking through the Body: An Essay on Understanding Metaphor." *Social Analysis* 14:127–49.

———. 1989. *Paths toward a Clearing: Radical Empiricism and Ethnographic Inquiry.* Bloomington: Indiana University Press.

Janson-Bjerklie, Susan, Sandra Ferketich, Patricia Benner, and Gay Becker. 1992. "Clinical Markers of Asthma Severity and Risk: Importance of Subjective as Well as Objective Factors." *Heart and Lung* 21:265–72.

Johnson, Mark. 1987. *The Body in the Mind.* Chicago: University of Chicago Press.

Jung, Carl. 1933. *Modern Man in Search of a Soul.* Translated by W. S. Dell and C. F. Baynes. New York: Harcourt Brace.

Kagawa-Singer, Marjorie. 1993. "Redefining Health: Living with Cancer." *Social Science and Medicine* 37:295–304.

Kaufman, Sharon. 1986. *The Ageless Self.* Madison: University of Wisconsin Press.

———. 1988a. "Illness, Biography, and the Interpretation of Self Following a Stroke." *Journal of Aging Studies* 2:217–27.

———. 1988b. "Toward a Phenomenology of Boundaries in Medicine: Chronic Illness Experience in the Case of Stroke." *Medical Anthropology Quarterly* 2:338–54.

———. 1994. "The Social Construction of Frailty: An Anthropological Perspective." *Journal of Aging Studies* 8:45–58.

Keesing, Roger. 1992. *Custom and Confrontation: The Kwaio Struggle for Cultural Autonomy.* Chicago: University of Chicago Press.

Kiefer, Christie. 1974. *Changing Cultures, Changing Lives.* San Francisco: Jossey Bass.

Kirmayer, Laurence. 1988. "Mind and Body as Metaphors: Hidden Values in Biomedicine." In *Biomedicine Examined,* ed. Margaret Lock and Deborah Gordon, 57–93. Dordrecht: Reidel.

———. 1992. "The Body's Insistence on Meaning: Metaphor as Presentation and Representation in Illness Experience." *Medical Anthropology Quarterly* 6:323–46.

————. 1994. "Improvisation and Authority in Illness Meaning." *Culture, Medicine, and Psychiatry* 18:183–214.

Kleinman, Arthur. 1988. *The Illness Narratives.* New York: Basic Books.

Kohli, Martin. 1986. "The World We Forgot: A Historical Review of the Life Course." In *Later Life: The Social Psychology of Aging,* ed. Victor Marshall, 271–303. Beverly Hills: Sage.

Laderman, Carol, and Marina Roseman. 1996. "Introduction." In *The Performance of Healing,* ed. Carol Laderman and Marina Roseman, 1–16. New York: Routledge.

Lakoff, George. 1987. *Women, Fire, and Dangerous Things.* Chicago: University of Chicago Press.

Lakoff, George, and Mark Johnson. 1980. *Metaphors We Live By.* Chicago: University of Chicago Press.

Langness, L. L., and Gelya Frank. 1981. *Lives: An Anthropological Approach to Biography.* Novato, CA: Chandler and Sharp.

Laqueur, Thomas. 1987. "Orgasm, Generation, and the Politics of Reproductive Biology." In *The Making of the Modern Body,* ed. Catherine Gallagher and Thomas Laqueur, 1–41. Berkeley: University of California Press.

LaRue, A., L. Bank, L. Jarvik, and M. Hetland. 1979. "Health in Old Age: How Do Physicians' Ratings and Self-Ratings Compare?" *Journal of Gerontology* 34:687–691.

Leavy, Morton L., and R. D. Weinberg. 1979. *Law of Adoption.* Dobbs Ferry, NY: Oceana.

Leder, Drew. 1990. *The Absent Body.* Chicago: University of Chicago Press.

Levin, David Michael. 1991. "Visions of Narcissism: Intersubjectivity and the Reversals of Reflection." In *Merleau-Ponty Vivant,* ed. Martin C. Dillon, 47–90. Albany: State University of New York Press.

Linde, Charlotte. 1993. *Life Stories: The Creation of Coherence.* New York: Oxford University Press.

Lock, Margaret. 1993. "Cultivating the Body: Anthropology and Epistemologies of Bodily Practice and Knowledge." *Annual Review of Anthropology* 22:133–55.

Lock, Margaret, and Nancy Scheper-Hughes. 1996. "A Critical-Interpretive Approach in Medical Anthropology: Rituals and Routines of Discipline and Dissent." In *Medical Anthropology: Contemporary Theory and Method,* 2d ed., ed. Carolyn F. Sargent and Thomas M. Johnson, 41–70. New York: Praeger.

Low, Setha. 1994. "Embodied Metaphors: Nerves as Lived Experience." In *Embodiment and Experience,* ed. Thomas Csordas, 139–62. New York: Cambridge University Press.

Lowenberg, June S. 1989. *Caring and Responsibility: The Crossroads between Holis-*

tic Practice and Traditional Medicine. Philadelphia: University of Pennsylvania Press.

Lowenthal, Marjorie Fiske, Majda Thurnher, David Chiriboga and Associates. 1975. *Four Stages of Life: A Comparative Study of Women and Men Facing Transitions.* San Francisco: Jossey Bass.

Luborsky, Mark. 1987. "Analysis of Multiple Life History Narratives." *Ethos* 15: 366–81.

———. 1990. "Alchemists' Visions: Cultural Norms in Eliciting and Analyzing Life History Narratives." *Journal of Aging Studies* 4:17–29.

———. 1993. "The Romance with Personal Meaning in Gerontology: Cultural Aspects of Life Themes." *The Gerontologist* 33:445–52.

———. 1994a. "The Cultural Adversity of Physical Disability: Erosion of Full Adult Personhood." *Journal of Aging Studies* 8:239–53.

———. 1994b. "The Identification and Analysis of Themes and Patterns." In *Qualitative Methods in Aging Research,* ed. Jaber Gubrium and Andrea Sankar, 189–210. Thousand Oaks, CA: Sage.

———. 1995. "The Process of Self-Report of Impairment in Clinical Research." *Social Science and Medicine* 40:1447–59.

Luborsky, Mark R., and Robert L. Rubinstein. 1987. "Ethnicity and Lifetimes: Self-Concepts and Situational Contexts of Ethnic Identity in Late Life." In *Ethnicity and Aging: New Perspectives,* ed. David Gelfand and D. Barresi, 35–50. New York: Springer.

———. 1990. "Ethnic Identity and Bereavement in Later Life: The Case of Older Widowers." In *Cultural Dimensions of Aging: Worldwide Perspectives,* ed. Jay Sokolovsky, 229–40. Brooklyn: Bergin and Garvey.

Luckmann, Thomas. 1991. "The Constitution of Human Life in Time." In *Chronotypes: The Construction of Time,* ed. John Bender and David E. Wellbery, 151–66. Stanford: Stanford University Press.

Luke, Helen M. 1985. *Woman Earth and Spirit: The Feminine in Symbol and Myth.* New York: Crossroad.

Lyon, Margot L. 1990. "Order and Healing: The Concept of Order and Its Importance in the Conceptualization of Healing." *Medical Anthropology* 12: 249–68.

MacIntyre, Alasdair. 1981. *After Virtue: A Study in Moral Theory.* Notre Dame: University of Notre Dame Press.

Manheimer, Ronald J. 1989. "The Narrative Quest in Qualitative Gerontology." *Journal of Aging Studies* 3:231–52.

Marsella, Anthony, George DeVos, and Francis Hsu, eds. 1985. *Culture and Self: Asian and Western Perspectives.* New York: Tavistock.

Marsella, Antony, and Geoffrey White. 1982. *Cultural Conceptions of Mental Health and Therapy.* Boston: D. Reidel.

Martin, Elmer P., and Joanne Mitchell Martin. 1978. *The Black Extended Family*. Chicago: University of Chicago Press.

Mathews, Holly F., Donald R. Lannin, and James P. Mitchell. 1994. "Coming to Terms with Advanced Breast Cancer: Black Women's Narratives from Eastern North Carolina." *Social Science and Medicine* 38:789–800.

Mattingly, Cheryl. 1994. "The Concept of 'Therapeutic Emplotment.'" *Social Science and Medicine* 38:811–22.

Mattingly, Cheryl, and Lindo Garro. 1994. "Introduction: Narrative Representations of Illness and Healing." *Social Science and Medicine* 38:771–74.

Mauss, Marcel. 1950. "Les Techniques du corps." *Sociologie et anthropologie*. Paris: Presses Universitaires de France.

———. 1985. "A Category of the Human Mind: The Notion of Person, the Notion of Self." In *The Category of the Person: Anthropology, Philosophy, History*, ed. Michael Carrithers, Steven Collins, and Steven Lukes, 1–25. Cambridge: Cambridge University Press.

McLaughlin, Judith, and Ib Zeeberg. 1993. "Self-Care and Multiple Sclerosis: A View from Two Cultures." *Social Science and Medicine* 37:315–29.

Merleau-Ponty, Maurice. 1962. *Phenomenology of Perception*. Translated by Colin Smith. New York: Routledge.

———. 1968. *The Visible and the Invisible*. Edited by Claude Lefort. Translated by Alphonso Lingis. Evanston, IL: Northwestern University Press.

Meyer, John W. 1986. "The Self and the Life Course: Institutionalization and Its Effects." In *Human Development and the Life Course: Multidisciplinary Perspectives*, ed. Aage B. Sorensen, Franz E. Weinert, and Lonnie R. Sherrod, 199–216. Hillsdale, NJ: Lawrence Erlbaum Associates.

———. 1988. "Levels of Analysis: The Life Course as a Cultural Construction." In *Social Structures and Human Lives*, ed. Matilda White, 49–62. Beverly Hills: Sage.

Miller, Alice. 1981. *Drama of the Gifted Child: The Search for the True Self*. New York: Basic Books.

Milligan, Sharon E. 1990. "Understanding Diversity of the Urban Black Aged: Historical Perspectives." In *Black Aged: Understanding Diversity and Service Needs*, ed. Zev Harel, Edward A. McKinney, and Michael Williams, 114–27. Newbury Park, CA: Sage.

Minkler, Meredith. 1990. "Aging and Disability: Behind and Beyond the Stereotypes." *Journal of Aging Studies* 4:245–60.

Mishler, Elliott. 1986. *Research Interviewing*. Cambridge: Harvard University Press.

Modell, Judith. 1994. *Kinship with Strangers: Adoption and Interpretations of Kinship in American Culture*. Berkeley: University of California Press.

Moore, Sally, and Barbara Myerhoff. 1972. *Secular Ritual*. Amsterdam: An Gorcum.

Moss, Miriam S., and Sidney Z. Moss. 1989. "Death of the Very Old." In *Disenfranchised Grief: Recognizing Hidden Sorrow*, ed. Kenneth Doka, 213–17. Lexington, MA: Lexington Books.

Mullings, Leith. 1995. "Households Headed by Women: The Politics of Race, Class, and Gender." In *Conceiving the New World Order: The Global Politics of Reproduction*, ed. Faye D. Ginsburg and Rayna Rapp, 122–39. Berkeley: University of California Press.

Murphy, Robert. 1987. *The Body Silent*. New York: Holt.

Murphy, Robert, Jessica Scheer, Yolanda Murphy, and R. Mack. 1988. "Physical Disability and Social Liminality: A Study in the Rituals of Adversity." *Social Science and Medicine* 26:235–42.

Murray, D. W. 1993. "What is the Western Concept of the Self? On Forgetting David Hume." *Ethos* 21:3–23.

Myerhoff, Barbara. 1979. *Number Our Days*. New York: Dutton.

Nachtigall, Robert, Gay Becker, and Mark Wozny. 1992. "The Effects of Gender-Specific Diagnosis on Men's and Women's Response to Infertility." *Fertility and Sterility* 57:113–21.

Neugarten, Bernice L. "Adult Personality: Toward a Psychology of the Life Cycle." In *Middle Age and Aging*, ed. Bernice L. Neugarten, 137–47. Chicago: University of Chicago Press.

———. 1969. "Continuities and Discontinuities of Psychological Issues into Adult Life." *Human Development* 12:121–30.

———. 1976. "Adaptation and the Life Course." *Counseling Psychologist* 6(1).

———. 1979. "Time, Age, and the Life Cycle." *American Journal of Psychiatry* 136:887–93.

Nora, Pierre. 1989. "Between Memory and History." *Representations* 26:7–25.

Nydegger, Corrine. 1986. "Role and Age Transitions." In *New Methods for Old Age Research*, ed. Christine L. Fry and Jennie Keith, 131–62. South Hadley, MA: Bergin and Garvey.

Office of Technology Assessment. 1988. *Infertility: Medical and Social Choices*. Washington, D.C.: U.S. Government Printing Office.

Okun, M. A., W. A. Stock, M. J. Haring, and R. A. Witter. 1984. "Health and Subjective Well-Being: A Meta-Analysis." *International Journal of Aging and Human Development* 19:111–31.

Oleson, Virginia, Leonard Schatzman, Nellie Droes, Diane Hatton, and Nan Chico. 1990. "The Mundane Ailment and the Physical Self: Analysis of the Social Psychology of Health and Illness." *Social Science and Medicine* 30:449–55.

Ortner, Sherry. 1973. "On Key Symbols." *American Anthropologist* 75:1338–46.

———. 1995. "Resistance and the Problem of Ethnographic Refusal." *Comparative Studies in Society and History* 37:173–93.

Palmer, Gary B., and William R. Jankowiak. 1996. "Performance and Imagination: Toward an Anthropology of the Spectacular and the Mundane." *Cultural Anthropology* 11:225–58.

Pandolfi, Mariella. 1990. "Boundaries inside the Body: Women's Sufferings in Southern Peasant Italy." *Culture, Medicine and Psychiatry* 14:255–73.

Parsons, Talcott. 1972. "Definitions of Health and Illness in Light of American Values and Social Structure. In *Patients, Physicians, and Illness*, 2d ed., ed. E. Gartly Jaco, 107–27. New York: Free Press.

Paul, Robert A. 1990. "What Does Anybody Want?: Desire, Purpose and the Acting Subject in the Study of Culture." *Cultural Anthropology* 5:431–51.

Peacock, James L., and Dorothy C. Holland. 1993. "The Narrated Self: Life Stories in Process." *Ethos* 21:367–83.

Pearlman, R. A., and R. F. Uhlmann. 1988. "Quality of Life in Chronic Diseases: Perceptions of Elderly Patients." *Journal of Gerontology: Medical Sciences* 43: M-25–M-30.

Pitcher, Linda. 1996. "Phenomenology: Towards an Anthropology of Embodiment." University of California, San Francisco. Unpublished manuscript.

Quinn, Naomi. 1991. "The Cultural Basis of Metaphor." In *Beyond Metaphor: The Theory of Tropes in Anthropology*, ed. James Fernandez, 56–93. Stanford: Stanford University Press.

———. 1992. "The Motivational Force of Self-Understanding: Evidence from Wives' Inner Conflicts." In *Human Motives and Cultural Models*, ed. Roy D'Andrade and Claudia Strauss, 90–126. Cambridge: Cambridge University Press.

Quinn, Naomi, and Dorothy Holland. 1987. "Culture and Cognition." In *Cultural Models in Language and Thought*, ed. Dorothy Holland and Naomi Quinn, 3–40. Cambridge: Cambridge University Press.

Ragone, Helena. 1994. *Surrogate Motherhood: Conception in the Heart.* Boulder, CO: Westview Press.

Register, Cheri. 1987. *Living with Chronic Illness.* New York: Bantam.

Reiser, Stanley J. 1985. "Responsibility for Personal Health: A Historical Perspective." *Medical Philosophy* 10:7–17.

Rhodes, Lorna. 1996. "Studying Biomedicine as a Cultural System." In *Medical Anthropology: Contemporary Theory and Method*, 2d ed., ed. Carolyn F. Sargent and Tom M. Johnson, 165–80. New York: Praeger.

Ricoeur, Paul. 1977. *The Rule of Metaphor: Multidisciplinary Studies of the Creation of Meaning in Language.* Toronto: Toronto University Press.

———. 1980. "Narrative Time." In *On Narrative*, ed. W. J. T. Mitchell, 165–86. Chicago: University of Chicago Press.

———. 1981. "The Metaphorical Process as Cognition, Imagination, and Feeling." In *Philosophical Perspectives on Metaphor*, ed. Mark Johnson. Minneapolis: University of Minnesota Press.

———. 1983. "Can Fictional Narratives Be True?" *Analecta Husserliana* 14:3–19.

————. 1984. *Time and Narrative.* Vol. 1. Chicago: University of Chicago Press.

Riessman, Catherine Kohler. 1990. "Strategic Uses of Narrative in the Presentation of Self and Illness: A Research Note." *Social Science and Medicine* 30: 1195–200.

————. 1991. *Divorce Talk.* New Brunswick, NJ: Rutgers University Press.

Riley, Matilda White, and Kathleen Bond. 1983. "Beyond Ageism: Postponing the Onset of Disability." In *Aging in Society: Selected Reviews of Recent Research,* ed. Matilda White Riley, Beth B. Hess, and Kathleen Bond, 243–52. Hillsdale, NJ: Lawrence Erlbaum Associates.

Robinson, Ian. 1990. "Personal Narratives, Social Careers, and Medical Courses: Analyzing Life Trajectories in Autobiographies of People with Multiple Sclerosis." *Social Science and Medicine* 30:1173–86.

Rosaldo, Renato. 1984. "Toward an Anthropology of Self and Feeling." In *Culture Theory: Essays on Mind, Self, and Emotion,* ed. Richard A. Shweder and Robert A. LeVine, 137–57. Cambridge: Cambridge University Press.

————. 1989. *Culture and Truth: The Remaking of Social Analysis.* Boston: Beacon.

Rosenwald, George C., and Richard L. Ochberg, eds. 1992. *Storied Lives: The Cultural Politics of Self-Understanding.* New Haven: Yale University Press.

Rosow, Irving. 1979. *Socialization to Aging.* Berkeley: University of California Press.

Rubinstein, Robert L. 1990. "Nature, Culture, Gender, Age." In *Anthropology and Aging,* ed. Robert L. Rubinstein, 109–15. Dordrecht, Netherlands: Kluwer.

————. 1995. "Narratives of Elder Parental Death: A Structural and Cultural Analysis." *Medical Anthropology Quarterly* 9:257–76.

Rubinstein, Robert L., Baine B. Alexander, Marcene Goodman, and Mark Luborsky. 1991. "Key Relationships of Never Married, Childless Older Women: A Cultural Analysis." *Journal of Gerontology, Social Sciences* 46: S270–77.

Rubinstein, Robert L., Janet C. Kilbride and Sharon Nagy. 1990. *Elders Living Alone: Frailty and the Perception of Choice.* New York: Aldine de Gruyter.

Ryff, Carol D. 1986. "The Subjective Construction of Self and Society: An Agenda for Life-Span Research." In *Later Life,* ed. Victor Marshall, 33–74. Beverly Hills, CA: Sage.

Sacks, Oliver. 1984. *A Leg to Stand On.* New York: Harper and Row.

Sahlins, Marshall. 1985. *Islands of History.* Chicago: University of Chicago Press.

Sandelowski, Marguerite. 1991. "Compelled to Try: The Never-Enough Quality of Conceptive Technology." *Medical Anthropology Quarterly* 5:29–47.

————. 1993. *With Child in Mind: Studies of the Personal Encounter with Infertility.* Philadelphia: University of Pennsylvania Press.

Sankar, Andrea. 1984. "'It's Just Old Age': Old Age as a Diagnosis in American and Chinese Medicine." In *Age and Anthropological Theory,* ed. David Kertzer and Jennie Keith, 250–80. Ithaca, NY: Cornell University Press.

————. 1987. "The Living Dead: Cultural Constructions of the Oldest Old." In

The Elderly as Modern Pioneers, ed. Philip Silverman, 345–56. Bloomington: Indiana University Press.

Scheer, Jessica, and Luborsky, Mark. 1991. "The Cultural Context of Polio Biographies." *Orthopedics* 14:1173–81.

Scheper-Hughes, Nancy. 1992. *Death without Weeping: The Violence of Everyday Life in Brazil.* Berkeley: University of California Press.

Scheper-Hughes, Nancy, and Lock, Margaret. 1987. "The Mindful Body: A Prolegomenon to Future Work in Medical Anthropology." *Medical Anthropology Quarterly* 1:6–41.

Schiefflin, Edward. 1996. "On Failure and Performance: Throwing the Medium Out of the Seance." In *The Performance of Healing,* ed. Carol Laderman and Marina Roseman, 59–90. New York: Routledge.

Schneider, David. 1968. *American Kinship: A Cultural Account.* Englewood Cliffs, NJ: Prentice Hall.

———. 1980. *American Kinship.* Chicago: University of Chicago Press.

Schroots, Johannes J. F. 1991. "Metaphors of Aging and Complexity." In *Metaphors of Aging in Science and the Humanities,* ed. Gary M. Kenyon, James E. Birren, and Johannes J. F. Schroots, 219–43. New York: Springer.

Shapiro, Michael, and Marianne Shapiro. 1976. *Studies in Semiotics.* Vol. 8, *Hierarchy and the Structure of Tropes.* Bloomington: Indiana University Publications.

Sharp, Sharon A. 1986. "Folk Medicine Practices: Women as Keepers and Carriers of Knowledge." *Women's Studies International Forum* 9:243–49.

Shweder, Richard A., and Edmund Bourne. 1984. "Does the Concept of the Person Vary Cross-Culturally?" In *Culture Theory: Essays on Mind, Self, and Emotion,* ed. Richard A. Shweder and Robert A. LeVine, 158–99. Cambridge: Cambridge University Press.

Smith, Robert J., and Michael C. Thornton. 1993. "Identity and Consciousness: Group Solidarity." In *Aging in Black America,* ed. James S. Jackson, Linda M. Chatters, and Robert Joseph Taylor, 203–16. Newbury Park, CA: Sage.

Snowdon, R., G. D. Mitchell, and E. M. Snowden. 1983. *Artificial Reproduction: A Social Investigation.* London: George Allen and Unwin.

Somers, Margaret R., and Gloria D. Gibson. 1994. "Reclaiming the Epistemological 'Other': Narrative and the Social Constitution of Identity." In *Social Theory and the Politics of Identity,* ed. Craig Calhoun, 39–99. Oxford, U.K.: Blackwell.

Sontag, Susan. 1978. *Illness as Metaphor.* New York: Farrar, Straus and Giroux.

Spence, Donald P. 1982. *Narrative Truth and Historical Truth: Meaning and Interpretation in Psychoanalysis.* New York: Norton.

———. 1986. "Narrative Smoothing and Clinical Wisdom." In *Narrative Psychology: The Storied Nature of Human Conduct,* ed. Theodore Sarbin, 211–32. New York: Praeger.

Stoller, Paul. 1980. "The Epistemology of Sorkotaray: Language, Metaphor, and Healing among the Songhay." *Ethos* 8:117–31.

———. 1989. *The Taste of Ethnographic Things.* Philadelphia: University of Pennsylvania Press.

———. 1994. "Embodying Colonial Memories." *American Anthropologist* 96: 634–48.

Strauss, Anselm L., Juliet Corbin, Shizuko Fagerhaugh, Barney G. Glaser, David Maines, Barbara Suczek, and Carolyn L. Wiener. 1984. *Chronic Illness and the Quality of Life.* 2d ed., St. Louis: C. V. Mosby.

Strauss, Claudia. 1992. "What Makes Tony Run? Schemas as Motives Reconsidered." In *Human Motives and Cultural Models,* ed. Roy D'Andrade and Claudia Strauss, 191–224. Cambridge: Cambridge University Press.

Tamir, Lois M. 1982. "Men at Middle Age: Developmental Transitions." *Annals of the American Academy of Political and Social Science* 464:47–56.

Taylor, Charles. 1989. *Sources of the Self: The Making of the Modern Identity.* Cambridge: Harvard University Press.

Terrell, John, and Judith Modell. 1994. "Anthropology and Adoption." *American Anthropologist* 96:155–61.

Teubel, Sarah J. 1984. *Sarah the Priestess: The First Matriarch of Genesis.* Athens, OH: Swallow Press.

Toch, Hans. 1965. *The Social Psychology of Social Movements.* Indianapolis: Bobbs Merrill.

Toombs, S. Kay. 1987. "The Meaning of Illness: A Phenomenological Approach to the Patient-Physician Relationship." *Journal of Medicine and Philosophy* 12: 219–40.

Turner, Bryan. 1984. *The Body and Society.* London: Basil Blackwell.

———. 1991. "Missing Bodies: Toward a Sociology of Embodiment." *Sociology of Health and Illness* 13:265–72.

———. 1992. *Regulating Bodies: Essays in Medical Sociology.* New York: Routledge.

Turner, Victor. 1969. *The Ritual Process.* Ithaca, NY: Cornell University Press.

———. 1974. *Dramas, Fields, and Metaphors.* Ithaca, NY: Cornell University Press.

———. 1980. "Social Dramas and Stories about Them. In *On Narrative,* ed. W. J. T. Mitchell, 137–64. Chicago: University of Chicago Press.

———. 1986. *The Anthropology of Performance.* New York: Paj Publications.

Tversky, Amos, and Daniel Kahneman. 1981. "The Framing of Decisions and the Psychology of Choice." *Science* 211:453–58.

Tymstra, Tjeerd. 1989. "The Imperative Character of Medical Technology and the Meaning of 'Anticipated Decision Regret.'" *International Journal of Technology Assessment in Health Care* 5:207–13.

van Gennep, Arnold. 1960. *The Rites of Passage.* Chicago: University of Chicago Press.

Vash, Carolyn. 1983. *The Psychology of Disability.* New York: Springer.

Wagner, Roy. 1986. *Symbols That Stand for Themselves.* Chicago: University of Chicago Press.

Watson, Lawrence C. 1976. "Understanding a Life History as a Subjective Document: Hermeneutical and Phenomenological Perspectives." *Ethos* 4:95–131.

Watson, Lawrence C., and Maria-Barbara Watson-Franke. 1985. *Interpreting Life Histories.* New Brunswick, NJ: Rutgers University Press.

Weigle, Marta. 1989. *Creation and Procreation: Feminist Reflections on Mythologies of Cosmogony and Parturition.* Philadelphia: University of Pennsylvania Press.

White, Hayden. 1980. "The Value of Narrativity in the Representation of Reality." In *On Narrative,* ed. W. J. T. Mitchell, 1–23. Chicago: University of Chicago Press.

Wiener, Carolyn. 1981. *The Politics of Alcoholism.* New Brunswick, NJ: Transaction.

Wiener, Carolyn, and Marylin Dodd. 1993. "Coping amid Uncertainty: An Illness Trajectory Perspective." *Scholarly Inquiry for Nursing Practice: An International Journal* 7:17–31.

Widdershoven, Guy A. M. 1993. "The Story of Life: Hermeneutic Perspectives on the Relationship between Narrative and Life History." In *The Narrative Study of Lives,* ed. Ruthellen Josselson and Amia Lieblich, 1:1–20. Newbury Park, CA: Sage.

Wikan, Unni. 1989. "Managing the Heart to Brighten Face and Soul: Emotions in Balinese Morality and Health Care." *American Ethnologist* 16:294–312.

———. 1990. *Managing Turbulent Hearts: A Balinese Formula for Living.* Chicago: University of Chicago Press.

———. 1995. "The Self in a World of Urgency and Necessity." *Ethos* 23:259–85.

Williams, Gareth. 1984. "The Genesis of Chronic Illness: Narrative Reconstruction." *Sociology of Health and Illness* 6:175–200.

Yanagisako, Sylvia, and Carol Delaney. 1995. "Naturalizing Power." In *Naturalizing Power: Essays in Feminist Cultural Analysis,* ed. Sylvia Yanagisako and Carol Delaney, 1–22. New York: Routledge.

Zola, Irving Kenneth. 1982. *Missing Pieces: A Chronicle of Living with a Disability.* Philadelphia: Temple University Press.

Index

259

Compositor: G&S Typesetters, Inc.
Text: 10/14 Palatino
Display: Snell Roundhand Script and Bauer Bodoni
Printer: Thomson-Shore, Inc.
Binder: Thomson-Shore, Inc.